The Lost Autobiography
of Samuel Steward

THE LOST AUTOBIOGRAPHY

of

SAMUEL STEWARD

*Recollections of an Extraordinary
Twentieth-Century Gay Life*

edited by

JEREMY MULDERIG

with a foreword by Scott Herring

The University of Chicago Press
Chicago and London

The University of Chicago Press, Chicago 60637
The University of Chicago Press, Ltd., London
© 2018 by The University of Chicago
Published 2018
Printed in the United States of America

27 26 25 24 23 22 21 20 19 18   2 3 4 5

ISBN-13: 978-0-226-52034-6 (cloth)
ISBN-13: 978-0-226-54141-9 (paper)
ISBN-13: 978-0-226-54155-6 (e-book)
DOI: https://doi.org/10.7208/chicago/9780226541556.001.0001

Library of Congress Cataloging-in-Publication Data

Names: Steward, Samuel M., author. | Mulderig, Jeremy, editor. |
Herring, Scott, 1976– writer of foreword.
Title: The lost autobiography of Samuel Steward : recollections
of an extraordinary twentieth-century gay life / edited by Jeremy
Mulderig ; with a foreword by Scott Herring.
Description: Chicago : The University of Chicago Press, 2018. |
Includes index.
Identifiers: LCCN 2017036831 | ISBN 9780226520346 (cloth :
alk. paper) | ISBN 9780226541419 (pbk. : alk. paper) |
ISBN 9780226541556 (e-book)
Subjects: LCSH: Steward, Samuel M. | Authors, American—
United States—20th century—Biography. | Gay men—
United States—Biography.
Classification: LCC PS3537.T479 Z46 2018 | DDC 813/.54 [B]—dc23
LC record available at https://lccn.loc.gov/2017036831

♾ This paper meets the requirements of ANSI/NISO Z39.48-1992
(Permanence of Paper).

To the memory of
Jon and Nancy Wallace

Words are easy, like the wind;
Faithful friends are hard to find.

Courtesy of the Estate of Samuel M. Steward

I was in no sense a case of multiple personalities—like the three faces of Eve or the extraordinary young man with some ten or twelve differing selves. But—although the simile is not a good one, nor very imaginative—I did in a sense have an old artichoke heart, and the various pen names I used in the things I wrote, my Sparrow name as a tattoo artist and later the Andros name as a writer, were like the separate leaves that are capable of being stripped away. But what was at the center?

SAMUEL STEWARD

CONTENTS

FOREWORD

The choicest task that awaits an author—besides finishing a book—is titling it. Sometimes the writer makes this decision from the get-go. At other times, a working title such as James Joyce's "Work in Progress" becomes *Finnegans Wake*. Or James Weldon Johnson commits to *The Autobiography of an Ex-Colored Man* after he entertains "The Chameleon." Or Djuna Barnes's *Nightwood* starts off as "Bow Down." What Jeremy Mulderig presents here is an expanded version of a remarkable but forgotten gay autobiography of the twentieth century, which, thanks to his meticulous editing, now earns its new title, *The Lost Autobiography of Samuel Steward*.

Mulderig's introduction notes that Samuel M. Steward originally considered various titles after he finished his manuscript in the winter of 1978, including "A Triple Life"—a reference to three of the many personal and professional identities that he adopted during his eighty-four years of living: his role as a university professor for twenty years, his alter ego as a tattoo artist (Phil Sparrow), and his pseudonym as a writer of pornography (Phil Andros). Other titles that Steward mulled over included "Things Past," "Three Lives in One," and, amusingly, "Three-Way." The allusions to his modernist literary heroes Gertrude Stein and Marcel Proust are clear enough and evidence Steward's lofty aspirations. A potential title such as "Three-Way" also reveals a campy worldview that he wielded throughout his writerly life and that Mulderig carefully excavated earlier with his wonderful edited collection of Steward's mid-twentieth-century essays, *Philip Sparrow Tells All: Lost Essays by Samuel Steward, Writer, Professor, Tattoo Artist* (Chicago: University of Chicago Press, 2015).

What if we approached this working title—"Three-Way"—as a thematic guide for understanding Steward's multiple personae? What does it mean to have a threesome with yourself? Or to imagine your triple life as a "Three-Way"? Steward's sexual contacts, which his memoir discusses at length, numbered well into the quadruple digits. But one of Steward's most important relations was with and to himself. I mean this self-relation both literally and figuratively. As we learn early in *The Lost Autobiography of Samuel Steward*, after departing from the small town of Woodsfield, Ohio, Steward prized his young-adult life in the greener urban pastures of Columbus. "I went to Columbus," he writes, "with the major purpose of bringing pleasure to others, mainly straight young men, and not to be concerned about pleasuring myself—for in bringing it to those I admired, I *did* please myself." Later in his autobiography he references "shafering"—his idiosyncratic term for masturbating—with Lord Alfred Douglas as well as with his Accu-jac device, a masturbation machine he owned during his later life in the Bay Area. "Along with [Jean] Genet—who first suggested it—let us form a cult of the solitary pleasure," he writes in his first chapter. Pleasing this solitary self, he engaged with the wider world of male same-sex desire.

Steward's focus on self-pleasure also applies to the various selves that his autobiography details. The link between autoeroticism and writing is an old saw but one still germane to this writing at hand. It is hard not to read Steward, drafting prose at age sixty-nine, taking supreme delight in reliving the exploits of Andros and Sparrow. Writing—itself "a cult of the solitary pleasure"—linked him to these two past lives as the sections of his memoir add up to a figurative three-way with his younger selves. Published in 1981, *Chapters from an Autobiography* enabled him to revisit these experiences in a compressed version. *The Lost Autobiography of Samuel Steward* shows in even greater depth how he imaginatively cruised the twentieth century that he lived and loved so intensively. Indeed, Mulderig's edition confirms Steward's to have been a life full of hindrances but also sincere pleasures of which he took full advantage. Between the pages of these lengthened chapters, we have a wide-eyed Steward meeting Stein and Alice B. Toklas in Bilignin, France; a Steward who became one of the most admired tattoo artists in the Midwest; an aging Steward who moved to Berkeley, California, and struggled with its youth-obsessed gay communities. He notes that his time spent in Berkeley was "a tumultuous period," and that is quite the understatement. With *The Lost Autobiography of Samuel Steward*'s references to major historical events such as World War II and what one anthropologist, Kath Weston, terms the Great Gay Migration to cities that started in the later 1960s, we have an account of a gay male who lived through every decade of the twentieth century. The act of recording these past events and prior selves clearly gratified him: referring to his pseudonym, Steward observes, "Phil Andros, springing full-grown from my temple, like Athena from the brow of Zeus, was a pleasant surprise, helping me to pass the time. In him and through him for several years, I relived not only the adventures of my own youth but those of several others I had known."

With Mulderig's edition, we get a chance to remember the last century vicariously. We get to join yet another "cult of the solitary pleasure"—reading about Steward's lives with our own singular selves. Interestingly, Steward may have anticipated this experience, since he conceived his writing as an emotional and erotic aid that would "bring pleasure to lonely old men in hotel rooms at night." Besides this poignant niche market, his chapters in *The Lost Autobiography of Samuel Steward* now have a much wider readership in the twenty-first century. This is Mulderig's generous gift. We have seen a lot of Steward, Andros, and Sparrow in the past decade thanks to Justin Spring's inspirational biography, the new Steward archives housed at Yale, Mulderig's edition of his midlife essays, and a slow but steady stream of related literary and cultural criticism. Mulderig's restored version of Steward's autobiography offers another important facet: his take on how his three lives became one particular way of being. As Mulderig claims, the book unquestionably "deserves to rank among the major queer autobiographies of the twentieth century."

So let this lost-and-now-found autobiography take its place with other much-praised memoirs that capture the pleasures and pressures of LGBT living not that long ago. *The Lost Autobiography of Samuel Steward* should sit on the same proverbial bookshelf next to Samuel R. Delany's *The Motion of Light in Water*, Alison Bechdel's *Fun Home* and its follow-up *Are You My Mother?*, Audre Lorde's *Zami: A New Spelling of My Name*, and, yes, his beloved Stein's *The Autobiography of Alice B. Toklas*. I think you will get much enjoyment from Steward's writing in these pages. After all, he made his mark—and several lives—out of that not-so-solitary undertaking.

Scott Herring
May 2017

ACKNOWLEDGMENTS

Everyone who writes on Samuel Steward owes a fundamental debt to Michael Williams, who rescued, sorted, and preserved eighty boxes of Steward's manuscripts, letters, journals, photographs, and miscellaneous documents after his death in 1993, and to Justin Spring, who later spent a decade of his life turning these materials into the biography that has established Steward's important place in twentieth-century gay history and literature. I am very grateful to Michael for his support of my plan for this book and for kindly permitting the use of documents and photographs from Steward's papers, and to Justin—whose encyclopedic knowledge of Steward's life I have frequently depended on—for his interest in this project and his comments on portions of the manuscript. My deep thanks also go to Douglas Mitchell at the University of Chicago Press, with whom I have been fortunate to work for a second time and without whose enthusiastic endorsement this book would not have been possible.

A number of colleagues and friends made contributions large and small but always important. Thanks go to Douglas Martin, who read the entire manuscript from the invaluable perspective of Steward's former student and friend, and to Andrea Bainbridge, Jonathan Gross, Barrie Jean Borich, Susan Solway, Eve Sinaiko, N. John Hall, and Mark Samuels Lasner.

I am very grateful to Catherine Roehr-Johnson, formerly of the Kinsey Institute for Research in Sex, Gender, and Reproduction, for her help in accessing the institute's collection of Steward's letters and journals. And the knowledge, helpfulness, patience, and good humor of the exceptional staff in the reading room of the Beinecke Library once again made working there a joy. Special thanks go to Adrienne Sharpe for her help in locating and reproducing photographs from the Samuel Steward Collection at Yale.

Finally, this book benefited in countless ways from the expertise of the editorial and production staff at the University of Chicago Press, among whom I particularly wish to thank Kyle Wagner for his meticulous attention to all manner of details, as well as Ashley Pierce, Tyler McGaughey, Christine Schwab, Isaac Tobin, and Amy Smith. My deepest gratitude to all.

J. M.

SOURCES CITED BY SHORT TITLE

Bad Boys Samuel M. Steward. *Bad Boys and Tough Tattoos: A Social History of the Tattoo with Gangs, Sailors, and Street-Corner Punks, 1950–65*. Binghamton: Harrington Park, 1990.

Chapters Samuel M. Steward. *Chapters from an Autobiography*. San Francisco: Grey Fox, 1981.

Dear Sammy Samuel M. Steward, ed. *Dear Sammy: Letters from Gertrude Stein and Alice B. Toklas*. Boston: Houghton Mifflin, 1977.

IDJ *Illinois Dental Journal.*

Kinsey Steward Collection Samuel Steward Collection, the Kinsey Institute for Research in Sex, Gender, and Reproduction, Indiana University.

Manuscript Samuel M. Steward. Clean typescript of unpublished autobiography, untitled, 368 pages (revised version of 237-page typescript with holograph corrections dated December 1, 1978). Yale Steward Papers, box 19.

OED *Oxford English Dictionary.*

Spring   Justin Spring. *Secret Historian: The Life and Times
                  of Samuel Steward, Professor, Tattoo Artist, and Sexual
                  Renegade*. New York: Farrar, Straus & Giroux, 2010.

Stein Letters   Gertrude Stein and Alice B. Toklas Papers, YCAL
                  MSS 77, series II, box 11. Yale Collection of American
                  Literature, Beinecke Rare Book and Manuscript Library,
                  Yale University.

Steward Letters   Gertrude Stein and Alice B. Toklas Papers, YCAL MSS
                  76, series II, box 126. Yale Collection of American
                  Literature, Beinecke Rare Book and Manuscript Library,
                  Yale University.

Yale Steward   Samuel Steward Papers. General Collection, Beinecke
Papers   Rare Book and Manuscript Library, Yale University.

INTRODUCTION

THE LOST AUTOBIOGRAPHY OF SAMUEL STEWARD

On August 21, 1978, a year before his seventieth birthday, Samuel Steward sat down at his typewriter in Berkeley, California, and began to compose one of the most remarkable gay autobiographies of the twentieth century. No one but his closest friends at the time knew the improbable details of his multifaceted life as a respected college professor of English, a sought-after Chicago tattoo artist calling himself Phil Sparrow, and the author of a series of distinctively literary erotic gay novels that circulated widely under his pseudonym Phil Andros in the 1960s and 1970s. A gay man who had discovered his sexuality as a boy in rural Ohio, he had had more than 4,500 sexual encounters during his life with eight hundred men, including all the members of his high-school basketball team, Rudolph Valentino, Lord Alfred Douglas, Roy Fitzgerald (later known to the world as Rock Hudson), a number of his university students, and very many sailors from the Great Lakes Naval Training Station north of Chicago[1]—all of which he meticulously documented in his "Stud File," an alphabetical card file of his lifetime sexual contacts that would amaze the sex researcher Alfred Kinsey when they met in 1949.[2] In 1965, he moved his tattoo business from Chicago to Oakland, California, where he became the tattoo artist of choice for the Hells Angels until his retirement in 1970.

The impulse to write down the details of this unusual life in 1978 may have originated in part from memories reawakened by the project he had completed just a year earlier: an edition of letters written to him by Gertrude Stein and Alice Toklas, which he prefaced with a 115-page memoir of the two summers he spent with them in France during the 1930s and his subsequent

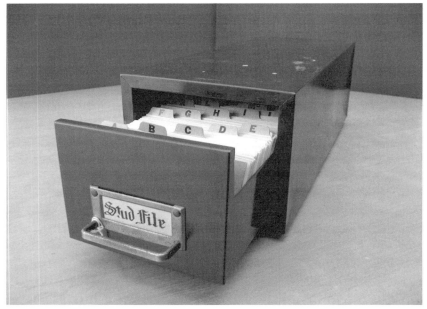

Steward's card file of his lifetime sex partners. (Yale Steward Papers)

visits with Toklas until her death in 1967.[3] But an incentive more pressing than a mood of reminiscence seems to have been the state of his health: "Faced with an operation of some magnitude," he explained later, "I wrote everything down in case I should die on the operating table or be seized with total amnesia caused by some new-fangled anesthetic."[4]

Steward completed the first draft, a 237-page typescript with substantial changes and corrections in ink, on December 1. With his penchant for record keeping, he noted in ink on the final page that he had produced an estimated 110,000 words in 102 days, for an average of 1,080 words per day. At the bottom of the page he jotted down possible titles, including "The Past and I," "A Triple Life," "My Wicked Ways," and "The Autobiography of Sam Steward, Phil Sparrow, and Phil Andros." Early in 1979, he produced a 368-page clean typescript of this first draft, incorporating the ink corrections and making final additions and changes.

By that time, though, Steward had begun to lose interest in his autobiographical project, and feeling that his text was too long and shapeless, he put it aside. The manuscript eventually came to the attention of his friend and the former Grove Press editor Donald Allen, who suggested a new plan: cutting the text by one-half and publishing what remained under the title *Chapters from an Autobiography* through his own Grey Fox Press in San Francisco.

The title appropriately echoed that of Mark Twain's serialized autobiographical fragments,[5] for as in Twain's texts, the episodic pieces of Steward's original manuscript that appeared in this short book, intriguing as they were, no longer constituted an autobiography or even a coherent narrative. Steward had taken this opportunity to recast many sentences and even to expand a few sections of the manuscript for publication, but the overall result was still a radical abridgment of the original text that swept away huge periods of his life. Gone from the manuscript were his nearly thirty years of living in Chicago, which included his teaching careers at Loyola University and DePaul University, as well as many details about his boyhood, college years, and later life in California. What remained in *Chapters from an Autobiography* was a collection of mostly abbreviated and disconnected episodes from the life of a man whom few people had even heard of in 1981, since nearly all of his previous publications had appeared pseudonymously.

Justin Spring's award-winning biography of Steward—*Secret Historian: The Life and Times of Samuel Steward, Professor, Tattoo Artist, and Sexual Renegade* (New York: Farrar, Straus & Giroux, 2010)—not only recovered the details of the often-astonishing story of Steward's life but also firmly established his place in twentieth-century gay history and literature. And my edition of Steward's entertaining columns written monthly for the *Illinois Dental Journal* in the 1940s—*Philip Sparrow Tells All: Lost Essays by Samuel Steward, Writer, Professor, Tattoo Artist* (Chicago: University of Chicago Press, 2015)—made widely available for the first time a collection of his essays notable for their wit and erudition as well as for their coded but clear gay sensibility. Until now, however, the story of Steward's life in his own words has appeared only in the truncated form of *Chapters*, little noted when it was published in 1981 and now long out of print and largely forgotten.

The Lost Autobiography of Samuel Steward: Recollections of an Extraordinary Twentieth-Century Gay Life integrates text from Steward's 110,000-word manuscript (now in the Beinecke Library of Yale University) with text from his 55,000-word published volume to create a single more coherent narrative of 85,000 words that deserves to rank among the major queer autobiographies of the twentieth century. An artful integration of the two texts is necessary because, in its current form, the full manuscript is no more satisfactory than the abbreviated published version. There is truth in Steward's own judgment that this text is overly long ("three times as long as a porno novel," he once noted[6]) and that some of its content contributes little to the narrative of his life ("I seemed to be trying to prove just how much I could remember," he confessed[7]). A lifelong recycler of his published work, Steward constructed some parts of the manuscript by pasting in autobiographical portions of his *Illinois Dental Journal* articles from the 1940s, often to predictably unsatisfactory effect. Moreover, because events and even chapters are manifestly in the wrong order, the chronology of Steward's life is difficult to grasp. People are confusingly referred to long before they are actually identified, paragraphs are often unfocused, and duplications in the text are numerous. There is, in short, much that should be reorganized or that can profitably be deleted. But the manuscript is also rich in significant details, perceptive self-analysis, and witty writing whose careful integration with text from *Chapters from an Autobiography* yields a compelling gay life story on the scale that Steward originally planned.[8]

Steward was well prepared to write an autobiography in 1978, for he had been writing shorter autobiographical pieces under various pen names for more than thirty years. The fifty-six *Illinois Dental Journal* essays that he published from 1944 to 1949 under the name Philip Sparrow—composed as a favor to his handsome personal dentist in Chicago, who was the journal's editor—were his first experiment in inventing a persona in nonfiction and imagining a specific audience of readers. After a few false starts, he succeeded in creating a Philip Sparrow who was a fully realized version of himself, and he found the subjects for his monthly essays in aspects of his actual life in the 1930s and 1940s—cryptography, food allergies, opera and ballet, alcoholism, teaching, Gertrude Stein, Marshall Field's department store, hoarding tendencies, becoming musclebound, turning forty, the wonders of Chicago, Paris, Algiers. In later years, Steward would hone his ability to create a distinctive voice in dozens of essays and stories that he published under various names in the early European gay magazines *Der Kreis*, *eos*, and *amigo* and later in *The Advocate*.

In both versions of his autobiography, the persona Steward creates is an engaging combination of candor, wit, and erudition. But in revising his original manuscript for impending publication as *Chapters from an Autobiography*, he made changes to the first two paragraphs that suggest he was giving fresh thought to the likely audience for the story he wished to tell. To the manuscript's opening scene of boys tobogganing in Woodsfield, Ohio,[9] he added two new sentences that subtly defined the readers he imagined: "Without knowing exactly why, I always managed to sit in front of the school's handsomest basketball player, who wrapped his long arms around me, holding me tight, and pressed his long legs close against each side of my body. I was about ten years old." Nothing else is—or needs to be—said in this paragraph, for the readers Steward envisioned will recognize the point of this detail and understand where this story is going. And as if to offer a preview of that journey, he added an even more explicit sentence to the manuscript's second paragraph, which described the domed bell tower atop the county courthouse in town: "Since my father at one time was county auditor, I had access to this mysterious region, and after finding out what I was and getting to the proper age, I used to take tricks up there." The manuscript's first two paragraphs had originally been only about Woodsfield, but revised as the opening paragraphs in *Chapters*, they are now about Steward and the story of his homosexuality, and they imply readers who are both empathetic and unshockable.

Having defined for himself an audience that will require no tedious justifications of his homosexuality, Steward proceeds with the story of his progress through worlds that are likely to be far outside most of his readers' experiences: a strict Methodist childhood in small-town America; Bohemian Columbus, Ohio, in the 1920s and 1930s; the French countryside around the home of Gertrude Stein and Alice Toklas; academic life, with its frustrations and occasional pettiness; the paralyzing fog of alcoholism; the underground universe of the tattoo artist; life among the Hells Angels motorcycle gang; the world of pornographic fiction writers in the 1960s and 1970s. Steward's homosexuality is of course never far out of view; in an unpredictable world, the centrality of sex—the ceaseless craving for yet another encounter—is the one constant in his life, and sexual episodes are woven through every phase of the story he tells. Occasionally, indeed, sex *is* the story, as when Steward writes an entire chapter about his most memorable sexual partners in Chicago (forthrightly acknowledging that he paid for many of them) or an account of willingly being filmed for two days at the Kinsey Institute with a sadist who beats and sexually dominates him (with Mrs. Kinsey on hand to change the sheets as necessary). The matter-of-fact tone in such sections is a striking indication of Steward's confidence in his readers' readiness to accept even the most extreme manifestations of his sexuality.

Though Steward's life was unconventional in many ways, much of it fell into a recognizable and persistent pattern of exhilarating highs and crushing lows. In graduate school at Ohio State, he idolized his advisor, Clarence Andrews, and was bereft when Andrews died unexpectedly in 1932. In May 1936, when he was just twenty-seven, his newly published first novel received a glowing review from the *New York Times*, but just a week later, the same book caused his dismissal from the teaching position he held because the university's president had heard that it was "racy." The friendship that he formed with Gertrude Stein in the late 1930s and the interest she took in his writing represented the high point of Steward's life, but their relationship was cut short by Stein's death in 1946, which plunged him into a period of deep depression. In 1949, he met and became close friends with Alfred Kinsey, the one person to whom he could safely reveal the details of his sexual life, only to be devastated by Kinsey's death seven years later. Steward's tattoo studio in Chicago flourished after he quit teaching in the 1950s, but the city's 1963 ordinance prohibiting tattooing anyone under the age of twenty-one decimated his business, which had catered to eighteen-year-old naval recruits, and forced him to move elsewhere to make a living. Steward does not dwell in the autobiography on this series of disappointments—he seems, in fact, remarkably resilient—but his narrative clearly presents them as profoundly life-altering events.

To his descriptions of people and events in this life, Steward brought a novelist's respect for descriptive detail, and the characters who populate his life story are drawn with Dickensian precision and wit. His best friend in college, for example, is a lesbian named Marie Anderson, a woman who "did not go unnoticed":

> [A] tall girl, about five-nine, and a heavy one, approximately two hundred, she moved with a swirl and a gazelle's grace. She had bright yellow hair in a longish bob which curled and swayed and swept back from her face. Her pencil-thin eyebrows were more active than swallows in flight; she could control them separately, draw one down and send the other up quizzically and then reverse the pattern. Her nose was short and well formed, and her full lips—painted always the most vivid of scarlets—were as mobile as her eyebrows.

At the other extreme is Randy Webb, "the nastiest-looking person I had seen for a long time," with whom he is forced to share a work space at the start of his tattooing career:

> He was a little old man with yellow-brown hair, dressed in filthy clothes and a dirty wool shirt, toothless because an irate customer on whom he had once put a five-legged black panther had swatted him and knocked his plates out. They broke on the floor and were never replaced. He had one of the worst complexions I ever saw in my life, the result of his inordinate wine drinking. His face was covered with rum-blossoms—big scarlet and purple and yellow pustules which he was fond of squeezing, popping out about a quarter teaspoonful of pus and matter. His nose veins were purple and broken in many places with resultant spots of purpura, and his eyes were red-rimmed and rheumy.

Steward's entire chapter on his two visits with Stein and Toklas is a masterful example of details chosen for their evocative value from the notes he made daily while staying with them in 1937 and 1939. In this typical passage, he selects inconsequential incidents that, woven together, humanize Stein and suggest the warm feelings he had for her:

> I remember her as a great and very human woman, an intricate yet simple and earthy personality, tremendously alive. I think of her on a rainy day in a small garage, down on hands and knees on the oily floor discussing the axle of her car with a young mechanic. I remember how we worked together in her garden, both bent over hoes as we weeded the tomatoes. I see her walking along the dusty roadways, switching her dog leash at the ragweed as she talked, and now and then shouting to Pépé, the little Mexican Chihuahua that Picabia had given her, to stop chasing chickens. I see her turn quickly away from the sight of a helpless calf with its legs tied for market, saying, "Let us not look at that." I hear her hearty laugh as she showed me how, with one quick movement, she had mastered the French peasant's trick of catching a napkin under both arms at once.

As the narrative of Steward's path from his boyhood in tiny Woodsfield to his adult life in Chicago and later in Berkeley, his autobiography might at first seem to be a retelling of the almost archetypal twentieth-century story of the sexually uncertain youth who flees his confining life in the country or the suburbs to discover himself and a world of men like him in the big city. In the wake of George Chauncey's landmark *Gay New York* (1994), studies of the gay history of other cities, including Chicago, have brought to light the previously undocumented urban sites of contact and support that attracted queer residents and newcomers in the early and mid-twentieth century.[10] Allen Drexel, for example, sees this community affirmation in the drag balls popular in Chicago during the 1930s and 1940s, especially the elaborate balls on the city's South Side, whose participants were mainly gay black drag queens. "For most gay men," he writes, "whether or not they actually attended in drag—and many did not—the balls were rare, critical opportunities to meet and socialize openly with one another, and in doing so, to reaffirm and celebrate a shared sense of cultural identity."[11] David K. Johnson found evidence for the same point in examining the gay life narratives collected by University of Chicago sociology students in the 1930s, when Chicago's gay population was already large and visible enough to be an object of study. His conclusions restate the gay trope of the city as a place of self-discovery and community:

[B]oth the leisure and work environments where gay men congregated provided crucial supports for the establishment of a gay identity. . . . In telling their stories, the gay men [who were interviewed] did not speak of an individual, private realization that they were homosexual, but rather highlighted their discovery of "queer life," which led to a new identity and often a new place of residence, wardrobe, circle of friends, and job. Prior to this discovery, they may or may not have been engaging in same-sex sexual activity, but they rarely understood themselves as different. Indeed, for many men, contact with the gay world and adoption of a gay identity were concurrent events.[12]

Such familiar descriptions of young gay men coming of age together in the city provide a backdrop against which Steward's life seems decidedly anomalous, for he appears in his autobiography as sexually self-aware from an early age and accustomed to a largely solitary life as an adult. His thoughts as he anticipates his move to Chicago in 1936 at the age of twenty-seven are revealing: "So, finally, I would be in a city large enough to absorb me, hide me, challenge me, and keep me happy—City of the Big Shoulders." Having perfectly understood—and very frequently acted on—his homosexuality since he was a teenager, Steward was drawn to Chicago not by a need for a supportive gay community but rather by the range of new sexual adventures that a large city would provide under the convenient cover of urban anonymity.

Steward does introduce a few gay friends in his autobiography—Marie Anderson, Kevin Kleeman, and Dino Bellini in Columbus; Richie Tucker, Doc Anthony, and Cliff Raven in Chicago[13]—but they quickly disappear from the narrative. Apart from his connection with Emmy Curtis, the Chicago relationships that he spends the most time describing are the sexual ones he paid for with (often heterosexual) hustlers. The single occasion on which we see Steward in a group of gay peers occurs near the end of the book, when he attends an annual Oktoberfest party given by two friends—"a pleasant little gathering of middle-aged queens." But at this event, significantly, he sits alone on a sofa catching snippets of the conversations that are swirling around him but of which he is not a part.

Steward had more friends than his autobiography suggests, but a constellation of factors clearly tended to isolate him during his life—his drinking, his unremitting and time-consuming quest for sex, his eventual disaffection with teaching, his solitary work as a tattoo artist, his impulsive move to California. Asked in a 1983 interview about the gay "social climate" in 1950s Chicago, Steward revealingly answered in terms of opportunities for sex, noting that "it was largely a matter of apartment living and apartment encounters."[14] In another interview a year later, he said that he found no visible gay community in Chicago when he arrived there in 1936; instead, he observed, "We all went our separate, very lonesome, very lonely ways to our neighborhood bars, seeing whom we could make."[15]

"Lonesome" seems an odd self-description from a man who had thousands of sexual encounters with hundreds of men, but in fact none of those connections ever resulted in a romantic relationship. "I was never in love," he writes at one point,

> perhaps because I preferred a multifold experience rather than a long commitment to a single idealized love object. . . . Had I the capacity for love, or was I intended to be a solitary with such poverty of spirit that I could never enlarge myself to take in another? Was I too much an egoist? The most dangerous of all egoists is the one skilled in what seems to be self-effacement, one whose outer kindness and gentleness really mask a complete and total centering on self, with a thorough indifference to others.

It is a telling passage, but does it express self-knowledge or self-pity? Or perhaps both? Late in the book, writing in a similar vein, Steward warns of the dangers of engaging too fully with the world, recommending instead the safety of "detachment," of living "untouched in the deeply emotional sense so that no person or thing or situation would ever have the power again to wound." Against the ebullient tone that dominates the autobiography, the unmistakable notes of deprivation and loneliness in these passages hint at a dimension of Steward's life that his autobiography largely evades.

But even though Steward's thousands of sexual encounters had nothing to do with love, it would be inaccurate to say that he filled his life with "meaningless" sex. Rather, every sexual act had meaning for him because it distanced him further from the narrowly religious upbringing he had rejected and affirmed the sexuality that was so central to his sense of self. Steward's Stud File—with its eight hundred carefully typed index cards documenting every sexual encounter of his life with name, date, place, endowment, activity, and (often amusing) supplementary notes—may look like an example of sexual braggadocio, but it was more than a flippant record of sexual conquests. Instead, in a lifetime of disappointments, it constituted a serious account of Steward's strivings for self-fulfillment, a tangible record of his persistent attempts to be who he felt he was meant to be.

Although Steward's autobiography introduced no formal innovations in the genre, he brought to the task of recounting the improbable events of his life the distinctive combination of a scholar's witty allusiveness and a novelist's grasp of narrative form, together with an engaging tendency toward self-deprecation and a droll sense of humor. Consistently fascinating is the apparent ease with which Steward inhabited and performed a range of disparate identities during his life, from dapper English professor to Skid Row tattoo artist, from respected budding novelist to underpaid pornographer. This is a man whose friends ranged from Gertrude Stein and her circle to Sonny Barger and his Hells Angels, a man who on one page converses in French with Thomas Mann about contemporary literature and on another offers a lively explanation of the best way to tattoo a penis. One arrives at the book's subdued last chapter with the sense of having witnessed a life of giant possibilities, some fulfilled, many not, all related by a writer who has sought simply to interest, charm, and entertain us.

At its core, *The Lost Autobiography of Samuel Steward* is a story of living life true to oneself, even if doing so is fraught with risk, even if it relegates you to the margins of society. Driven by his sexuality, refusing to be bound by social convention, and by nature adaptable to setbacks, Steward makes his way through unfamiliar worlds with apparent satisfaction at his frequent good fortune in life and a stoic acceptance of events that turn against him. The result is a curiously uplifting life story that is always compellingly readable and often unexpectedly funny.

CONSTRUCTING THE TEXT OF
THE LOST AUTOBIOGRAPHY OF SAMUEL STEWARD

The task involved in producing this new edition of Steward's autobiography might more precisely be described as constructing rather than merely editing the text. Confronted with two versions of the same story, one twice as long as the other, both problematic for different reasons, I have carefully drawn from both accounts—combining, deleting, and rearranging sentences, paragraphs, and chapters as necessary—to create a more coherent and complete narrative than either offers by itself.

The actual process of developing this final text has of course been less neat and objective than the last sentence might suggest, for autobiographical texts are themselves always fraught with subjectivity. Autobiographers inevitably compose rhetorical rather than strictly factual presentations of themselves and their worlds, and autobiographical "truth" is especially elusive when the writer is as linguistically sophisticated as Steward. Indeed, the two versions we have of his life story illustrate the uncertain foundation of all autobiographies, where the authentic "feel" of the narrative may have at its core either accurate or distorted recollection, factual or artful intent, perceptive self-analysis or blatant self-delusion. A telling example of this fluidity is provided by a paragraph early in Steward's autobiography in which he lists a few remembered incidents from his childhood. In the manuscript, he includes a recollection of his father striking his mother for spilling a jar of ketchup; in the published text, this detail has disappeared. Did Steward remove this sentence because it clashed with the other largely benign childhood recollections in the paragraph or because it presented his father in too negative a light? In either case, fact—if indeed it is a fact—would seem to have been trumped by rhetoric in the final text. And more to the point for this project: should this detail be included or not?

Another key passage from Steward's manuscript offers an example of the way that even pure fiction can masquerade as autobiographical truth. In his manuscript, Steward claims to have sensed in March 1954 that he was about to be fired from his teaching position at DePaul University because of the tattoo business he was operating on Chicago's Skid Row when he was not in the classroom, so when called to a meeting in the dean's office, he went prepared with a resignation letter that he submitted before he could be dismissed. The meeting was hostile, with outbursts like "Hold it just a minute, Fatty" (Steward) and "Just a minute, damn it" (the dean). But in his personal journal, written contemporaneously with the event,[16] Steward described the incident quite differently: though he had had a poor relationship with the dean, his firing that March came as a surprise that sent him staggering back to his office in a state of shock. And subsequent journal passages in which Steward nervously contemplates having to leave teaching and make his living as a full-time tattoo artist clearly suggest that the autobiography's account, composed more than two decades later, is an imagined rendering of the scene as he might have wished that it had played out.

Given the uncertainties that are inherent in all autobiographies, the best outcome one can aspire to in trying to derive a satisfactory text from Steward's two versions of his life—even when the attempt is based on a knowledge of the known facts of Steward's life and a vigilant sensitivity to context and language—is a final text marked by clarity and coherence rather than objective truth. But the possibility of making widely available a full version of Steward's autobiography nonetheless validates this effort, for it is by any measure an unusual story and one that he obviously wanted to tell. Once he had agreed to publish only excerpts from his original manuscript, however, there was no longer any use for the more than 50,000 words that he had to remove, and thus there was seemingly no possibility that a complete narrative of his life in his own words would ever reach a reader. What had begun as a grand attempt to document the story of a most unusual gay life ended as another of Steward's unfinished works.

One key principle has guided this project from the outset: apart from very minor changes in wording necessitated by occasional syntactic or logical problems, my final text consists only of Steward's own words and sentence structures. Thus, for example, a given paragraph in my text may be constructed with sentences taken from two or more other paragraphs, but its coherence is entirely due to my logical ordering of Steward's own sentences and not to any rewriting on my part to make them fit together. In the interest of providing a seamless integration of the two sources and giving the reading experience preference over the behind-the-scenes editorial process, however, I present the final text here without brackets, ellipsis points, or other typographical devices indicating where the narrative draws on one source or the other. To have indicated all such textual moves would have inevitably shifted the focus from Steward's own story of his life to the minutiae of the process by which this form of the story came to exist.

No autobiography is comprehensive, and from his letters and voluminous journals, we now know that Steward omitted many incidents and people from this story of his life, that his fascination with masochistic sex ran far deeper than he suggests here, and that he suffered from extended periods of doubt and depression that are masked by the generally sunny tone of the autobiography.[17] In my annotations, I have tried to provide useful context and background and have identified allusions to people and texts that indicate the breadth of Steward's knowledge, but I have not attempted to create a parallel narrative of his life that corrects and completes the story he tells. Undoubtedly, the choices of inclusion and exclusion that I have made in developing this version of Steward's autobiography are no more free of subjectivity than the choices he himself originally made in composing it. Against that inescapable reality, I can say only that the final text of his autobiography in this volume represents a rigorous, line-by-line comparison of its two sources and that it reflects on every page my deliberate search for completeness and balance, for narrative sense and rhetorical effectiveness, and for faithfulness to Steward's voice as a writer.

WORKING WITH STEWARD'S TEXTS

Steward composed the first version of his autobiography in a conventional way, tracing his life from childhood to the present with a chronology that is discernible, if often incorrect and confusing. But cutting that 110,000-word manuscript by about one-half for publication posed a challenge: if the published version will contain only selected "chapters" from the original autobiography, which chapters can be done away with, and what connections will exist among those that remain?

Steward addressed the task of condensing and reorganizing his manuscript with several strategies. First, he cut large sections of the text: The manuscript's opening two chapters—on his early interest in theater and ballet and on spiritualism and the occult—were eliminated, perhaps because they constituted a rather peculiar way to begin the autobiography and couldn't be fitted in elsewhere (something I also found to be true). Also deleted were chapters and parts of chapters on medical topics—his allergies and his alcoholism, the syphilis he contracted in the late 1920s, his operation for testicular cancer. He slashed the over-long account of his boyhood in Ohio from 14,000 words to 6,000 and the story of his years at Ohio State from 9,600 words to 4,700. Most radically, after devoting only a page and a half to his hiring by Loyola University in 1936, he dropped all further discussion of his teaching career, which actually continued for twenty more years, first at Loyola University and subsequently at DePaul University, where for several years in the 1950s he lived a perilous double life as an English professor and a Skid Row tattoo artist.

Steward then dealt with the matter of coherence among the remaining pieces of his manuscript by simply abandoning chronology in the second half of the book. The first four chapters trace his life from childhood through graduate school and his early teaching positions up to his move to Chicago in 1936 and his first meeting with Gertrude Stein in 1937. But after this point, Steward stripped out the narrative connections between chapters as they had appeared in the manuscript and now presented the formerly linked chapters as separate stories about various loosely related aspects of his life: his tattooing career; his friendship with Alfred Kinsey; his pornography authorship as Phil Andros; his most memorable sex partners in Chicago.[18]

Steward's third revision strategy was to shrink the text that remained by deleting details and reducing dialogue and commentary. The resulting prose may be quite readable, but when compared with the corresponding text in the manuscript, it appears markedly less precise and vivid. However, the condensed text in *Chapters* cannot simply be ignored in favor of the manuscript, for in the process of shortening that text for publication, Steward often improved it by rewriting sentences and even adding new details. Consequently, when both sources address the same events or topics, the best final text is often the manuscript text enhanced by the changes he made as he was cutting it down for use in *Chapters*.

An analysis of Steward's two versions of a passage about his summer work at Glacier National Park in 1935 illustrates his editing strategy and also demonstrates why a satisfactory final text must draw on both sources. The manuscript version of this episode below consists of 630 words; the underlining indicates the material that he subsequently deleted in order to reduce the passage to 342 words for publication.

MANUSCRIPT (630 WORDS)

It was all my own little kingdom for a while, after my superior left. Into this idyllic summer burst Clayton like a small whirlwind—brash, young, handsome, arrogant. From the first there was a personality clash—and all kinds of attempted rearrangements. The two of us did not get along together at all, and the rest of the summer was filled with scores and draws—a hundred incidents and annoyances, the battle between us becoming a kind of deadly game. I remembered Blake's poem, "A Poison Tree," and tried to find the apple with which to do him in—maintaining a false and sunny simplicity while I stabbed him in the back. And he did the same to me but less cleverly. We were two good Christians being nice to each other.

My search for the ultimate stratagem was complicated by the fact that we both shared the same cabin—but I had one advantage. I did not drink on duty—and he did; moreover, he could not hold his liquor well, had blackouts, and was several times caught by Mrs. Barley, the hotel manager. By the end of his first four weeks there, everyone was aware of the feud between us; and most of them blamed him for it. People saw through his clumsy tricks, and ended by siding with me. I let them.

And there was one other complication. Despite my dislike of his dirty tricks, his brashness and arrogance and all the rest, I found him extremely attractive physically.

He kept on creating ruin for himself—racing the horses down the mountainside from Sperry Glacier, which made the cowboy foreman, old Angus, madder than hell; and drinking too much. One night he was put off the dance floor during the square dance, drunk, and that was the night that I helped him to bed and ministered unto him.

Unfortunately, he did not have the memory blackout that night which he should have had, and the next day he told Mrs. Barley, who sent for me.

"I'll get right to the point," the ancient white-haired little lady said; there was no nonsense about her. "Clayton said that after the dance last night you made homosexual advances to him."

It rocked me to hear her use the word; she looked so sweet and grandmotherly that you wouldn't have believed it to be in her vocabulary. Still,
in the hotel business . . .

"That's outrageous!" I said violently.

"Please," she said. "Everyone knows about the feeling between you and
Clayton this summer. And I'm no fool. If you really dislike each other as
much as you obviously do, the last thing he should have accused you of
would be that. It wasn't sensible. I told him so. I said I thought he was just
trying to do you damage."

I opened my mouth to speak. She held up her hand.

"I also told him," she said, "that we could manage to do without his services from this evening on. He can pack and take the six-thirty bus to the
station. If I were you, I would arrange to have someone in your cabin while
he packs." She looked at me. "Why not Bull? You seem to get along with him
very well. I'll excuse him from his duties between six and seven. That might
be the easiest way for all of us."

And then her bittersweet old face actually crinkled into a smile. She
stood up behind the desk and extended her hand. "It's a real pleasure to
have you here," she said. "Everyone thinks you're a gentleman. And that includes me."

We shook hands, and I smiled and thanked her.

Bull moved into the vacant bunk in my cabin, and the rest of the summer was very interesting.

The *Chapters* version of this incident is not simply shorter; with less explanation of the clash between Steward and Clayton, no mention of Clayton's
drinking and blackouts, and only half of the dialogue with Mrs. Barley (who
is not named), and without Steward's characteristically appropriate literary
allusion and the charming surprise that the diminutive Mrs. Barley knows
the word *homosexual* in 1935, the text as published reads more like a sum-
mary of the event than a retelling of it. Yet Steward also added the two new
passages underlined below, both of which would quite nicely fill gaps in the
manuscript text. (He also changed the line "'That's outrageous!' I said violently" to the more visual "I sputtered with histrionic rage.")

CHAPTERS (342 WORDS)

It was all my own little kingdom for a while, until brash young handsome
Clayton burst like a small whirlwind onto the scene. He was loud and bossy;

we didn't get along. It was a classic case of personality clash, which eventually turned into backstabbing as the summer went on. The whole hotel was aware of our feud, although it was a quiet one with no loud arguing.

One of the major difficulties was that we had to room together in a very small log cabin. The other was that physically Clayton was very attractive to me — a heavy sexual aura, extremely handsome with black curly hair, and a body with excellently-defined musculature. Watching him undress from my lower bunk bed created both temptation and desire in me. And one evening when there was a dance in one of the buildings, Clayton broke all the rules, got drunk and danced with the "dudes," and was put off the floor.

I was in bed when he came to the cabin drunk much later, and had to help him get undressed. It was too much for me. He could not climb up into his own bunk, so he slept in mine — and so did I, moving to the upper one in the early dawn. Put another card into my Stud File.

The next day Clayton went to the manager and accused me of making homosexual advances to him, and the manager called me in. She was a tiny grandmotherly woman with white hair. She told me what he had said.

I sputtered with histrionic outrage. She silenced me with her hand.

"It's nonsense, I know," she said. "Anyone who has watched you two squabble all summer would know that homosexual advances would be the last thing you would make. Clayton was drunk and obnoxious, and I have already asked him to leave. Why don't you ask Bull to be there while he packs?"

I did — and Clayton left, furious. Bull moved into the cabin, and the rest of the summer was very interesting indeed.

My final text of 570 words mainly follows the manuscript but incorporates the new text added to the *Chapters* version. I deleted the puzzling phrase "all kinds of attempted rearrangements" and a few other small items, and I borrowed the short sentence "He was loud and bossy" and the phrase "very small log cabin" from the *Chapters* text. Of the two endings, I chose the one in *Chapters* for the effective briskness of Steward's final five sentences, even though doing so meant forgoing the handshake and final compliment that Steward received from Mrs. Barley in the manuscript:

FINAL TEXT (570 WORDS)

It was all my own little kingdom for a while after my superior left and before brash young handsome Clayton burst into this idyllic summer like a small whirlwind. From the first, there was a personality clash. He was loud and bossy. The two of us did not get along together at all, and the rest of the summer was filled with scores and draws—a hundred incidents and annoyances, the battle between us becoming a kind of deadly game. I remembered Blake's poem "A Poison Tree" and tried to find the apple with which to do him in—maintaining a false and sunny simplicity while I stabbed him in the back. And he did the same to me but less cleverly. By the end of his first four weeks there, everyone was aware of the feud between us, and most of them blamed him for it. People saw through his clumsy tricks and ended by siding with me. I let them.

My search for the ultimate stratagem was complicated by the fact that we had to room together in a very small log cabin. But I had one advantage: I did not drink on duty—and he did. Moreover, he could not hold his liquor well, had blackouts, and was several times caught by Mrs. Barley, the hotel manager. And there was one other complication. Despite my dislike of his dirty tricks, his brashness and arrogance and all the rest, I found him extremely attractive physically—a heavy sexual aura, extremely handsome with black curly hair and a body with excellently defined musculature. Watching him undress from my lower bunk bed created both temptation and desire in me.

One night he was put off the dance floor during the square dance, drunk, and that was the night that I ministered unto him. I was in bed when he came to the cabin and had to help him get undressed. It was too much for me. He could not climb up into his own bunk, so he slept in mine—and so did I, moving to the upper one in the early dawn. Put another card into my Stud File.

Unfortunately, he did not have the memory blackout that night which he should have had, and the next day he told Mrs. Barley, who sent for me.

"I'll get right to the point," the ancient white-haired little lady said; there was no nonsense about her. "Clayton said that after the dance last night you made homosexual advances to him." It rocked me to hear her use the word; she looked so sweet and grandmotherly that you wouldn't have believed it to be in her vocabulary.

I sputtered with histrionic outrage. She silenced me with her hand.

"It's nonsense, I know," she said. "Anyone who has watched you two squabble all summer would know that homosexual advances would be the last thing you would make. Clayton was drunk and obnoxious, and I have already asked him to leave. He can pack and take the six-thirty bus to the station. If I were you, I would arrange to have someone in your cabin while he packs." She looked at me. "Why don't you ask Bull to be there? You seem to get along with him very well."

I did—and Clayton left, furious. Bull moved into the vacant bunk in my cabin, and the rest of the summer was very interesting indeed.

Besides highlighting the contributions that both of Steward's texts make, this example illustrates my goal of constructing a new text by moving or deleting—but not altering—his original words. In the sections that follow below, I demonstrate how closely I was able to adhere to that principle as I dealt with several different kinds of editorial problems.

Repositioning Sentences

One curious source of confusion in Steward's prose in his autobiography— stemming, perhaps, from the fact that it was composed on a typewriter— is that sentences that manifestly belong in one paragraph have somehow ended up in another. Usually this problem can be solved without altering any words simply by repositioning the misplaced sentences. In the following straightforward example, the underlined sentence about Hatcher's books belongs not in the paragraph about the Hatcher myth but in the following one about the Hatcher reality. (Here, as elsewhere, I've altered Steward's sometimes idiosyncratic punctuation.)

MANUSCRIPT, 113–14

[T]he stories about Hatcher were even more vivacious than those about Claire. Harlan had, it was said, been a Kaintucky mountain boy, who showed up at some tiny Ohio college barefoot in a raggedy Huck Finn costume—and had astounded everyone by his brilliance and the way he sailed through college. He was never able to divest himself of this absurd rumor, and seemed not to care about it at all. He had written three novels: Tunnel Hill [1931], Patterns of Wolfpen [1934], Central Standard Time [1937], and a book of literary criticism: Creating the Modern American Novel [1935].

Actually, Harlan was born in 1899 in Ohio, reared in Kentucky, graduated with the usual degrees (BA, MA, PhD) from The Ohio State University—with some time at Chicago and a year in Europe. He was as brilliant as Andrews, no doubt, but his personality was quieter. Yet he was a stalwart in the fight for academic freedom in actuality and in theory; and he harmed himself at Ohio State by taking up the cause of a professor fired without reason by the regents.

FINAL TEXT

[T]he stories about Hatcher were even more vivacious than those about Claire. Harlan had, it was said, been a Kaintucky mountain boy who showed up at some tiny Ohio college barefoot in a raggedy Huck Finn costume and had astounded everyone by his brilliance and the way he sailed through college. He was never able to divest himself of this absurd rumor and seemed not to care about it at all.

Actually, Harlan was born in 1899 in Ohio, reared in Kentucky, graduated with the usual degrees (BA, MA, PhD) from The Ohio State University, with some time at Chicago and a year in Europe. He had written three novels — *Tunnel Hill* (1931), *Patterns of Wolfpen* (1934), *Central Standard Time* (1937) — and a book of literary criticism, *Creating the Modern American Novel* (1935). He was as brilliant as Andrews, no doubt, but his personality was quieter. Yet he was a stalwart in the fight for academic freedom in actuality and in theory, and he harmed himself at Ohio State by taking up the cause of a professor fired without reason by the regents.

Sometimes sentences that clearly belong together in one paragraph are found scattered among two or more other paragraphs. In this example, the underlined sentences are about Steward's free time while working in Glacial National Park in 1935; the other sentences describe his job.

MANUSCRIPT, 166–67

On days when there was no sun, the Garden Wall turned grey and silver and its reflection shimmered in the green-black waters of Lake McDonald. You were free to take a saddle-horse ride when you didn't have to work, or to go fishing in the noisy streams in the afternoon.

Only in the evenings, every evening, did you have to put on a suit and try to sell saddle-horse trips to the dude tourists, pack trips into the wilderness, complete with authentic cowboy guide. For this small restriction of your freedom you were paid a few bucks a week. You ate in the main dining room, slept in a small cabin, and in general enjoyed your paid vacation. And for fun — there was always trying to make Bull, a tall, grey-eyed butch bellboy.

"Information clerk" was a misnomer — my real duties were selling those trips at outrageous fees. You developed quite a line as you learned more about the work and talked to the dudes — low and sexy to the gals, man-to-man to the guys—about the wonders of solitude, of sleeping under the million stars, of coffee brewed over an open fire, and steaks sizzling. You never said anything about the mosquitoes, the ever-present wood-ticks, the dangers of spotted fever and you soft-pedaled the extraordinary price of the tours.

Reorganized with one paragraph about his job and the other about his free time, the passage is much clearer:

FINAL TEXT

On days when there was no sun, the Garden Wall turned grey and silver, and its reflection shimmered in the green-black waters of Lake McDonald.

"Information clerk" was a misnomer. My real duties—only in the evenings, every evening—were putting on a suit and trying to sell saddle-horse trips at outrageous fees to the dude tourists, pack trips into the wilderness, complete with authentic cowboy guide. You developed quite a line as you learned more about the work and talked to the dudes—low and sexy to the gals, man-to-man to the guys—about the wonders of solitude, of sleeping under the million stars, of coffee brewed over an open fire and steaks sizzling. You never said anything about the mosquitoes, the ever-present wood ticks, and the dangers of spotted fever and snakes, and you soft-pedaled the extraordinary price of the tours.

For this small restriction of your freedom, you were paid a few bucks a week. You ate in the main dining room, slept in a small cabin, and in general enjoyed your paid vacation. You were free to take a saddle-horse ride when you didn't have to work or to go fishing in the noisy streams in the afternoon. In the chalet, the fire burned every evening in a fireplace large enough to sit inside on rough log benches. And for fun, there was always trying to make Bull, a tall, grey-eyed butch bellboy.

A more complicated example of confusion caused by misplaced sentences is Steward's powerful but disjointed chapter tracing his battle with alcoholism, a chapter whose incoherence may perhaps reflect his difficulty in engaging this subject. The passages below appear on pages 83–84 and 88 of the manuscript and are separated by a lengthy but irrelevant excerpt from one of his *Illinois Dental Journal* essays that I deleted. The sentences I used in constructing a new, more chronological version of this passage—again with no changes in the original wording—are underlined and numbered according to their sequence in my revised text. (Some of the remaining sentences were used elsewhere.)

MANUSCRIPT, 83–84, 88

How is it possible to collapse nearly seventeen years of drinking into a small space? How tiresome it would be to try to recall and list all the mistakes and dreadful events—Emmy's broken finger, the loss of friends, the insults, the time I slapped my sister. And there were the mornings when with a towel around your neck you seized the towel-end and shot-glass together and pulled, to steady the alcohol on its way to your mouth. (2) <u>These were the vacant years, the empty years, when the blackouts steadily increased— until sometimes I had to take to marking the calendar with crosses, the way a convict might in prison, so that I could remember what day it was—and whether I had to teach at that time.</u>

They tell you in Alcoholics Anonymous and elsewhere that each drunk has his own "bottom" to hit, and that these "bottoms" are layered at all levels—the very lowest being the gutters of Skid Row, or jail, or periods in the psychiatric wards. As for my own "bottom"—well, (4a) <u>I somehow usually made it back to my apartment, though in what condition of befuddlement and befouling I hate to recall—but I never landed in jail for drunkenness, nor did I miss classes, nor did I lose my position</u> as a professor. At the university in Chicago at which I was teaching, among the Jesuits, there were too many drunks at the time on the faculty for my case to be outstanding. In a room where all are eating garlic, so to speak, no one can smell another. At any rate, I always showed up for class (4b)—<u>even though I strongly suspect that I was perhaps the only professor who ever fell asleep in class while he was lecturing; usually it was the students who nodded off. And though it was a nap of perhaps only three or four seconds, it was nonetheless enough to startle me into complete wakefulness for the rest of the period—especially when I saw the wide eyes of the handsome basketball player locked quizzically on me when I awoke. . . .</u>

[Twelve unrelated paragraphs]

(1) <u>By the time I reached Chicago and started teaching there in the autumn of 1936, I was fairly established as a secret drunk. Things grow steadily worse for the next ten years, until I was consuming—at home in my apartment—a quart a day, to which must be added the shots I had en route to and from class.</u> (3) <u>It was a period filled with dreadful scenes, the gradual loss of friend after friend, the deterioration of my health and sleep patterns, the</u>

inexorably growing loss of memory, and the slow ruin of my potency and my body. Yet (5) at this distance removed from such a dark night of the soul, I do not wish to recover in memory the frightfulness of it. I have pulled down the window shade and done my best to expunge it completely. Moreover, it would be of interest only to another ex-lush. Behind the shade the details have not festered nor reached out to trouble me; they are viewed with regret and a sense of loss for the seventeen years which might have permitted me to become a writer, a thing I much wanted at one time. But they are not mourned and wept over. They have really and truly been mostly forgotten, save when—with sadly shaking head—I recall some dreadful episode, and say to myself "God, how awful I was!" For of the cutely named six stages of drunkenness—jocose, amorous, bellicose, morose, lachrymose, and comatose—I was familiar with every one, but especially two, three and six. But oh, when I drank, I was a prince of the world; I commanded fire and flames!

FINAL TEXT

By the time I reached Chicago and started teaching there in the autumn of 1936, I was fairly established as a secret drunk. Things grew steadily worse for the next ten years, until I was consuming—at home in my apartment—a quart a day, to which must be added the shots I had en route to and from class. These were the vacant years, the empty years, when the blackouts steadily increased—until sometimes I had to take to marking the calendar with crosses, the way a convict might in prison, so that I could remember what day it was—and whether I had to teach at that time. It was a period filled with dreadful scenes, the gradual loss of friend after friend, the deterioration of my health and sleep patterns, the inexorably growing loss of memory, and the slow ruin of my potency and my body. I somehow usually made it back to my apartment, though in what condition of befuddlement and befouling I hate to recall. But I never landed in jail for drunkenness, nor did I miss classes, nor did I lose my position—even though I strongly suspect that I was perhaps the only professor who ever fell asleep in class while he was lecturing. And though it was a nap of perhaps only three or four seconds, it was nonetheless enough to startle me into complete wakefulness for the rest of the period—especially when I saw the wide eyes of the handsome basketball player locked quizzically on me when I awoke.

At this distance removed from such a dark night of the soul, I do not wish to recover in memory the frightfulness of it; I have pulled down the window shade and done my best to expunge it completely. Moreover, it would be of interest only to another ex-lush. Behind the shade, the details have not festered nor reached out to trouble me. They are viewed with regret and a sense of loss for the seventeen years which might have permitted me to become a writer, a thing I much wanted at one time, but they are not mourned and wept over. They have really and truly been mostly forgotten, save when—with sadly shaking head—I recall some dreadful episode and say to myself: "God, how awful I was!"

Integrating Sources

The Glacier National Park episode discussed at the beginning of this section provided an example of my editing practice when integrating complementary passages from the manuscript and *Chapters* texts. The situation is more complicated—and the editorial decisions admittedly even more subjective—when the two sources constitute competing rather than complementary texts. A revealing example of such a case is the pair of paragraphs in which Steward lists some seemingly random childhood reminiscences.

MANUSCRIPT, 34–35

Not much of my childhood remains in my memory. When I was three or four, I remember how my arm pained me when my mother held my hand as I walked beside her, thus pulling it straight up. And when we lived for a while in Richmond, Virginia, because my father in one of his innumerable jobs worked for the International Harvester Company, I went across the street to a vacant lot and set fire to it. People came with brooms to swat it out; I do not remember any fire engines. From the Richmond period I also recall the first grade, when I stood and asked to go to the toilet—at which Miss Munday, the teacher, put her finger vertically across her lips and held one finger up in the air. The toilet was in the basement; the stalls were dank and green with slime. I remember also in Richmond my mother dropped a jar of homemade tomato catsup and the lid came off, spilling the catsup all over the kitchen floor, at which my father hit her across the face. I also recall reading a child's book while I lay flat on my stomach; a few feet away my baby sister, five years younger, was on the potty, and a bit of shit exploded from her tiny behind, to fall precisely on King Arthur's face. And once, I was roller-skating on the street near a telephone pole, the kind that had climbing spikes sticking out the sides; a begoggled motorcyclist rounded the corner from Monument Avenue, hit the curb, flew thirty feet into the air, and punctured his skull pan on a spike. He hung there a moment and then his body fell to the ground, dead, with brains and blood scattered all over the sidewalk. This accident haunted my nightmares for a long time.

For publication, Steward condensed the paragraph and also made it somewhat less grim by altering the first sentence, deleting the toilet and ketchup incidents, and changing "shit" to "poop."

CHAPTERS, 2

Luckily, not much of my childhood remains in my memory, but I think it was sheltered and pleasant enough. When I was three or four, I remember how painful it was when my mother held my hand as I walked beside her, for my arm was pulled straight up. In Richmond, Virginia, where we lived for a while because my father had one of his innumerable jobs there, I went across the street to a vacant lot and set fire to the dry grass. I also recall lying on my stomach reading a child's book about King Arthur while a few feet away my sister Virginia, five years younger, was on the potty, and a bit of poop exploded from her tiny behind, to fall directly on King Arthur's face. And once I was roller-skating on the street near a telephone pole, the kind that had climbing-spikes out the sides; a motorcyclist with goggles rounded the corner from Monument Avenue too fast, hit the curb and flew into the air. His skullpan was punctured on a spike. He hung there a moment and then fell to the ground dead, with brains and blood splattered all over the sidewalk. This accident furnished me with nightmares for a long time.

But "sheltered and pleasant enough," Steward's opening addition to the published text, presents an idea not borne out by the details that follow in either version of this paragraph, and the phrase seems particularly unconvincing as the description of the life of a child whose mother died when he was six, whose alcoholic and drug-addicted father was mostly absent, and whose aunts raised him while at the same time attending to the endless work of operating a rooming house. Striving for a logical middle course between the manuscript and the published text, my integration of these two paragraphs follows the shorter published version but deletes "sheltered and pleasant enough," includes the telling incident of the spilled ketchup, and parenthetically adds a sentence from an otherwise deleted manuscript chapter that bears directly on the content of this paragraph. Again, all the words are Steward's.

Not much of my childhood remains in my memory. I remember how painful it was when my mother held my hand as I walked beside her when I was three or four, for my arm was pulled straight up. In Richmond, Virginia, where we lived for a while because my father had one of his innumerable jobs there, I went across the street to a vacant lot and set fire to the dry grass. (I could not have known then that "between jobs" was the family's way of covering the fact that my father had twice taken the Keeley cure for alcoholism and opium addiction and had also dabbled in laudanum and morphine.) I remember also in Richmond my mother dropped a jar of homemade tomato catsup and the lid came off, spilling the catsup all over the kitchen floor, at which my father hit her across the face. I also recall lying on my stomach reading a child's book about King Arthur while a few feet away my sister Virginia, five years younger, was on the potty, and a bit of poop exploded from her tiny behind, to fall directly on King Arthur's face. And once I was roller-skating on the street near a telephone pole, the kind that had climbing spikes out the sides; a motorcyclist with goggles rounded the corner from Monument Avenue too fast, hit the curb, and flew into the air. His skull-pan was punctured on a spike. He hung there a moment and then fell to the ground dead, with brains and blood splattered all over the sidewalk. This accident furnished me with nightmares for a long time.

Editing Syntax

When it was diction or syntax itself that created confusion in a passage, minor adjustments in wording were unavoidable. In this case, for example, the problem in the original text is that Eva and the landlady seem to be different people:

CHAPTERS, 130

My landlady's ancient father died, and Eva's daughter got her a long-haired dachshund, a feisty little beast name Fritz. And after two years Eva died.

The ancient father of my landlady, Eva, died, and her daughter got her a longhaired dachshund, a feisty little beast name Fritz. And after two years, Eva herself died.

In the following example, the three words underlined in the revision were necessary to eliminate the confusing passives at the start of the original text. After that, I rearranged Steward's own sentences to reveal more clearly the paragraph's underlying cause-effect structure: his new business practices produced more customers.

MANUSCRIPT, 264–65

After Randy was shaken out of his money-tree and the shop made as clean and inviting as it could be, the trickle of customers began to increase until it was a stream, a river, and on some Saturdays a torrent. I gave out cards to everyone who got tattooed; there were instructions printed on the back and address and so on on the recto. Always to sailors in those days I gave several cards to pass around at Great Lakes. And I kept my prices at approximately one-half of what the others charged.

It worked. . . .

FINAL TEXT

<u>With</u> Randy shaken out of his money tree, <u>I made</u> the shop as clean and inviting as it could be. I gave out cards to everyone who got tattooed; there were instructions printed on the back and address and so on on the recto. To sailors in those days I always gave several cards to pass around at Great Lakes. And I kept my prices at approximately one-half of what the others charged. It worked: the trickle of customers began to increase until it was a stream, a river, and on some Saturdays a torrent.

Sometimes, as in the following case, the confusion in the text was more complicated and required a bit more editorial intervention. The Supreme Court case that Steward alludes to but does not mention by name is *Memoirs v. Massachusetts* (1966), but the syntax misleadingly suggests that he is citing *Roth v. United States*. In the context of the narrative, moreover, the only relevant point about this case is the last one, which crucially altered the definition of obscenity laid out in the earlier *Roth* decision. The paragraph is clarified with the deletion of the irrelevant material and the addition of just six words (underlined).

CHAPTERS, 115

In the United States in the mid-1960s, a case came before the Supreme Court, one intended to settle the question of obscenity, the famous Roth decision of 1957, in which the nine quarrelsome old men came to the conclusion that obscenity had three criteria: (1) it had to appeal to the prurient interest of the average man; (2) it had to violate contemporary community standards; and (3) it had to be utterly without any redeeming social value.

FINAL TEXT

In the United States in the mid-1960s, a case came before the Supreme Court, one intended to settle the question of obscenity <u>addressed by</u> the famous Roth decision of 1957. The nine quarrelsome old men <u>now</u> came to the conclusion that obscenity <u>required a work</u> to be utterly without any redeeming social value.

Copyediting

Edits like the following, which would fall under the rubric of copyediting, also naturally involved minor changes in wording (added words underlined; deleted words struck out).

PARALLEL CONSTRUCTION ERRORS

<u>They wanted</u> not only ~~did they want~~ the skull with wings but other designs.
Either I would have to become a master of argot or ~~have~~ <u>I would need</u> someone in my shop . . .

SMALL EDITS FOR CLARITY OR CORRECTNESS

In ~~the~~ <u>my</u> seventeen visits to her . . .
As an undergraduate, ~~there was~~ <u>I had</u> little time for writing.

Other Editorial Considerations

A few final notes are in order about idiosyncratic features of Steward's prose. In most of his writing, Steward employs square brackets where parentheses would be normal, and in this work, he also sometimes ends a paragraph with ellipsis points, seemingly to suggest his wistfulness or the paragraph's deliberate incompleteness. To avoid any confusion between these marks and the marks traditionally used to indicate editorial insertions or deletions, I have changed all of Steward's square brackets to parentheses in the final text and have deleted most of his ellipsis points when they appear at the end of a paragraph.

I have also standardized mechanics, including Steward's somewhat irregular punctuation, according to the *Chicago Manual of Style*, 16th edition. For example, his characteristic commas between compound predicates ("I grew more and more irritated with the double game Winthrop played, and felt that I had to interfere") have been cut; by the same token, when Steward omits the comma that is normal in a compound *sentence*, I have in most cases inserted it.

Steward almost always introduces restrictive relative clauses with *which* rather than the now-preferred *that*, but since that usage was accepted at the time he wrote and changing it would involve altering words in the text, I have let it stand.[19] A few of his other stylistic idiosyncrasies have also been preserved. He has a tendency here, as in earlier writings, to assemble multiple adjectives before a noun without separating coordinate modifiers with a comma: "a square-jawed handsome blond giant," "a decaying ghostly gothic mansion." This feature is so characteristic, and its effect often so rhythmically interesting, that I have not tampered with the absence of punctuation. Steward's characteristic preference for some British spellings ("criticise," "timbre") has also been retained. He is fond of em dashes, and I have let them stand unless a colon or comma clearly seems called for to prevent confusion. (He does occasionally forget the second em dash to close a parenthetical insertion, and in those cases I have replaced his comma with the missing dash.) Here, as in other writings, Steward uses "coupla" to mean "couple of," a usage that he seems to have acquired from Gertrude Stein's conversation.

Finally, typos and related errors (for example, "provided over" for "presided over") have been silently corrected; similarly, a very few apparently dropped words have been supplied.

A NOTE ON NAMES AND TITLES

Steward did not wish his autobiography to compromise the privacy of anyone with whom he had had a sexual encounter, and to protect the identities
of some figures as he prepared *Chapters from an Autobiography* for publication, he occasionally omitted last names that appear in the manuscript, replaced last names with initials, or (as in chapter 13) used pseudonyms. In
developing this text, I have adapted Steward's practice in this way: names
that Steward published in *Chapters* appear in the same form in this volume,
but names that are found only in the unpublished manuscript have been replaced in this text with pseudonyms. In nonsexual contexts, Steward identified people in the manuscript and in *Chapters* sometimes by a full name,
sometimes by a first name and final initial, and sometimes by a first name
alone. In these cases, I have followed his choices despite their apparent in-
consistencies.

With the exception of chapters 8 and 15, chapter titles are taken or adapted
from Steward's original titles in the manuscript or in *Chapters*.

NOTES

1 Spring quotes Steward writing in 1977, at age 68, that he had documented 4,541 separate encounters with 801 men (380). Steward described his boyhood visit to Valentino's Columbus, Ohio, hotel room in a 1989 interview with Carl Maves ("Valentino's
Pubic Hair and Me," *The Advocate*, June 6, 1989, 72–74). In *Chapters*, Steward noted
that in high school he had sex with "four members of the football team, all of the
basketball, three of the track" (12) and described his 1937 meeting with Lord Alfred
Douglas (44–51). His encounter with Roy Fitzgerald (Rock Hudson), when the two of
them were working in Marshall Field's department store in December 1946, is documented in Steward's Stud File; see also Spring, 94n. Steward observed that during his
years at DePaul "there were a half-dozen contacts between certain handsome male
students and their beloved teacher" (Manuscript, 251), three of which are also documented in the Stud File. He later estimated that over the years in Chicago he had had
sex with "a coupla hundred" sailors (quoted in Spring, 85).

2 Steward's original Stud File card index is in the Yale Steward Papers.

3 *Dear Sammy: Letters from Gertrude Stein and Alice B. Toklas*, ed. Samuel M. Steward
(Boston: Houghton Mifflin, 1977).

4 *Chapters*, ix.

5 Twain described the plan for his autobiographical chapters, serialized in 1906–7 in
the *North American Review*, by saying, "I shall talk about the matter which for the
moment interests me, and cast it aside and talk about something else the moment

its interest for me is exhausted. . . . It is a system which is a complete and purposed jumble" (*Chapters from My Autobiography* [Oxford: Benediction Classics, 2011], 2).

6   *Chapters*, ix.

7   Ibid.

8   The text that I constructed in this volume draws on approximately 75 percent of the manuscript and 85 percent of *Chapters from an Autobiography*.

9   The corresponding first paragraphs of the narrative are in chapter 1 in *Chapters* but chapter 3 in the manuscript.

10   George Chauncey, *Gay New York: Gender, Urban Culture, and the Making of the Gay Male World 1890–1940* (New York: Basic Books, 1994). Of course, there are and always have been many gay lives that do not revolve around city life. For recent discussions of some of those stories, see, for example, Will Fellows, *Farm Boys: Lives of Gay Men from the Rural Midwest* (Madison: University of Wisconsin Press, 1996); John Howard, *Men Like That: A Southern Queer History* (Chicago: University of Chicago Press, 1999); Mary L. Gray, *Out in the Country: Youth, Media, and Queer Visibility in Rural America* (New York: NYU Press, 2009); Scott Herring, *Another Country: Queer Anti-Urbanism* (New York: NYU Press, 2010); and Colin R. Johnson, *Just Queer Folks: Gender and Sexuality in Rural America* (Philadelphia: Temple University Press, 2013). For a wide-ranging examination of queer life in twentieth-century Chicago, see St. Sukie de la Croix, *Chicago Whispers: A History of LGBT Chicago before Stonewall* (Madison: University of Wisconsin Press, 2012).

11   Allen Drexel, "Before Paris Burned: Race, Class, and Homosexuality on the Chicago South Side, 1935–1960," in *Creating a Place for Ourselves: Lesbian, Gay, and Bisexual Community Histories*, ed. Brett Beemyn (New York: Routledge, 1997), 137.

12   David K. Johnson, "The Kids of Fairytown: Gay Male Culture on Chicago's North Side in the 1930s," in *Creating a Place for Ourselves*, ed. Brett Beemyn, 113–14.

13   See "A Note on Names and Titles" below.

14   "Alfred Kinsey and Homosexuality in the '50s," interview with Samuel Steward by Len Evans, ed. Terence Kissack, *Journal of the History of Sexuality* 9 (2000): 479–80.

15   "Steward on Sex: The Author of 'Phil Andros' Looks Back," interview with Samuel Steward by Eric Rofes, *The Advocate*, December 11, 1984, 90.

16   Which actually occurred in March 1956.

17   On Steward's depression, see, for example, Spring, 90–91, 94–95.

18   Steward had already edited and published several of these chapters as separate magazine articles. See Spring, 391.

19   Even the *Chicago Manual of Style* did not explicitly address the distinction between *that* and *which* until the 14th edition (1993).

Chapter One

WOODSFIELD, OHIO

1909–27

In winter, the snow sometimes fell thick in Woodsfield, melted for a day under a feeble sun, and froze again during the night. Then it was possible to take a toboggan holding about five persons, go to the top of Reservoir Hill at the north end of town, get on, and with a wild whooping go sliding down the street through town, a mile and a half, to the Catholic Church at the south end. Without knowing exactly why, I always managed to sit in front of the school's handsomest basketball player, who wrapped his long arms around me, holding me tight, and pressed his long legs close against each side of my body. I was about ten years old.

Woodsfield, Ohio, was the county seat, in those days a sleepy little town. It still is. It has grown worse; it has been arrested in time. It had a narrow-gauge railroad and a county courthouse with a huge round dome in which were set four clock faces, and beneath the dome a columned structure housing a large bell that struck the hours. Since my father at one time was county auditor, I had access to this mysterious region, and after finding out what I was and getting to the proper age, I used to take tricks up there.

Woodsfield sprawled considerably for a small town; the little white houses were spaced far apart. There were many trees shading the brick streets—not macadam or asphalt, but honest red paving bricks. There was no west side to the town; it lay north, south, and east—and curiously enough, the wealthiest families were not bunched together but existed side by side with the average ones. The Monroe Bank was run by the Mooney family, who had the largest yard in town and a beautiful house with four two-story white columns in front and a porch that ran almost entirely around the house. It was situated next to the Shafer house; the Mooneys and Shafers were related. Oh, how

The Morris House in Woodsfield, Ohio. (Courtesy of the Estate of Samuel M. Steward)

grand they were, this "society" of Woodsfield! Yet it was the Monroe Bank that was the first bank in town to fail, taking with it the savings of innumerable farmers from the surrounding countryside. Many of the townspeople were secretly pleased when the bank failed—provided, that is, they did not lose much money—for they saw the disaster as bringing the Mooneys down a peg . . . and that of course was as it should be in a democracy. Puttin' on all them airs. Served 'em right.

I lived in a two-story boarding house that my Grandfather Morris built. Its small rooms were rented out to traveling salesmen, and there was a dining room where three meals a day were served. Thus my maiden aunts made a living for themselves and their parents—a rather cheerless existence of cooking and serving, making beds and washing, and tending the garden when there was time for it.

The Morris House was about a half block from the town square and the courthouse. Diagonally across the street from our house was the Methodist Church with its square bell tower, and alongside the church ran an alley down a small incline which led over to Paul Street. The alley was the path I took to grade school. For those days, the schoolhouse must have been a magnificent building—all of red brick, set in a wide lawn with trees (and right next to the Mooney house, too, from which it was separated by a high impenetrable hedge).

a two-story boarding house. The house survives, in the form of a somewhat ramshackle apartment building, at 131 North Main Street in Woodsfield.

Woodsfield was a WASP town, certainly—white, Anglo-Saxon, and Protestant. There was an abundance of Catholics—"Catlickers" they were called—and all the good Methodists, Presbyterians, Baptists, and the rest tried to ignore them and were even a bit frightened of them. For were not the basements of their church and rectory and convent stacked with rifles and ammunition against the day when the Catlickers would take over the world? And were there not secret subterranean tunnels leading from the priest's house to the nuns' house, where vile things happened at night? Oh my yes . . . and we believed it all.

There was one Jewish family—Mike Schahet, who had a daughter Lily. His presence was tolerated in town because he was a junk dealer—real junk, that is, the metal and rubber kind—and thus beneath the notice of everyone. And there was one black family, who lived across the street from my Aunt Tillie; curiously (and some thought it a disgrace) my Aunt Matilda's married name was Cooper, and that too was the name of the Negro (we did not call them black in those days), who happened to be a chiropractor. He had a wife and daughter. When I was eight or nine, playing on Aunt Tillie's front lawn one afternoon, I saw a car drive up—an old Model T Ford sedan, with isinglass window curtains up in place. It belonged to the town butcher (I recognized it), and out jumped four men in white sheets and peaked hats—the dreaded Ku Klux Klan! They ran into the Negro Cooper's house and brought him struggling into the car and drove off with him, leaving me paralyzed with shock. The next day his wife and child left, and none of them was ever heard from again; their house and furnishings were sold at auction. Thus Woodsfield maintained its purity.

Actually, cross burnings in empty fields and Klan Konclaves were common in Monroe County; I had seen many. Years later, while I was working on a rewriting of the *World Book Encyclopedia*, we received a new article on Ohio from one of the "authenticators," and in it occurred a sentence somewhat like this: "The southeast corner of Ohio is possibly one of the most backward and culturally deprived sections of the United States, worse even than Appalachia." We had to take out the sentence—but I knew what he was talking about.

Eventually, the railroad was removed, and finally the bus line, and after that, you reached the town only by private car or taxi. The physical isolation of Woodsfield was indicative of its artistic, aesthetic, and intellectual isolation as well. But Monroe County had proudly named itself the "Switzerland of Ohio," and the scenery *was* pretty—lots of wooded green hills and the Ohio River, blue-green in those days. And later on, the farm boys proved handsome, and the town boys as well, as stalwart and ruddy as the real Swiss.

Not much of my childhood remains in my memory. I remember how painful it was when my mother held my hand as I walked beside her when I was three or four, for my arm was pulled straight up. In Richmond, Virginia, where we lived for a while because my father had one of his innumerable jobs there, I went across the street to a vacant lot and set fire to the dry grass. (I could not have known then that "between jobs" was the family's way of covering the fact that my father had twice taken the Keeley cure for alcoholism and opium addiction and that he had also dabbled in laudanum and morphine.) I remember also in Richmond my mother dropped a jar of home-made tomato catsup and the lid came off, spilling the catsup all over the kitchen floor, at which my father hit her across the face. I also recall lying on my stomach reading a child's book about King Arthur, while a few feet away my sister Virginia, five years younger, was on the potty, and a bit of poop exploded from her tiny behind, to fall directly on King Arthur's face. And once I was roller skating on the street near a telephone pole, the kind that had climbing spikes out the sides; a motorcyclist with goggles rounded the corner from Monument Avenue too fast, hit the curb, and flew into the air. His skull-pan was punctured on a spike. He hung there a moment and then fell to the ground dead, with brains and blood splattered all over the sidewalk. This accident furnished me with nightmares for a long time.

Once in Richmond we went to a carnival. There was a peaked building with the flags of all nations running to the top, at which point the Confederate battle flag waved in the breeze.

"But where is the American flag?" I asked my father. "Shush," he said. "We are in Richmond."

There was a bully in our block. He used to pick me up by the ears. That hurt.

"Damnyankee," he said.

"Ow," I screamed. He would hold me for about twenty seconds.

My mother died in Richmond, of an intestinal obstruction. I was once permitted to go see her in the hospital. "Oh Sammy," she said. "I'm all cut up inside." This gave me a vivid picture of her belly cut into tiny pieces, and I wept. I was six. After her death, I was taken back to Woodsfield, where I lived until I was about seventeen.

The trip home was made in the company of my aunt Elizabeth, a large kind

---

Keeley cure. Treatment for alcoholism and other addictions offered by Dr. Leslie Keeley (1839–1900) and his successors at his institute in Dwight, Illinois, and at its many branches throughout the country. Patients received injections of dubious efficacy, but Keeley's assertion that alcoholism is a disease was ahead of his time.

Steward at age five or six with his mother. (Courtesy of the Estate of Samuel M. Steward)

bosomy woman who never married. I had a lot of aunts. Elizabeth, Minnie, and Amy were the spinsters. Amy—a talented artist—died of dropsy. Aunts Elizabeth and Minnie brought up my sister and myself, along with Grandmother Morris. We all lived together in the old Morris House. I grew up thus in a house filled with women, and it must have had some effect on me. My father didn't count, for he was a weak man and often absent traveling.

As a child, I had the usual diseases, plus some not so usual—a broken eardrum (treated with laudanum and pepper on a pledget of cotton) and rheumatic fever, which without antibiotics lasted a long time and was very painful, making it difficult to walk. I was much babied and coddled. I had mumps, chicken pox, measles four times, and a broken nose. The nose accident occurred when I ran into a board extending across a sidewalk, running with my head down. For two or three weeks, I had two of the blackest eyes ever, and all my classmates in the third grade tried to find out who had socked me.

A fight? Not I, not ever. Once some bully picked on me when I was nine, and I ran screaming to my father.

"Teach me how to fight," I sobbed.

"Sorry, son—I can't," he said lamely. "You just have to make your hands into fists and keep them in front of your face. But the important thing is you must stand your ground."

Stand my ground, hell! Ever afterward, I ran from that particular oppressor and never stood my ground for any physical fight. After a while, I learned to talk my way out of difficulties and have used that method ever since.

Most of the townspeople thought me smart for my age. Perhaps I was. But I remember more disasters than triumphs. In second grade, Miss Goddard asked me to stand and read a passage. It should not have given me trouble, but it concerned a horse and had the word "Whoa" in it, which I pronounced "hoo-ay."

"Sit down, Samuel," she said, and called on Harriet Claugus.

Harriet had just come in from the country outside Woodsfield; she was considered a hick by all of us third-grade sophisticates. With her loping walk, her monkey mouth with buck teeth, her braids and receding chin, she was the object of our cruel laughter.

A year after "hoo-ay," Miss Griffith in the fourth grade asked, "Who can give us an example of an exclamation in grammar?"

Harriet's hand went up. "Write it on the board, Harriet," said Miss Griffith.

Harriet wrote: "Pshaw, the building fell down."

Miss Griffith frowned. "That's not a strong enough word for such an event."

I put up my hand. "Yes, Samuel," Miss Griffith said. "What would you say?"

"God damn it, the building fell down," I said.

The effect was magical. Miss Griffith had a fit of coughing and hustled me out of the room to see the principal, who sent me home with a note, even though I tried to explain it was only something I had heard my father say. My Grandmother Morris, a very tiny woman but remarkably strong for her size, washed out my mouth with soap on a toothbrush. Sixty years later, I can still taste it.

The change that came over me from grade school to high school was amazing, both to my family and to the teachers. The meek mild little mama's boy, the potential sissy, may have remained that on the outside, but inside there was a curious change to a twelve-year-old devil. The only reason that I have ever been able to find for this alteration reached me years later, when I happened to read Edgar Allen Poe's short story "The Imp of the Perverse." In that not-very-good tale, Poe nonetheless investigated what may have been one of the most profound observations he ever made—that there is something within a man which causes him to do exactly the opposite of what he should do for his own self-preservation. A man's reason violently deters him from the brink; *therefore* do we most impetuously approach it. We perpetuate an action merely because we feel that we should *not*. In the story, a man had committed a murder and got away with it—yet slowly working within him was the compulsion to reveal his dark deed, so that finally he ran down the street shouting the details of his crime to the world—and was caught.

It has been observed by the psychologists and the psychiatrists too that the personality which has been kept repressed, as mine had been by the strict Methodist upbringing my aunts had given me, and kept within the strictest lines and boundaries really goes wild—hog wild—when it finally breaks away. And although I was still living within the family walls, the rebellious spirit was growing daily stronger. Perhaps I was not, like the man in Poe's story, seeking to ruin myself by becoming a "bad boy," but at any rate, I was reaching out for freedom.

And it is amazing to me that such a reaching out for freedom has lasted so long in my life and been the motivating force behind what must have seemed to many an urge to destroy myself. I had to be free; I could not take orders for long. And I suppose, looking backward and making the roughest of counts, considerably less than a third of my years has been spent in a situation where it was necessary for me to take orders. Whether consciously or not, I seemed to arrange my life so that most of it was spent in freedom, as my own master.

By the time I reached the eighth grade in school, at the advanced age of fourteen, one might think that some of the delights of sex would have unfolded for me.

Not so. One afternoon, the principal, W. J. Crawford, a dour-faced man, gathered all the eighth-grade boys in a room. The knowledgeable ones knew what was coming. I didn't.

Cyril Dougherty poked me in the ribs. "This is the day we learn all about life," he said.

"Uh, ha ha, yes," I said.

The only thing remembered from that talk was that the principal spoke of the danger of "touching oneself *down there*," which he said while one hand vaguely swung in the segment of an arc in front of his own crotch. The room was hushed.

As we marched down the sidewalk after school, Cyril said, "Imagine— Clark Loper didn't know what ole W. J. was talkin' about." And laughed.

"Ha ha," I said. Neither did I. But that hour's talk by W. J. caused me a great deal of private agony. In my sheltered little-boy Methodist way, I imagined that the slightest brushing against my penis with my hand not only was a religious sin but would lead equally to blindness and pimples, kidney disease, bed-wetting, stooped shoulders, insomnia, weight loss, fatigue, stomach trouble, impotence, genital cancer, and ulcers. Many nights thereafter, I prayed secretly to God to keep me from sin and any inadvertent "touching of myself" which might occur during the night while I was asleep. It was during this period that I experienced my first wet dream, a frightening occurrence which caused me to leap from bed and run to my father's bedroom—for he was then temporarily staying in a room at the Morris House. He comforted me, took me to bed with him, and explained as best he knew how that this was a usual thing for growing boys. But he did not at that time, or ever, instruct me in anything sexual nor give me one word of sexually oriented advice. As for my spinster aunts—well, they were dears, but they may still have believed in storks and cabbage plants, for all I knew.

And then wicked Bill Shafer, a redheaded friend related to the Mooneys, showed me what old W. J. was really talking about. He introduced me to fantasyland and showed me a new device for my solitary hours with his none-too-specific instructions: "You just keep going back and forth on it, like this, and you'll see what will happen."

Wicked Bill, delightful Bill—thanks a lot forever and ever! Alone in the Morris House bathroom, I kept going back and forth on it, and suddenly my whole body began to tingle, and the tingling raced from head to feet. My breathing stopped, and like a strongly pulled bow, my body bent almost double over the toilet to release the four magic drops. Then with senses reeling, heart racing, panting, I fell back against the door until the black-red specks stopped dancing before my eyes.

Marvel of marvels! Was it sinful? Who cared? Say rather it was the toy that would forever be with me. Whether in green pastures or beside still waters—my rod and my staff would comfort me, enliven my darkest hours with visions that would delight, satisfy, and soothe, that would excite, fulfill my deepest desires, and respond to all my questions about the meaning

Whether in green pastures. Cf. Psalm 23:2, 4.

of life. Along with Genet—who first suggested it—let us form a cult of the solitary pleasure.

The next step was wondering what to do about this great advance toward manhood. I was aware of how babies were produced, but I learned nothing from any of my family. Rather, it was from an animated drawing film— very unusual for the early 1920s—which in black and white illustrated in diagrammatic and highly stylized fashion the male and female organs, the introduction of the seed, the growth of the fetus, and all the rest. This film was shown by the proprietor of the only picture show in town—an old man named (I think) King—and was open only to males one day and to females the next. As I remember, the female showing never took place.

Try to imagine a small town in Ohio in the 1920s—a narrow-minded citizenry, bigoted, sexually naive, Protestant (with all the shallow morality that entails)—and a parent in such a place who hears one night from his son that during the preceding afternoon he was shown a sex film!

The uproar was tremendous, and old man King was nearly lynched. Even at the current time, he would stand hardly a chance of surviving the night. He was scolded, reprimanded, and censured by all the church groups, the men's luncheon groups—by everyone, in fact, except those of us who had seen the film, which was clear, straightforward, and certainly not obscene.

So, now knowing for certain that neither storks nor cabbages had anything to do with it and aware of what vasty powers lay down there in my groin, knowing also that most of my peers carried around some contraceptives in a small box, I bought some of them from a young barber named Charlie, the town's "agent"—and "agent" meant only one thing in those days: a guy who sold rubbers. These neatly rolled rubbers (not pressed together on their diameters nor sealed in foil) came in small tin boxes on which in raised embossments appeared the phrase "Three Merry Widows" and in an arc at the bottom edge, "Agnes. Mabel. Beckie." (A thousand years later, wandering through a flea market at Alameda, California, I saw one of these boxes for sale for twenty-five cents. With pounding heart, I bought it. "Do you know what this is?" I asked the longhair who had sold it to me. He peered at it and me from behind his false-face of a full beard and mustache. "Haven't the foggiest," he said. I told him. "My god," he said, "I shoulda charged more.")

Genet. Jean Genet (1910–86), French political activist and writer of gay-themed novels and poetry from the perspective of marginalized figures in society. Steward refers to *Our Lady of the Flowers*, Genet's first novel, written while he was in prison for burglary in 1942.
what vasty powers. Cf. Shakespeare, 1 *Henry IV*: "I can call spirits from the vasty deep" (III.i.52). A favorite Steward word.

I was not yet brave enough to do anything with Agnes, Mabel, or Beckie except try them on and then go through the shafer ritual. But that seemed to be enough for the time being.

My peers and classmates were all interested in girls, so far as I knew, and I felt that it was necessary for me to be interested in them too. Among my classmates there were two girls who had scarlet reputations. One was Gwendolyn, a flamin' red-hot mama. She played jazz piano wonderfully well, much better than I ever could, although I rippled a mean "Rustle of Spring." But Gwendolyn snubbed me. She preferred Ralph Truex, a dark Heathcliff sort of man with curly black hair and a sexual aura. I preferred him too, but didn't know why. My fantasies during shafer time placed Ralph on top of Gwendolyn—but she was a blur, whereas I could see every hair on his ass and every muscle in his legs and back.

My Aunt Minnie sighed. "Why can't you take up with a decent girl like Kathryn?"

Kathryn was an intellectual rival. We were the two smartest students in first-year high school. Everyone thought we would get married and produce brainy children. I took Kathryn to a couple of movies and then walked her home. She thanked me prettily. I clumsily tried to kiss her goodnight but missed her lips and hit her eye. She said, "Ow," faintly, and we didn't try it again.

Then there was Edith, another fast one according to rumor. In Edith's front parlor one night we got pretty far. In order to keep myself from getting a disease and also from messing up my trousers, I put on both Agnes and Mabel at the same time, figuring that afterward I could remove Mabel and wear Agnes until I got home to wash. Unfortunately, the mechanics of getting both on made Edith titter and ask what in the world I was doing. Hearing that, I was immediately deflated. Nothing thereafter could be done. Burning with anger and shame, I fled the house, up the alley past Milligan's confectionary, and home. It was then, as if by magic and in the privacy of my bedroom, that my manhood asserted itself, and the shafer ritual was most satisfactorily performed.

Having thus tried the town trollops and its only certain virgin and finding myself wanting, I turned to higher things.

---

the shafer ritual. Here and below, Steward humorously uses Bill Shafer's name as a substitute for "masturbation."

"Rustle of Spring" (1896). Popular solo piece for piano by the Norwegian composer Christian Sinding (1856–1941).

Heathcliff. Handsome, brooding, mysterious character in the novel *Wuthering Heights* (1847), by Emily Brontë (1818–48).

What fifteen- or sixteen-year-old has not at some time developed a crush on a teacher? In this case, the victim was a charming lady named Starner—and she was affectionately known to all of Woodsfield High School as "Buddy" Starner. I am not sure that I ever knew her first name, although I presume she had one. She was small and blonde, with peach-bloom skin and blue eyes, and she taught shorthand and typing. I believe that I even took a typing course just to be near her, only to discover that the class was conducted by a person named Gatten, as homely as Buddy Starner was pretty. Claiming that typing aggravated a cyst on my wrist (which had already developed because of my piano practice and been smashed once by a Woodsfield doctor with a heavy book), I fled from the class.

Luckily, Miss Starner was not averse to socializing with the students, and in those days it seemed all right, because her morals were impeccable. Consequently, I spent many hours with her in the rooms she rented above a grocery store. There she had the use of a piano, and she would listen to me play "The Rosary" by Ethelbert Nevin over and over—always with a dreamy faraway look. Had I been wiser or more sophisticated, I might have seen that it reminded her of someone, probably a lost love.

Buddy Starner became my ideal, thus, although I had no idea what to do with her. I was too timid to kiss her or even try—and anyway she was too old for me, being probably then twenty (ancient!) to my fifteen or sixteen. But she seemed to appreciate my dumb and fawn-eyed adoration; furthermore, my aunts liked her and invited her to the Morris House to visit and smiled indulgently at my crush. She was an eminently respectable person to them.

So had things gone on, I might still have been sitting in Buddy Starner's parlor playing "The Rosary" for her when we arrived in our nineties. But Fate stepped in.

One afternoon when I was not expected at her rooms, I stopped by on my way from school. The door was partly open. And I looked through. There standing on tiptoe was my beloved Buddy Starner enfolded in the arms of that much-admired dark Heathcliff man, Ralph Truex, who was kissing her in a more prolonged embrace than any I had ever seen on the silver screen. I was destroyed, but my reasoning made me conclude that if both Buddy and I liked Ralph, and if Ralph and I had both fallen for her, then probably Ralph and I had similar tastes; if he likes Buddy, then he might like me too. It was a curious circular rationale, and I was not wise enough at the moment to understand its real meaning or to see the fallacy in my thinking.

"The Rosary" (1898). Popular short piece for piano and voice by the American composer Ethelbert Nevin (1862–1901).

I confronted her later and asked if she were going to marry him.

"Heavens no!" she said with a cascade of silver bells. "He's only eighteen." Then she changed the subject. "Coach Johnson asked me the other day why you didn't try out for the track team."

"I can't run all that fast."

"He said he saw you running up the alley the other night, and you went like the wind."

A compliment from the coach pleased me, even if he had seen me leaving Edith's place, for he looked a lot like Ralph Truex—the same black curly hair and, seen once in the gym showers, a sturdy well-muscled body with a fan of black hair on his chest. I went to see him and he talked me into trying out. I did, my specialty becoming the hundred-yard dash. The coach was delighted with me, and I hungered for his approval.

But when spring came and it was time for the athletic teams of Woodsfield High School to assemble for the yearly picture, I refused to get into my track costume and join them. "Why not?" said Coach Johnson.

"I just don't want to," I said, feeling my face grow red.

What was the reason? A modesty of sorts? The same feeling that causes a bride to undress herself in the bathroom on her wedding night? A feeling that my legs were too thin? A certainty that with his piercing black eyes Coach Johnson would lay bare my heart and see what was there—that he would know something I myself was not yet able to realize?

"Come see me this afternoon after football practice and we'll talk about it."

Nervous, I went to his office in the basement of the school. There was a sign on his door saying: "Am in the showers. C. L. J."

In the showers! The note did not say "Come see me" nor "Wait for me."

With dry mouth and pounding heart, not knowing what he meant me to do, I finally went toward the showers with hesitant feet, urged on by some deep power.

Standing outside the steamy door, I heard water running and a tuneless humming. I pushed the door and went in, around the corner to the three shower stalls.

"Hullo there!" the coach called in a loud cheery voice. My knees were weak.

"H-hul-lo," I managed to answer.

We were alone in the room. His muscular tanned body turned actively under the shower as he soaped himself, his arms and chest. The hair of his strong wide chest was now streaming downward under the water, his black curly hair atop his head flattened down the sides of his handsome face, strong-jawed, dark-browed. I tried to moisten my dry lips with my tongue, and my eyes traveled down the length of his superb body, the sturdy thigh muscles, the well-developed calves. I could hardly bring myself to look at his genitals, swinging free. But in his ministrations to himself with the soap under the shower, he turned his attention to them, soaping them, extending his penis by pulling at it, washing it.

The room began to turn faintly opalescent in the corners, my breathing grew short, and then with a rush the black spots came from all inside edges of the room-cube and blotted out my sight.

I had fainted. It did not help me much to be revived and see the coach bending over me naked, water from his body dripping on me, the smile replaced by a worried frown.

"What happened, Sammy?" he said.

"I-I g-guess I must have fainted," I said in great embarrassment.

"Does this happen to you often?" he said, concerned.

"No-no," I managed. "I'll be all right." Then I got to my feet and summoned enough courage to look at his naked body but did not dare let my eyes go below his heavily muscled glistening shoulders. "I f-forgot to eat lunch," I said—although I had had a large one at home.

"Well, get something in your stomach," the coach said gravely. "Right away. We'll postpone our talk until later."

I wonder if he knew, if he was playing games with me. I'll never be sure. I guess it wouldn't matter anyway; he would be eighty now.

It was gradually becoming clearer to me what I wanted. Just what influence the continuing disapproval of my aunts had upon me in turning my attention from women to men I do not know. I do know, however, that "choice" had no part in it. When I discovered what I wanted, every corpuscle, every instinct I had, drove me unerringly in that direction. No fag-baiter ignoramus, no born-againer bigot is ever going to tell me I had a choice. I was different—a queer alone in a world of gash-hounds—or so I thought at the time.

Little things helped me along my alternate path.

The Saturday-night loafers were sitting on the railings in front of Bertram's confectionery store, perched thereon with feet resting on a bottom rail and their buttocks snug against the top one. I had wedged myself in the line, even though the age of sixteen was considered too young for that crowd. But we

gash-hounds. Men driven by unrestrained sexual interest in women.

all wanted to hear Danny Evers, nineteen, recount his adventures at Buckeye Lake.

I had been to Buckeye Lake only once, at about the age of six. It was halfway from Zanesville to Columbus, a distance from Woodsfield of about ninety miles, and it was the only amusement resort in central Ohio. All I can remember is the few buildings I saw and a flat-bottomed rowboat which Uncle Joe rented for the next day.

But Danny had spent four whole days alone at Buckeye Lake, returning with many souvenirs—a bamboo Charlie Chaplin cane which he twirled most skillfully and an electric bow tie which lighted up on the ends when he pressed the tiny switch in his pocket.

All of us were much impressed with those items, but we had really gathered to hear of his amorous adventures, which he enjoyed relating in great detail—a new girl every night, all very cheap (two dollars), and there were lots of whores to choose from at the resort.

He was a great raconteur and left nothing undescribed, so that several of the boys sitting on the railings grew restive and reached to squeeze themselves. But all I remember is one or two sentences from his description of the "hot mama" he had saved until last.

"—see, we were both naked and she gave me a tongue-bath all over, and then she sucked my dick, and—"

It was like a revelation from above or below, a sudden burst of light and illumination which told me that this was what I wanted to hear. And try. Up to that moment the only contact I had had with other boys was in the mutual ritual—my hand on his armament, and his on mine.

At the end of the railing line sat Jeff Kinney, one of my newly acquired hand-rape partners (manus + turbare: Webster). I slid off the railing and approached him. We were the same age, but he was a big guy—so big he played football for the high-school team—guard, or something which demanded size and weight. There was a high rose in his cheeks, and he wore his hair in a pompadour, then much in fashion.

"Hey," I said in a low tone, "come with me; I want to show you something."

He slid off the railing, and together we sneaked into the Morris House, up the stairs to the attic door, and on into the airless attic. I had stopped in my room to get my flashlight. We were very soft-footed, because we could not know who was beneath us at that hour.

And so it was there on a sheeted mattress, amidst the dust and cobwebs, that the morning stars sang together for the first time for me. To Jeff I ap-

the morning stars sang together. Cf. Job 38:7.

plied an Agnes and went to work—and since that was the first time such a thing had ever happened to either of us, it was all over in less than two minutes. Jeff, panting, drew his trousers back on, and stealthily we left the scene.

So began my criminal life, punishable by the laws of the sovereign state of Ohio—at that time—by about twenty years of imprisonment. I guess. Each time. Total incarceration in Ohio: between five and six thousand years.

Now I knew what I wanted, but hardly how or why. And then a second event occurred, so unusual and bizarre and coincidental that it would not be believed in a work of fiction. Passing a room in the Morris House vacated by a salesman, I saw a book under the bed. It had evidently been stolen from the state library in Columbus—so the card in the front flap indicated. Stamped on the inside front cover was a word in large blue capitals: "Restricted." I felt my chest pressed in as if by huge metal bands, for the title page read: Studies in the Psychology of Sex, by Havelock Ellis. Volume II: Sexual Inversion.

The book opened the wide tall doors of the world for me, for it seemed that Ellis had gathered all sex together in one place. Not only did I discover that I was not alone in a world of heteros—I also found many new things to do. I created a secret hiding place for the volume under the attic stairs and read and read and read. It was an important thing to learn that I was not necessarily insane; and it was delightful for me to have in hand a manual of the erotic—for there was little in that volume that was left untreated. Here lay the magical world of sex, plus a kind of instructional how-to volume. Here were listed the names of the great and near-great who had been part of this band in the past: the legendary Greek and Roman heroes, the Theban band, Leonardo, Whitman, Tchaikovsky, Erasmus, Aretino, Michelangelo, Cellini, Marlowe, Shakespeare, Bacon, Edward FitzGerald, Symonds, Rimbaud, Verlaine, Proust, and Oscar Wilde. No, you did not have to be homosexual to be great—if you were great, maybe you were also homosexual.

Wilde was immediately available to me; there was a *Complete Poems* of his in the town library—remaining there no doubt because one of the things that made it comparatively easy to be a homosexual in the 1920s was the relative lack of sophistication, at least in the small towns. In the opening sonnet, I found these magic lines from "Hélas!":

> Lo, with a little rod
> I did but touch the honey of romance—
> And must I lose a soul's inheritance?

Havelock Ellis (1859–1939). British physician whose *Studies in the Psychology of Sex* (7 volumes, 1897–1928) was the first comprehensive study of human sexual behavior.

Just how a teacher in those days might explicate the meaning of those lines I do not know — but their sense was immediately clear to me. Romantic that I was, I went about the business of touching the honey of romance. But with this difference: not with my rod, but with theirs.

And who was "theirs"?

For the most part, I easily found willing bodies to practice on — four members of the football team, all of the basketball, three of the track — and curiously, none of them taunted me, nor was I openly called fairy or sissy or pansy or queer. I think that the healthy young Ohio animals enjoyed it all too much to jeopardize their not having it again by publicly making fun of me. And there were many others: Ted, who spread his heavy young thighs on a red velvet curtain which I put over the bed in the house of "Aunt" Lulu and "Uncle" Thurman, gone to Florida for the winter. Kenny — a crop-headed crewcut blond in a Model T Ford at the foot of Gooseneck Hill — an appreciative sort, the first one to kiss me after the labors were done. And the cousins Earl and Carl — Carl with the dusky brown-rose complexion, the first to reciprocate.

And Fred, Ted's brother — smooth and sophisticated, the town sheik with his slicked-back hair and handsome well-made body — spending his weekends in Wheeling, West Virginia, going from one whorehouse to another. He was very "jam," by which we then meant butch. I chanced to meet Fred on a wet and drizzly evening in front of the post office. Chanced? I had been stalking him since early afternoon. Light poured from the window full on his face. He wore a yellow rain slicker and no hat — very daring for those years.

And how to get this hero for myself?

A direct approach — no euphemisms. Right straight out with the four-letter words, the language of love in the 1920s. I told him what I wanted to do.

He cocked one eyebrow. I saw the little hairs of it glisten in the light with tiny water beads of drizzle. He smiled crookedly. "I heard you were up to that," he said. "What's in it for me?"

My first hustler. "Well," I said, swallowing with difficulty. "I could probably get you a quart of red wine" . . . steal it from Clem Rausch's cellar, but I did not add that.

"Okay," he said. And so it was up to the courthouse tower, a few feet above the stained-glass skylight and a few feet under the great bell, with Fred astride a beam. Fred came just as the clock struck eight, and the double surprise nearly knocked both of us off the perch.

Another favorite trysting place was the new cemetery — the old one being too close to the streetlights. I favored a tombstone of the proper height so that I could stand and my conquest could sit. Was there some kind of obscure challenge at work, to make me select such a place? An affirmation of aliveness, of sex and joy, in the midst of death? Years later, the chill came on me when I read the last sentence of Thomas Mann's *The Magic Mountain*: "Out of this universal feast of death . . . may it be that Love one day shall mount?"

And if romantic encounters in the graveyard were an affirmation of aliveness, what were those in the semicircle of Sunday-school classrooms upstairs at the Methodist church? Probably a matter of convenience — no more. I doubt very much that my feelings about God at that age were complex enough to compel me to cock a snoot at the deity by performing deeds that were specifically damned by St. Paul in the New Testament and a block of Jewish lawmakers in the Old Testament because they held the birthrate down. It was simply that I had a key to the church, where I could practice on the great blowpipe organ (that permission was eventually withdrawn from me because I insisted on playing music from *The Desert Song* and other popular tunes on the sanctified and holy pipes). Many were the pagan delights enjoyed in those small rooms or on the mattresses in the church gym below.

But in this universal feast of love, as Thomas Mann neglected to put it, there was a mistake made with results which I should have foreseen.

Made careless by a succession of triumphs with my classmates, I wrote a note to a salesman in the Morris House and left it in his room. I can see him now as I looked down from between the rungs of the upstairs banister railing, the white skin and copper-colored hair, the smooth and polished muscles as he returned from the washroom, clad in trousers and sleeveless undershirt, to the privacy behind his solid wooden door. What exactly was in the note I do not remember, but undoubtedly it was clear enough. I recall but one sentence, the last one: "I would certainly like to 'meat' you." Whether that use of *meat* was currently popular or my own invention of the moment, I do not remember either.

In the morning, at breakfast, my aunts were puzzled. "Mr. Rensaleer left this morning," said one. "He seemed to be mad about something."

Thomas Mann (1875–1955). German novelist and essayist, and winner of the Nobel Prize for literature in 1929. *The Magic Mountain* (*Der Zauberberg*, 1924) is Mann's wide-ranging and symbolic novel about a young man's seven-year stay in a sanatorium and the inhabitants he comes to know.

The Desert Song (1926). Operetta by Sigmund Romberg (1887–1951) with a plot of swashbuckling heroism set in North Africa and book and lyrics by Oscar Hammerstein II, Otto Harbach, and Frank Mandel. A huge success on Broadway, it spawned several film adaptations.

High-school photograph of Steward. (Courtesy of the Estate
of Samuel M. Steward)

"Didn't even eat breakfast," said the other. "He was supposed to stay three
more days. Always did stay a week before this."

I did not know it at that moment, but my salesman had taken the note to
Bill Bayes, proprietor of the only restaurant in town, and shown it to him;
and Bayes had immediately called my father. The worst had happened.

For some years, I had tried to love my father, but it never worked. We
fought continually. The propagandizing of my aunts against whomever he
looked upon as a possible new bride had affected me; they somehow felt that
he should remain true all his life to the memory of my mother. An additional
strain was that I had earned my own way during the high-school years, since
with his meager salary, he could not support either myself or my sister. And
finally, the superintendent of schools had given both my father and myself
the same IQ test—which had just then been invented. When the weighting

of scores was adjusted by our ages, it was discovered that my result topped his. I do not believe he ever forgave me and was jealous of that small detail the rest of his life; he often referred to it, but never in my hearing.

When he came home from work that evening — a Friday — he was glowering. "What are you doing tomorrow?"

It was Saturday; I was working in Uncle Will's grocery store. I told him. He took three dollars from his pocket "Tell your uncle you're sick," he said. "We're going to take a ride tomorrow."

"I get only two," I said, and handed one bill back. He took it.

We started early. He was silent, and I was terror-stricken. The eighteen miles down to Fly and the Ohio River were the most miserable I had spent until then. We drove through the lovely green countryside without a word, up and down the hills of our local Switzerland, ending with the final breakneck curving road that led down to the river — green and cool in those days. He turned right when we reached the bottom, drove about a mile or so in the direction of New Matamoras, and then pulled the prim little buggylike Model T Ford runabout to the side of the road and stopped. He turned to me. I must have been white-faced. I looked straight ahead.

"Now then," he said. "What's all this about your wanting to do something vile with that Rensaleer fellow?"

"Who told you?" I countered.

"None of your gah-damned business," he said. "I want to know what the hell a son of mine means by writing love letters to another man."

"I think," I said, drawing on my new vocabulary from Havelock Ellis, "that I am homosexual."

"Homosexual? What the hell's that?"

"It refers to the love that dare not speak its name," I said, remembering Wilde. "It is the same emotion that Socrates felt, and Michelangelo. It—"

"Don't give me any of your smart-aleck high-school rhetoric!" he bellowed. "Are you a cocksucker or not?"

"I've never done anything like that," I said, batting my eyelashes. "I just feel . . . well, I feel *drawn* to men."

"What men?"

"Well, Coach Johnson," I said, "and maybe Ralph Truex . . ."

"Did you ever . . . *touch* those men?"

"Why, I suppose I have," I said innocently. "I've shaken hands . . ."

"Goddamnit, you know what I mean!" he roared.

"No, not that way," I said, making myself tremble a little.

So it went for a half hour. When I saw that he *wanted* to believe that I had not actually sinned, the game became fairly easy, for I was already schooled in duplicity. I pretended to be chastened, to be horror-struck at the enormity of it (he told me of the Ohio law — twenty years' penalty), and to show a firm purpose of amendment, as a good Catholic might say.

I was protected in another way — Midwest American views on homosexuality in the 1920s were very quaint and were based on the assumption that all people raised in civilized Christian countries knew better than to fall in love with, or bed, persons of the same sex. Knowing better, then, the fundamentalist mind made two breathtaking leaps of illogic: people did not do such things, and therefore such things must be nonexistent. By and large, homosexuality and fellatio were considered so unbelievable and impossible that although one might be teased for being a sissy, no one could believe that any person actually engaged in the "abominable sin." This kind of thinking protected us all during the 1920s and '30s, and we lived happily under its shadow and cover. Only when the audience grew more sophisticated did our danger (the knowledge of our actual existence) and our long ordeal begin once more.

Having found the role my father wanted me to play, I worked it to the hilt, falling in easily with his suggestion that perhaps I should go to see a professional whore — that such an experience might start me on a heterosexual (he said "normal") path. That evening I met one of my favorites, Carl, and took him to the high-school building, where on the glass bubbles that formed part of the gymnasium ceiling, outside under the stars, we had a romantic encounter. When it was over, I told Carl about the day's experience, knowing that he would keep quiet. After all, he was almost as deeply involved as I.

"Tell you what," he laughed. "Next weekend we'll drive to Wheeling and visit a real whore."

"I don't particularly want to," I said.

"Oh, come on — try it once," he said. "It'll be fun."

"I'll probably be thinking of you while I'm with her," I said, with a sudden flash of insight.

Carl laughed. He had the biggest collection of beautiful white teeth I had ever seen, shining against his dusky skin.

"That's all right, too," he said. "Maybe I'll be thinking of you. Your mouth."

I left a note for my father asking for the loan of five dollars, to do "what we were talking about last week." We had to communicate by notes since he was working nights.

The next morning, I found his reply: "If you think for one minute I'm going to give you any money to go to Wheeling to get the clap or syff, you're badly mistaken." No "Dear Son," no signature, no money. I borrowed five from an aunt and we went anyway. But we pulled off on a road the other side of Barnesville, because Carl had got so warmed up thinking about the coming encounter that he had to be cooled off.

The visit to the whore was a sad little experience. Carl went into one room with a girl, myself into another. It took me a long time—and finally the girl herself had an orgasm. My own was brought about by thinking of Carl, as I had foreseen. Afterward, the girl squatted above a round white enamelware basin on the floor filled with a pale blue solution, copper sulfate I presumed, and with both hands splashed the liquid vigorously into herself.

Outside, Carl was talking to his girl. "What took you so long?" he asked. "I was done in five minutes."

"I wanted her to get her money's worth," I said archly.

They laughed.

My father never mentioned the episode again. As for myself, after the shock wave passed, I went on just as blithely as before. In the summer of 1927, my two aunts, in their sixties, sold the Morris House and bought a modest home in Columbus, Ohio, to put my sister Virginia and myself through high school and the university by taking in students as roomers. I severed all emotional contacts with Woodsfield. True, I went back now and then to bury a relative, but all neural connections between the town and myself had been forever destroyed. I was a stranger in a strange land when I returned. Whether word of my obliquity had been passed around I neither knew nor cared.

So farewell, Woodsfield, farewell! I could perhaps stay within your limits forever, going on and on, filling volume after volume like old Proust sitting with shrunken shanks in his tub of tepid bathwater, gargling it and spitting it out and gargling again—all that dreadful curdled residue of the past.

But there must be an end to childhood—and to gargling. The birth of desire had taken place in me, and the patterns that I needed to survive were firmly imprinted by the time I left the town: concealment and pretense, duplicity, a guise of wide-eyed innocence—and a kind of "passive aggression" that was not expected in such a shy-seeming young man. I went to Columbus with the major purpose of bringing pleasure to others, mainly straight young

---

Proust . . . in his tub. Steward alludes to a passage in chapter 1 of *Eyeless in Gaza* (1936), by Aldous Huxley (1894–1963), in which the novel's character Anthony Beavis mocks the focus on childhood in *À la recherche du temps perdu* (1913–27, most recently translated as *In Search of Lost Time*), by Marcel Proust (1871–1922).

men, and not to be concerned about pleasuring myself—for in bringing it to those I admired, I *did* please myself. In all the encounters since then, until—as Sophocles said—age released me from the tyranny of the mad master, sexual desire, I did the asking, and more often than not, succeeded.

Another aim? Oh, yes—nearly forgotten: to get an education.

Sources: *Chapters*, 1–17; *Manuscript*, 4, 33–77.

---

as Sophocles said. In Book I of Plato's *Republic* (360 BCE), Sophocles, asked about sexual passion in old age, is said to have replied, "Most gladly have I escaped the thing of which you speak; I feel as if I had escaped from a mad and furious master" (Jowett translation).

Chapter Two

UNIVERSITY YEARS

1927–34

Take a green sprout from a town of eighteen hundred and transplant him suddenly in the course of one summer to a metropolis of about three hundred and fifty thousand (in those days)—and what do you get? Stars in the eyes, a feeling of belonging to an important place, the development of inquisitiveness, a desire to live–live–live! Columbus was the Big City to me, wholly aside from the excitement of entering The Ohio State University in the fall.

How romantic the campus and its life all seemed! The buildings crouched around the green and grassy Oval, beginning with the medieval armory on the right as you entered the grounds—a turreted and castellated red brick building which looked as if it had been transplanted directly from Camelot. The library was at the far end; midway on the left side was the old ivy-covered geology building housing the campanile, which was played every day at noon. Remembering all of it transports me back a couple of centuries and a thousand beddings to another continuum in time—to a few hazy dim and golden wonder years, a green campus, frats and dances and a life of genuine excitement.

The university population was in those years something like twelve or fifteen thousand—far from the city-state size it has acquired today, but still large enough—and I was one unit in an entering class of more than three thousand, twice the population of Woodsfield. I had one small advantage, however. My two aunts had sold the Morris House in May and moved to Columbus the following month; thus I had three months of getting used to the city and the university before freshman week and did not feel as utterly strange as did many of the new students.

53

My aunts' house on 17th Avenue had three floors, ten rooms, of which about six were rented out to two boys each. That meant a dozen boys—and two bathrooms, one of which had to be added. There was quite a rush in the mornings. Among the various inhabitants of the rooms over seven years, I should say that there were romantic encounters with about half of them— lean and lanky tennis players; hunky muscled coal miners' sons from Bellaire, Ohio; rosy-cheeked farmer boys from Delaware; and shy Hungarians and blond Poles from Cleveland.

Under the same roof lived my two aunts, my sister Virginia, and myself, and occasionally George "Morris"—a thirty-fivish ne'er-do-well the aunts had adopted when they administered the Children's Home in Woodsfield. Aunt Minnie was the thin-lipped dragon of the family, the one who could pronounce "boozin'" with such terrifying inflection; she disapproved of nearly everything I did. Aunt Elizabeth, whom we called "Aunt Bebe," was a plumper, more quivery sort of person—always too ready to forgive her half nephew and niece—and it was she I was fonder of, for she was mother and confidante to me, the all-embracing warm and human personality that I was later to find repeated in almost exact duplicate in Gertrude Stein. The two aunts were completely different in personality; and they reminded me later of the good cop and the bad cop interrogating a suspect—save that Aunt Bebe never pried. I think, poor dear, she really preferred not to know what Sammy did.

And then there was Virginia, my sister, five years younger, who was so smart she skipped a grade and was thus ready to enter high school when I did college. Poor kid—the aunts were great mothers to her, but they knew nothing beyond the facts of menstruation and the physical changes in a young woman. It fell to me—when I was nineteen and she fourteen—to enlighten her about the Facts of Life. This I did with great earnest description, telling her in the process that I considered myself homosexual until something better came along and detailing for her the pitfalls ahead of young girls who know nothing about contraception (and were of course forty years too early for the pill). She took it all quite seriously and later in life admitted freely that it was I who had kept her from making any large mistakes.

I did not burst upon the academic scene with the flash and exuberance of a splendid rocket emitting golden stars in a brief path across the heavens. But although it was unknown to me at the time, my arrival did occasion

---

My aunts' house. The house, since demolished, was at 47 17th Avenue, directly across High Street from the university campus.

something of a stir amidst certain arcane circles. Part of the entrance requirements was the writing of an essay on your choice of subject, so that
you might be placed in the proper class level of freshman English. I chose
Walt Whitman as a topic and let fly with all the accumulated but undigested
wisdom—and none of the caution—of an eighteen-year-old who had read
Havelock Ellis and also through him investigated John Addington Symonds
and found out about Horace Traubel and Peter Doyle. Moreover, instead of
writing on *Leaves of Grass* in general, I chose the homosexual "Calamus" section in particular. I analyzed Whitman's praise of the "manly love of comrades," connecting it with his duties as a Civil War nurse, quoted *The Invert*
(by "Anomaly") on why inverts made such good nurses, and damned the high
schools for teaching nothing of Whitman's but "O Captain, My Captain" and
the lilac poem.

This amazing little essay, I later learned, landed in 1927 in the midst of
a staidly closeted English department with the disruptive force of several
pounds of TNT. It was discussed for days, and none of the overly cautious
teachers would touch me with a long pole in an "advisorial" capacity. It remained for the bravest and most foolish of them, a professor named Billy
Graves, to undertake the benevolent supervision of the young firebrand from
the sticks.

Billy was portly and blue-eyed and grey-haired, much beloved by women's

John Addington Symonds (1840–93). Homosexual English poet, biographer, and scholar
best known for his monumental study of the Renaissance (1875–86) and for his study and
defense of male same-sex relationships in ancient Greece (*A Problem in Greek Ethics* [1873]).
Horace Traubel (1858–1919). Friend, literary executor, and author of the first biography of
Walt Whitman (1819–92).
Peter Doyle (1843–1907). Streetcar conductor in Washington, DC, whom Whitman encountered as a passenger in 1865, beginning a romantic relationship that lasted until Whitman moved to Camden, New Jersey, in 1873.
"Calamus." Set of poems that extol the bonds and the physical expression of what Whitman called "adhesiveness" between men, first published in the 1860 edition of his *Leaves
of Grass*.
The Invert. *The Invert and His Social Adjustment* (1927), a call for society's understanding
and acceptance of homosexual attraction, published anonymously by "Anomaly." The term
invert was an early term for homosexual first used by Havelock Ellis in 1897 (*OED*). See
note on page 45.
lilac poem. "When Lilacs Last in the Dooryard Bloom'd" (1865), an elegy inspired by the
assassination of Abraham Lincoln.
Billy Graves. William Lucius Graves (1872–1943) began teaching English at Ohio State in
1896; he was married to Anice Colburn (1900–1974), twenty-eight years his junior.

clubs everywhere as a speaker. My aunts were charmed that such a well-known figure would take an interest in their nephew—dinners out, symphonies, auto trips, gifts of handsomely bound volumes of poesy, postcards and letters from England whither he went every summer—even coming to our modest house for a chicken dinner and improvising brilliantly on our old upright piano.

Unfortunately, I came to be more and more scornful of Billy's old-maid quality as my "sophistication" increased. He was not a practicing homosexual with me (nor I believe with anyone), and our only "romantic encounter" was one night when I slept in the same bed with him at his house and he caressed my shoulders and chest and back—on which latter, alas, he found some adolescent pimples. I was all too conscious of them and of the way his hand drew back when he touched them.

After that, we had very little to do with each other. Later, during my seven years at college, I heard that one of his fraternity brothers took a swing at him for an attempted caress. And I remember that an obsessed female graduate student began to chase him everywhere (I once saw him disappear from her, panic-struck, into the men's toilet, where she could not follow). After some years, like a sad old Ulysses, he ended the pursuit by marrying the woman—and thereupon retired. Whether he was caught in fragrant delicious with a boy, or whether he was simply worn out with running, I never heard.

My first top-level English class was conducted by a bright-eyed little woman with black hair in a boyish bob and the flightiest Eastern or British accent I had ever heard until then. Her name was Doris P. Buck, and she showed up for the first class on crutches, having broken her ankle returning by ship from Europe. She was an intellectual, married to a professor of architecture—and her stories and verse are still to be seen occasionally in the magazine of *Fantasy and Science Fiction*. I had to work like hell for an A in her class, but I got one. Just how much my bringing a new novel or play to class once in a while had to do with the grade, I'll never know—but I remember how her eyes lighted up as she looked at a copy of Édouard Bourdet's lesbian play, *The Captive* (lavender binding, yellow letters), which I had

in fragrant delicious. Steward puns on the phrase *in flagrante delicto* ("in the very act of committing the offence" [*OED*]).

Doris P. Buck (1898–1980). Prolific author of science fiction stories and poems and a co-founder of the Science Fiction Writers of America who began teaching English at Ohio State in 1927, the same year Steward enrolled.

The Captive. English translation by Arthur Hornblow Jr. of a play about lesbian love by the French dramatist Édouard Bourdet (1887–1945). Opened on Broadway in 1926; closed by police raid in 1927.

with me one day, and how fascinated she was with a copy of *Fantazius Mallare* which I borrowed to carry to class. Duplicity? Skill? *Gracian's Manual* put into practice? Or was I really worth an A? My undergraduate average was 3.96 out of 4.00, and I made Phi Beta Kappa at the end of my junior year. If I were skilled enough to fool between sixty and seventy-five professors in my undergraduate career into giving me A grades, perhaps I never fully realized my own calling—to be a second P. T. Barnum or Yellow Kid Weil.

One of my best friends on campus was my huge friend J. Marie Anderson. She had swooped down on me one day and made me her own. In a rather drab and colorless student body, Marie Anderson did not go unnoticed—a tall girl, about five-nine, and a heavy one, approximately two hundred, she moved with a swirl and a gazelle's grace. She had bright yellow hair in a longish bob which curled and swayed and swept back from her face. Her pencil-thin eyebrows were more active than swallows in flight; she could control them separately, draw one down and send the other up quizzically and then reverse the pattern. Her nose was short and well formed, and her full lips—painted always the most vivid of scarlets—were as mobile as her eyebrows. She accentuated her bulk by wearing a capelike overgarment with sleeve slits. She was a true lesbian, in love with a rather plain and pleasant girl named Alice, but her real passion was Garbo, whom she sketched endlessly in charcoal.

One day as my sophomore year approached, Marie said to me, "M'dear, you ought to take a course from Claire Andrews. He's teaching a general lit-

---

Fantazius Mallare. Novel (1922) by Ben Hecht (1894–1964), a leading writer of the so-called Chicago Literary Renaissance. The story of a mad artist consumed by "an intolerable loathing for life, an illuminated contempt for men and women" (29–30), it was seized by government officials for obscenity on the basis both of the text and of the book's nude illustrations by Wallace Smith (1888–1937).

Gracian's Manual. The Art of Worldly Wisdom (1647) by the Spanish Jesuit Baltasar Gracián y Morales (1601–58), a guide in the form of maxims to success in life.

Yellow Kid Weil (1875–1976). Renowned Chicago con artist.

Garbo. Greta Garbo (1905–90), celebrated (and possibly lesbian) Swedish-born star of silent films in the 1920s whose award-winning work in American talking films of the 1930s and early retirement made her a film legend.

Claire Andrews. Clarence E. Andrews (1883–1932) started teaching in the Ohio State English department in 1915. His wide-ranging books include *Richard Brome: A Study of His Life and Works* (1913), *The Writing and Reading of Verse* (1918), *Old Morocco and the Forbidden Atlas* (1922), *The Innocents of Paris* (1928), and the anthologies *From the Front: Trench Poetry* (1918) and *Victorian Poetry* (1924). The film version of *The Innocents of Paris* (1929), directed by Richard Wallace, was based on the story "The Flea Market" in Andrews's book.

erature course this fall, and he rarely teaches anything open to sophomores. I'm going to sign up for it. Why don't you?"

"Is he really all that good?"

She made a *moue*. "He's the best there is," she said flatly. "There is no one on the whole damned campus who can approach him."

And so I signed up for Andrews's class.

Marie was right. I was fascinated by him from the first. He was a slim elegant man reminding me of Edwin Arlington Robinson's "Richard Cory," who "glittered when he walked." Always perfectly groomed, blue eyes twinkling behind glasses with narrow horn rims, tie neatly knotted beneath a carefully trimmed mustache, he was the very model of the cosmopolite professor. He taught for six months of every year and then for the other six would disappear into the darkly romantic life of Paris, which he loved, and where he attended Gertrude Stein's salon many times. He had written several texts and currently was enjoying the popularity brought to him by his book *The Innocents of Paris*, an extended love song to the city and the vehicle for Maurice Chevalier's first American movie, the one which contained the popular song "Louise." With what a thrill we sat in the darkened Loews Ohio Theater and saw the screen credit "From the book by C. E. Andrews," realizing that the very next day we would be sitting in a class taught by the same man. Of such things was high glamor created in the 1920s!

Andrews was infinitely more discreet than Billy Graves, and besides, he lived with a youngish painter of not very much talent named David Snodgrass, who took care of his needs. Try as I would, I could not penetrate the barrier around this idol of mine. Occasionally he would ask a group of three or four students to his home when there was a visiting dignitary or literary luminary, and then he would serve sherry. Thus at his charming balconied house in Arlington, among his thousands of books, we sat and listened to William Butler Yeats, Louis Untermeyer, and a few others. But I could never get closer than that.

I wrote a short novel (imitative of Mann's *Death in Venice*, I fear) about Billy Graves. Andrews read it and scolded me for my preoccupation with sex.

"Richard Cory." Frequently anthologized poem (1897) by Edwin Arlington Robinson (1869–1935) about a man whose personal bearing and social status everyone admires.

Maurice Chevalier (1888–1972). French cabaret singer made famous by a series of starring roles in Hollywood musicals during the 1930s.

Death in Venice. Novella (*Der Tod in Venedig*, 1912) by Thomas Mann about a writer who visits Venice and is enthralled by and then obsessed with a beautiful boy staying with his family at the same hotel.

"Can't you write about anything else, Mr. Steward?" he asked in some exasperation.

"I find all else uninteresting, Dr. Andrews," I said, with one of his twinkles.

"Hm-m. Well, you are perhaps too advanced for your time," he said, smiling.

His classroom manner was impeccable. He could set us quivering with delight at some wordplay or send us into shock with a few remarks. There were no secrets skipped over in his classes. He was the first I knew to speak openly about Oscar Wilde, the decadents of the 1890s, Byron, Shelley, and the rest. His lectures were scrupulously planned and impeccable jewels of organization, filled with bon mots and sometimes the dubious luxury of a high-level pun.

When he died of pneumonia on December 12, 1932, my world was darkened—even shattered. The fact that I have carried the date in my head for nearly fifty years (and have forgotten so many others) should indicate his importance to me: in actuality, I *inhaled* him, I worshiped his intellect and understanding, and I patterned my teaching career around him. I also altered my handwriting. I had earlier changed it to imitate that of Doris Buck, but when Andrews died, I used his handwriting for the rest of my life. It occasionally frightened people who had received letters from him to receive one from me, long after his death.

I even sought out the nurse who had been on duty at the hospital and asked her if he had uttered any last words that she could remember. She must have thought me mad. But she told me that he had been delirious and had been speaking "some foreign language," which I surmised was his beloved French. And having been the previous year temporarily converted to Catholicism in my search for the Great Unknown, I managed to be alone with his body at the funeral home long enough to slip in the breast pocket of his suit a tiny rosary enclosed in a small bone container that screwed apart to hold it. Later, I told a Catholic sponsor about this, who said, "Well, I don't suppose it would hurt . . . but it probably won't do him any good either."

It does not make me happy to remember that about six months after his death, David Snodgrass got in touch with me. He had sold the house in Arlington and was living in a shabby section of Columbus. He had disposed of most of Andrews's valuable library but said that he wanted to return to me

David Snodgrass got in touch with me. In the manuscript, Steward writes that the inscribed copy of his book was returned to him by a friend who found it in a used bookstore and that Snodgrass invited him over to offer him some other books from Andrews's collection (112–13).

the copy of *Pan and the Fire-bird*, the short stories I had done in Andrews's class, which had been published. I had inscribed Andrews's copy in French to the "dear father of these stories."

Snodgrass got me drunk on gin and then crowed at me, "And I suppose that all the time you thought your sainted Claire Andrews was above such low sins of the flesh! Well, let me tell you, dearie—he liked a good fuck as much as anyone, more so I expect, and I was just the one to ram it to him!" He seized on me with a wide monkey mouth, wet and smelling of liquor and onions, sucking at my lips with octopus force, bruising them and making them bleed. He threw me on the narrow bunk bed and screwed me—and I endured it, thinking that the same cock which impaled me had been the one to bring pleasure to Andrews and was therefore tolerable—my last and only link with my dead idol.

Snodgrass died about six months later also of pneumonia and left me wondering what had become of Emily Dickinson's amethyst cross, which Andrews had owned. Only one of the faculty went to the funeral.

Andrews's premature death—he was in his early forties—left me desolate. Of less importance, I was now without a guide on the faculty under whom to do my doctoral dissertation, which I began in 1933 and finished in 1934. The only other professor with whom I was *sympathique* was Harlan Henthorne Hatcher, a tall, good-looking man with a rather prognathous jaw, married to a woman somewhat older than himself. Hatcher was as close-mouthed about his past as Andrews had been—and the stories about Hatcher were even more vivacious than those about Claire. Harlan had, it was said, been a Kaintucky mountain-boy who showed up at some tiny Ohio college barefoot in a raggedy Huck Finn costume and had astounded everyone by his brilliance and the way he sailed through college. He was never able to divest himself of this absurd rumor and seemed not to care about it at all.

Actually, Harlan was born in 1899 in Ohio, reared in Kentucky, graduated with the usual degrees (BA, MA, PhD) from The Ohio State University, with some time at Chicago and a year in Europe. He had written three novels— *Tunnel Hill* (1931), *Patterns of Wolfpen* (1934), *Central Standard Time* (1937)— and a book of literary criticism, *Creating the Modern American Novel* (1935). He was as brilliant as Andrews, no doubt, but his personality was quieter. Yet

Harlan Henthorne Hatcher (1898–1998). Hatcher began teaching at Ohio State in 1922 and earned his PhD in English in 1927, the same year that Steward enrolled. He later served as dean of the College of Arts and Sciences and as vice president; in 1951, he was named the eighth president of the University of Michigan.

he was a stalwart in the fight for academic freedom in actuality and in theory, and he harmed himself at Ohio State by taking up the cause of a professor fired without reason by the regents. Eventually he went into administration and ended by reigning as president of the University of Michigan for many years. Under him as an advisor, I prepared a master's thesis on "Mutability in Spenser" — and then, since there were no jobs available during the Depression years, went on with him to do my doctoral dissertation on "Provocatives of the Oxford Movement and Its Nexus with English Literary Romanticism," a helluva long thing in which I uncovered the fact that Cardinal Newman — and indeed most of the Oxford group in the mid-nineteenth century — was homosexual. Newman even asked to be buried in the same grave with his friend, Ambrose St. John, and had the walls of his private chapel hung with pictures of his male friends rather than those of the saints.

Such a little tidbit, released on a faculty committee in 1934, was almost as much of a bombshell as my early essay on Whitman, and a couple of Jesuits outside the university heard of it and reprimanded me. I think that the non-Catholic members of my oral examining committee enjoyed my revelations — but one French member voted against me because I had forgotten the name of Atala's grandfather, a heinous crime, since I had minored in French. It was also necessary for me to defend myself against a suggestion from an examiner that in my dissertation I went just so far — and then when confronted with Catholic doctrine went no farther. He was intimating that the work was not scholarly because of my recent conversion to Catholicism.

I had gone into the Church by the back door, as a kind of spiritual experiment in my search for answers — which had gone on since my very early years. First of all, I learned from Wilde's *The Picture of Dorian Gray* about

---

uncovered the fact that Cardinal Newman . . . was homosexual. John Henry Newman (1801–90) was a well-known Anglican priest and theologian and a leading figure in the Oxford Movement, which sought to restore elements of pre-Reformation Christianity to the Church of England. A prolific writer on doctrinal and educational issues, Newman converted to Catholicism in 1845, was ordained a Catholic priest in 1846, and became a cardinal in 1879. Similar suggestions about the sexuality of Newman and his Oxford Movement band had also been made by Geoffrey Faber in his *Oxford Apostles: A Character Study of the Oxford Movement* (1933), which Steward cites in his 1934 dissertation.

Atala. Central character in the popular novella *Atala, ou les Amours de Deux Sauvages dans le Désert* (1801), by François-René de Chateaubriand (1768–1848).

a book in which "in exquisite raiment, and to the delicate sound of flutes, the sins of the world were passing in dumb show before him," a book filled with "metaphors as monstrous as orchids," a "poisonous" book about strange purple sins.

This book was *Against the Grain* by Joris-Karl Huysmans. Its sensuality and erudition fascinated me, enchanted me, for it described the life of the senses in terms of mystical philosophy, and the exploits of its hero, Des Esseintes, seemed to range from the ecstasies of a medieval saint to the confessions of a modern sinner. That was the first step. The second was taking a course in the Reformation under a sly and witty professor named Walter Dorn, whose innuendoes and crafty indictments of the Catholic Church called up the Imp of the Perverse in me once again and made me stubbornly determined to find out more about Catholicism.

How richly colorful the vestments of the Church seemed when I first attended a mass! Romantic that I was, the panoply, the incense, the Latin—all worked a spell on me. And I remembered Browning's "The Bishop Orders His Tomb at Saint Praxed's Church," which in about a hundred and twenty-five lines contained more of the spirit of Renaissance Italy than all the volumes of Symonds's *History of the Renaissance* and images such as

> I shall lie through centuries,
> And hear the blessed mutter of the mass,
> And see God made and eaten all day long,
> And feel the steady candle-flame, and taste
> Good strong thick stupefying incense-smoke!

Then, having developed a passionate admiration for Huysmans, I read his *Down There*, a study of Satanism and the Black Mass in Paris. Drawn

---

"in exquisite raiment." These passages, from chapter 10 of Wilde's *The Picture of Dorian Gray* (1891), are generally assumed to refer to the novel *À rebours* (1884), by the French novelist Joris-Karl Huysmans (1848–1907), translated as *Against the Grain* or *Against Nature*.

Walter Dorn (1894–1961). Specialist in eighteenth-century Prussian history who taught at Ohio State from 1931 to 1956.

"The Bishop Orders His Tomb at Saint Praxed's Church." Dramatic monologue (1845) by the Victorian poet Robert Browning (1812–89) that exposes the worldliness of the bishop as he contemplates his death and burial.

Down There . . . The Oblate. English titles of a series of novels by Huysmans that trace the conversion to Catholicism of an autobiographical character named Durtal: *Down There* (*Là-bas*, 1891), *En Route* (1895), *The Cathedral* (*La cathédrale*, 1898), and *The Oblate* (*L'Oblat*, 1903).

ever deeper into the writing of the French aesthete, I then went through *En Route*—about the beginning of his climb back from atheism to the Church; *The Cathedral*—a study of Chartres; and finally, *The Oblate*—detailing the experiences of his last years as an "oblate" dedicated to the monastic life.

That did it. By the time I had thoroughly absorbed Huysmans, I was a Catholic. And this strange odd period of stop-and-go in celibacy and sin lasted for a year and a half.

All of the events of the early years at the university were turned even more dramatic by the fact that we were living in the 1920s, the Age of Discovery, and things were happening all around us that made life even more exciting. In a curious way, the 1920s were an opening, yet the primary struggle was against the forces which wanted to keep the period closed—puritanism and hypocrisy and optimism, the three-footed stool on which America rested. So we watched the birth of jazz and Dixieland, breaking the mold of Stephen Foster; we looked to our midsections as the glow from Freud filtered down to illuminate our crotches; we struggled against censorship—powerful forces under Anthony Comstock and the New York Society for the Suppression of Vice. We hunched over our crystal radio sets, fiddling with the cat whisker to try to tease some night music from the star crackle and the static; we drank bathtub gin and homemade red wine. We read Dreiser and Anderson and Hemingway, sat through endless hours of O'Neill's tragedies, read smuggled copies of Joyce's *Ulysses*, adored Garbo and Stravinsky, listened in awe to the first "talkies," cheered Lindbergh's flight, and wept with the beauty of the Ballet Russe de Monte Carlo.

Anthony Comstock (1844–1915). Driving force behind the Comstock Law of 1873, which criminalized using the US mail to distribute materials whose content was deemed "obscene" under a very broad definition of the term (Comstock targeted documents related to birth control with particular relentlessness). Congress repealed most of the law's provisions in 1971.

crystal radio sets. Early twentieth-century radios, often sold in do-it-yourself kits, that consisted mainly of an antenna wire, a crystal, and a tuning coil. They needed no power source, but their weak signals could only be heard with headphones.

Joyce's Ulysses. Until it was ruled not obscene in the 1933 case *United States v. One Book Called Ulysses*, the 1922 novel by James Joyce (1882–1941) could not legally be published in or imported into the United States.

Ballet Russe de Monte Carlo. Ballet company founded in 1932 as the successor to the Ballets Russes, the great Russian ballet company that traveled the world from 1909 to 1929. Steward describes his infatuation with the Ballet Russe in his *IDJ* essay "On Balletomania" (June 1945).

Who introduced me to the Bohemia in Columbus? I think it was Marie. "You must come with me down to Long Street," she said one day.

"What on earth for?" It was a dismal part of town, close to the bus station.

"Because," said Marie.

"A woman's answer," I said, a reply calculated to annoy her.

"At number 31 East," she said, "there is an old building, a three-story one, which is absolutely honeycombed, m'dear, honeycombed with small apartments and studios, and if you want really to know what life is like in a Midwest Bohemia, you'll come with me to find out."

That did it for me. I had been reading Ben Hecht's *Count Bruga* and knew all about New York's Bohemia and Greenwich Village. I doubted that a Midwest one could come up to it.

But in a way, it did. The building was old and evil-smelling—disinfectant, mold, and stale urine. The stairways were twisted and crazy and the walls flaking with calcimine so old that you could not tell if the original color had been blue or green. And there were many turnings; it was a kind of rabbit-warren of rooms and hallways that became very confusing to a first-time visitor. At intervals, unshaded light bulbs dangled from ceiling cords like strangled felons. Their feeble light made our shadows grotesque on the walls.

Marie took me first to meet Jon Gillespie on the third floor, an artist and a poet of sorts. When we knocked at his door and he let us into his studio, he was holding his bowl of supper in one hand—two small wieners lying atop a shredded wheat biscuit, but whether it was meat sauce or water moistening the odd combination I could not tell. He had sunken pale eyes, high cheekbones, and hollow cheeks. Lank yellow hair, unshorn for a long time, fell over one eye.

Jon was in love with Russell Griffin, who also lived on the third floor. He, too, painted—not very well. Russell was a square-jawed handsome blond giant who first introduced all of us to the music of Erik Satie and played his *Gymnopédie* over and over on an old 78 record he had bought in Paris. *Gymnopédie* he translated as "Dance of the Naked Boys"—perhaps taking a small liberty in transferring the meaning from French to English.

Russell, in turn, was in love with Thelma Walley, a large-nosed charming intellectual who freely went to bed with Russell, whom she much admired, and just as freely bedded with this or that girlfriend. Having heard from un-

Count Bruga. Hecht novel (1926) about Bohemian life in New York's Greenwich Village in the 1920s. See also note on *Fantazius Mallare*, page 57.

Erik Satie (1886–1925). Eccentric but influential French composer whose three piano compositions *Gymnopédies* (1888) made use of unconventional harmonies and dissonances.

impeachable sources that she and Russell frequently had to do with each other, I once asked Tee for the same favor. Still bent on "normalizing" myself? Or just experimenting? I am inclined to think the latter. To my dismay, her eyes widened and in seeming horror she said, "Oh, no, dear — I don't do things like that." To be thus turned down — and lied to in addition — enabled me to sever most of my ties with Tee Walley. We remained good friends, but the first fine careless rapture had fled.

On the second floor of the crazy building on Long Street lived Bobby Creighton, who had a frizzed-out short bob of yellow hair, which she thought gentlemen preferred, but the yellow also had black roots. She was very free with her body, and it was not unusual for her to entertain guests while completely nude, or so nearly — in see-through negligee — that she might as well have been naked. Her library was fantastic for those times, and she was kind enough to lend me many esoteric items — the early poetry of Pound, the work of Joyce and Stein and e. e. cummings, the suppressed drawings of Félicien Rops, the work of Huysmans (*Against the Grain* and *Down There*, the latter almost unavailable anywhere in English). My education bounded ahead. She had a copy of Ben Hecht's *Fantazius Mallare* with the illustrations by Wallace Smith, a book much in the news at the time, for Covici-McGee had been fined for publishing it in 1922. Wallace Smith had been fined for illustrating it (the major basis for the judgment being the frontispiece of a male figure copulating with a huge gnarled "female" tree) — but Ben Hecht had gone free. Just why this had happened was the subject of much debate, for Ben Hecht's text, the fantastic journal of a madman, was fully as obscene by the standards of the day as were the drawings of Wallace Smith.

Once Marie had introduced me into this charmed circle, I found my way there alone almost every weekend, and sometimes even during the school nights. Red wine was plentiful, and I managed to contribute my share even on my severely curtailed money. I was so much a part of the circle, indeed, that once I went with Bobby Creighton to Lima, Ohio, to visit someone and remember waking up in bed with her and a handsome young man (she had slept between us) who was slowly, leisurely screwing her in the morning and paying no attention to me whatsoever. I caressed his moving buttocks. Alas, he was quite resistant to my importuning.

Hovering in and out of this group was a number of persons from the university besides Marie and myself: Virginia Cooley, the tall cool imperturb-

---

Félicien Rops (1833–98). Belgian printmaker whose work was known for its erotic themes.
Covici-McGee. Chicago publishing house and bookstore founded in 1922. See also note on *Fantazius Mallare*, page 57.

able tawny beauty queen, a liberated soul like the rest of us; Carolyn Whitcomb, a totally deaf and very ugly girl, but an accomplished lip-reader (it used to amuse me to "talk" to her without making any sounds, using only the lip movements, which she understood perfectly); Robert von Riggle, the sandy-haired flamboyant creature who was always floridly onstage; and a shy dark little boy named Ted Carl Wilson.

T. C. Wilson had been published; his poetry had appeared in *Poetry: A Magazine of Verse*, edited in Chicago by Harriet Monroe. For this reason, he was much admired and sought out—but he resisted all of it. No one ever knew whether he was homosexual or not, although gossip had paired him with everyone from Russell Griffin on down or up. It was known, however, that he was very friendly with Benjamin Musser, the poet laureate of New Jersey. As poet laureate, he had in my opinion written only one good line in all his life: "I cannot live away from water."

Somehow—whether through T. C. Wilson or Marie Anderson, who was a good friend of Wilson's—I made the acquaintance of Tessa Sweazy Webb, the poet laureate of Ohio. Both Musser and Webb wrote what you might expect—dull sentimental poems about God and life and flowers, the sort of thing Ella Wheeler Wilcox and Edgar Guest turned out in vast quantities to soothe the plebian mind.

At any rate, one evening I was invited downtown by Tessa Webb to the Chittenden Hotel to hear Benjamin Musser read his poems and lecture on poesy; he lived in Margate City and was making a tour to promote himself and his magazine, *Contemporary Verse*, as well as its unimportant offshoot, *JAPM*, the initials for "Just Another Poetry Magazine." On the evening he read, I hopped a streetcar to go downtown, slipped on the entry step, stumbled, and tore a large hole in the knee of my trousers. There was not time to go home to change, so I went on. And since I arrived late, all the back seats were filled; I had to sit in the very front row, where the combination of

---

Ted [Theodore] Carl Wilson (1912–50). Poet and Marxist critic whose work led to friendships with many of the leading poets of the 1930s. Interrupted by service in World War II, his career foundered, and he died shortly thereafter.

"I cannot live away from water." Title of a 1929 poem by Benjamin Musser (1889–1951). Steward also quotes this line in his *IDJ* essay "On Chicago" (August 1946) and in his erotic novel *The Boys in Blue*, where Phil, the narrator, calls it "the only good line of poetry that old Ben Messer [sic], one of my earliest scores, had ever written" (Phil Andros [Samuel Steward], *The Boys in Blue* [San Francisco: Perineum Press, 1984], 139).

Ella Wheeler Wilcox (1850–1919) and Edgar Guest (1881–1959). Authors of popular but unsophisticated and frequently mocked verse.

Margate City. Oceanfront town south of Atlantic City, New Jersey.

a torn trouser leg and (as Ben later said) my "ethereal face" hardly allowed his eyes to roam anywhere else. T. C. Wilson, sitting a few seats away, looked angrily at me all through the evening.

That, I thought as I left, after having been presented to His Royal Highness, King of Poetasters, is that. I expected to hear nothing more of the whole episode.

To my surprise, however, a few weeks later Ben Musser wrote me a cordial letter asking me to submit some verse to him for possible appearance in his magazine. I remember that I turned out one called "Virgina [sic] to Harlotta," ostensibly written from one woman to another. But the only lines I recall from it are the last two:

> Weave me a spell, O bow-boy, so that he
> Embracing her sends his caress to me!

—a statement which should take care of any reasonable doubt arising anywhere.

"And lo! from that chance meeting," as Huysmans wrote in À rebours, "there sprang a mistrustful friendship that endured for several years."

Mistrustful in several ways. On my first visit to Margate City, Ben read me with much cackling humor a verse of his beginning:

> I am in love with six young men
>   I love them tenderly.
> Oh, I can be faithful now and then
>   But they've all been false to me.

—and went on to name them: Parker Tyler, Charles Henri Ford, Ted Carl Wilson, myself, and a coupla others whom I have forgotten. Thus I saw that I was not the only shepherd of his eclogues, and it annoyed me.

It was not a match calculated to endure.

Still, it was exciting while it lasted.

I must have irritated him by referring rather frequently to the fact that he was forty and I twenty. And once, suspecting that he was steaming open and reading the letters that I sent back to Marie, I put a small piece of chew-

---

"And lo! from that chance meeting." The line appears in chapter 9 of Huysmans's *Against the Grain.*

eclogues. A poetic form originating in classical literature in which shepherds converse in an idyllic pastoral setting.

ing gum under the flap of the envelope. Sure enough, he showed up with the letter, trailing filaments of gum, and demanded that I open it and read it to him. I resisted for quite a while, using all the best arguments, but finally gave in. He was not pleased to hear his demands described as those of a "lecherous old skeleton with bird claws" nor his mouth referred to as "sunken like an old woman's." It took a lot of sweet talk to get out of that situation with a whole skin; I had to turn accusatory and confront him with all sorts of sins against privacy, trust, and Boy Scout ethics.

Ben published a poem or two of mine in his magazine *Contemporary Verse*, and in 1930, he subsidized the publication of my *Pan and the Fire-bird* by Henry Harrison, a small New York publisher, the vanguard of the vanity presses. His introduction was extravagant; he called me "the golden boy" and "heir to Theocritus" and said he knew me twenty-five hundred years ago, when I was an "engrossing young Greek." Then he confused matters by additionally calling me "a gorgeous Renaissance personality." This was all very intoxicating stuff for someone barely twenty-one years old.

Ben was married to a fairly wealthy woman — and he sent me money. He paid for my trips east, and for the first time in my life I flew in an airplane. This must have been in 1928 or 1929, on TAT, Transcontinental Air Transport (later to become TWA). The trip went from Columbus to somewhere in New Jersey or perhaps Philadelphia, and I remember one of the excursions quite vividly. There was a storm with much thunder and lightning; we were flying just under the clouds, so that when you looked out the window you saw the low uneven level of the cloud line, out of which jagged lightning thrust itself in bursts that were alarmingly near. And the plane itself was hardly weatherproof — designed perhaps for fair weather only. It leaked directly over my seat. A steward brought a tarpaulin of some sort to put over my lap, since there were no empty places available in the twenty-four-seat plane. The meals aboard those early flights were simply a sandwich or two wrapped in wax paper — cheese or salami. The coffee came out of a large thermos jug — and when that was empty, there was no more, not even water to drink.

But it was fun, and after all you had the feeling you were a pioneer doing

---

trailing filaments of gum. Cf. "trailing clouds of glory," line 64 in "Ode: Intimations of Immortality" (1804), by William Wordsworth (1770–1850).

Theocritus. Third-century BCE Greek poet regarded as the creator of bucolic, or pastoral, poetry.

Transcontinental Air Transport. Airline founded in 1928 that merged in 1930 with Western Air Express to form Transcontinental & Western Air (T&WA). After 1950, the airline was known as Trans World Airlines; it went bankrupt in 2001.

a daredevil thing. Only two years previously, Lindbergh had flown the Atlantic—and here you were, flying from Columbus into the magic world of intellect and creativity, guest of the poet laureate of New Jersey! Could anything be more exciting than that?

It was not always the airplane; sometimes I went by train. And on one of those train trips, a Pullman porter crawled into my berth one night, stayed a while, and left me feeling peaceful and very drowsy. But alas! Three weeks later in Margate, a small indurated lesion appeared on the glans of my favorite plaything, and guess what it was! Yeah. The pox. Lues. *Le siflis.*

Given my loathing of uncleanliness, the shock nearly unraveled me. Even today, it would probably do the same, although fortunately this catastrophe has been experienced only once. I felt myself teeming with millions, billions, of spirochetes—and indeed I undoubtedly was—in my sweat, tears, blood, saliva, urine, everything. I had to tell Ben about the porter. His reaction was intense displeasure.

"I never want to see you again," he shouted.

"Nor I you, you old fart!" I retorted elegantly.

That particular visit was to have been a triumphal one, to celebrate the publication of *Pan and the Fire-bird.* But the chancre spoiled all that. I was hustled back to Ohio, my arm-crook aching from the first shot of Neosalvarsan, the arsenical discovered by Dr. Paul Ehrlich, his "magic bullet," formula 606. And Ben had his own shot—which laid him low, because his liver was none too good to begin with.

I wired ahead, and Marie Anderson met me at the station. She made as if to embrace me and kiss me.

"Don't touch me!" I shouted and backed away from her, bursting into tears.

Such was the beginning of a three-year ordeal—weekly shots of Neosalvarsan from a doctor, Joe Griffith, who had been a classmate of my father's.

Lindbergh. Charles Lindbergh (1902–74), the first person to fly solo across the Atlantic Ocean, in 1927.

Lues. From Latin, "a plague or pestilence; a spreading disease, *esp.* syphilis (*Lues venerea*)" (*OED*).

formula 606. Salvarsan, an arsenic-based compound developed in 1907 by the German scientist Paul Ehrlich (1854–1915), which along with its less toxic variant, Neosalvarsan (formula 914), remained the best treatment against syphilis until the development of penicillin in the 1940s. It exemplified Ehrlich's search for a "magic bullet," that is, an agent that would attack disease-causing organisms without harming healthy organs and tissue. Because of the potentially deadly effects of arsenic if brought into contact with the body's tissues, however, the drug had to be carefully injected directly into the bloodstream.

And my father had to know, too; I must credit him for not condemning me overmuch, and at this point I cannot remember if he asked me how I got it. It would have been very unlikely for him to do so, considering the embarrassment he always felt about things sexual. I believe that he quoted my grandfather's statement to those boys who didn't know where they had picked up something: "It's like backing into a buzz saw, ain't it? You can't tell which tooth bit you."

And so I left the sacred forest of physical delights for quite a while. Without trying to seem noble about it, I must confess that I was very scrupulous about infecting anyone. I went weekly for my shot—noting the sharp overwhelming smell of ether that occurred subjectively (the doctor could not smell it) when the arsenic first hit the bloodstream each time. I suffered various side effects—such as the purpura that once occurred in my mouth and on my back and the ulcer in the bend of my arm when the medico got a couple of drops of the compound outside the vein. Finally, after many months, there was a program of rubbing a mercury ointment into armpits and groin, and after that a "shelling of the woods"—a course of saturated solution of potassium iodide, rising daily in number of drops to a peak and then reducing—the whole thing lasting about three weeks. The drug caused the skin on one's back to erupt in what looked like Job's boils.

The kids today who can have their syphilis cured in a matter of weeks with penicillin are hardly aware of their happy state. Without seeming to be puritanical or too much of a moralist, I suggest that a great deal more care might be taken nowadays in physical relationships if penicillin did not exist. It was one hell of a thing to go through in 1930.

Yet I am not sure that the whole episode traumatized me too much. One can get used to anything, even weekly shots for three years. My romantic encounters were curtailed for several months, until the tests showed me free of bugs. During that time, I made no new friends—and I am sure that my old friends wondered just what the hell had happened to turn me into a noncooperating celibate. It was hard for me to find excuses—sometimes almost impossible except for a blunt "No." I could not very well say that I had got religion or been born again: too many of my acquaintances knew that I was not religious at all. Still, the shock must have indeed been great; until this day I have never told anyone the details of my experience. Shame has deep roots, particularly when they have grown in Methodist soil.

Once the interruption was ended, my life went on much the same as before—new acquaintances made, patterns unfolding, ties and cross-ties looming in the ever-widening circles of mutual friends and contacts. The telequeen network was developing rapidly.

One of the gathering places—for of course there were no bars, since Prohibition was still in effect—was the apartment of Merle Dean, back in an alley near the public library, heavily wooded and with shrubbery growing. It seemed always a delightful rendezvous and Merle was a good host, always with something on hand to drink.

It was there that I met two persons at different times whom I was to know for many years. One of them was Kevin Kleeman, a small guy with red curly hair and a kind of ambling bowlegged walk—but much in demand because of his considerable endowment. He worked as an assistant manager for a drugstore chain and eventually came to stay with my aunts at 47 17th Avenue, very close to the campus.

For many years, Kevin and I were "sisters"—the camp word for persons who were extremely close friends but did not indulge in romantic encounters. He was extremely sensitive about the fact that he had never been to a university, and he considered himself less fortunate because less "educated." It did not, however, make a bit of difference in his popularity, which was measured with a different kind of gauge. Like a couple of old maids, we exchanged confidences, discussed our "problems," nudged each other as we passed handsome persons on campus and graded them A, B, C, or D according to the size of what they showed. And I comforted him when he came screaming to me the time his hair caught on fire from the alcohol shampoo he had used too close to an open stove.

It was not until perhaps 1933 that Kevin and I had anything really to do with each other emotionally, and then we fell into each other's arms with loud exclamations of pity for ourselves and for the jolly good times we had deprived ourselves of in the past.

The second person was a handsome guy named Dino Bellini, with sleek black hair and a heavy beard mark and heavy hair on forearms and chest. We camped a lot together, and he really became my best friend in the years from 1929 to 1934. We went places together, cruised together, and in an age which still remembered the "sheik" type, Dino proved very popular. He had a considerable artistic talent, and one of the sketches I wrote in *Pan and the Fire-bird*, "Amor Profanis," is derived from an ink drawing that he did for me.

Like Kevin, Dino and I did not touch each other for many years. Then suddenly we did, and it was a repetition of the Kevin Kleeman experience.

But alas, something came between us. Dino had a large square-cut amethyst ring set in silver, of which he was very proud. It disappeared, and he believed that I had taken it. This conviction was underlined for him by the enlargement of a couple of snapshots which Marie Anderson took of me at that time; she wanted to preserve an image of me with a small anchor-beard which I wore for a month or two. In one of the prints she posed my hands folded together on my knee — and pulled from her finger a large square-cut ruby ring which she had been wearing and put it on my finger.

About two months later Dino saw the picture — in black and white; color was too expensive — and accused me of swiping his ring. In vain did I try to explain about Marie Anderson's ruby, but he was convinced it was his lost "bitch badge," as we called such costume jewelry in those days. I tried to get in touch with Marie, who by then had gone on to New York; my letter was returned marked "Addressee Unknown."

And that — unfortunately — was that. Dino never believed that I had not stolen his amethyst ring. Should he be alive and should he see this — how's about it, old cock? *I didn't take the goddamned ring.*

Or as we used to say: "Come home, Miss Mitchell — all is forgiven."

Sources: *Chapters*, 18–30; Manuscript, 16, 93–123.

Chapter Three

OUT OF THE NURSERY, INTO THE WIDE WIDE

1934–36

Clutching my brand-new PhD, I was now ready to go out into the world to bring light and culture and English grammar to mankind. It was June 1934. The Depression was five years old, and you took what job you could get. Through the placement office, there was a hurry-up call for a summer-session teacher at Davis and Elkins College in Elkins, West Virginia.

"Are you available," they said, "and do you want it?"

"Yes, indeed," I said, and off I went.

It was like going back to Woodsfield—perhaps worse. In Ohio, I had grown up gradually with the narrow attitudes, becoming somewhat hardened to them. Then came the freedom of Columbus. But in Elkins I was suddenly thrust deep into bigotry once again after the comparative liberalism of the university.

The president of the college, a man named James Allen, looked like a political caricature—his ears were phenomenal, standing out from his head like Dumbo's; his voice was nasal and filled with a mountain twang. He was authoritarian, and his mind was closed. As an instance of his character, when his dog bit me, he promptly had the ownership transferred to his black gardener. He was married to a white-haired FFV—First Families of Virginia—woman named Parke, who at fifty promptly fell in love with me, made me her confidant, and told me in the long afternoons how wickedly her husband treated her. She was almost the first woman who found me "motherable," as Gertrude Stein was later to say. Parke served me liquor and wine, although

president of the college. Contemporary photographs of James E. Allen (1876–1950), president of Davis and Elkins College from 1910 to 1935, suggest that Steward only slightly exaggerates the size of his ears.

the *mores* of the town and of her husband made it necessary for this gesture to be kept very secret.

The two of them rattled around in a decaying ghostly gothic mansion called Halliehurst, perched farther up the hill from the college. It was all of sagging wood, with a creaking two-story porch running halfway around it. Inside, there was an echoing wood-paneled dining room containing a long table that could have seated thirty, complete with servants' bell under the carpet at the host's foot! Hollywood might have used it for a horror film.

It was an odd time. I lived "downtown" at the YMCA, which that summer was filled with earnest young Mormon missionaries bent on proselytizing anyone who would pause—and I often found time to listen, especially to the handsomest ones, whose scorn of the human body was such that they frequently went to and from the showers draped only in a scanty YMCA towel. Although they talked long and solemnly about "secret abominations" and the "abominable connections" of man and woman or man and man and of "works in darkness," these young zealots seemed genuinely fascinated by the evil stalking the corridors in the person of the young sinner who taught at the wicked college up the hill. Several of them sinned repeatedly with this ungodly man.

The students of that summer session were mostly sincere females bent on acquiring a BA so they could teach in the high schools of West Virginia. A sample of education in Elkins: One of my courses was the tragedies of Shakespeare. I was one day endeavoring to explain in delicate terms the meaning of "cuckold," when a lank-haired, flat-heeled, bespectacled pimply girl in the front row said, "Dr. Steward, does that word mean the same as 'w-h-o-r-e' that I see a lot in Shakespeare?"

Try to get out of that one. I ignored the greasy sniggers from the boys in the back row. "No," said I, "that word *may* refer to the wife who makes a cuckold of her husband" and fled to the next topic.

Being a Catholic, especially a new one, in Elkins had its drawbacks. One night the college dean invited a group of us to dinner, and afterward we talked a lot, sitting on the porch swing and in rocking chairs, with the smell of honeysuckle strong in the twilight air and the swing chains squeaking near the ceiling. Somehow the conversation shifted to religion. I sensed that I was being evaluated, considered for a full-time teaching position during the regular school year. They expressed themselves in one way or another about God's mercy, salvation, being born again, and such like. Then one of them fell to damning the Vicar Apostolic, who had been so designated by Rome to undo the frightful incests and intermarriages of Appalachia, for interfering in "the folkways of the mountain people," and that led to a sudden burst of all the misinformation which as a child I had heard and absorbed in Woods-field—the stockpiling of guns and ammunition for the day of the Catholic takeover, the secret tunnels between sacristy and convent, the importing of scarlet women and clothing them as nuns, and on and on until darkness had completely fallen.

During this time, I was quite silent, and finally the dean in his oily Presbyterian tones with the minor-third inflection at each sentence end said, "And what faith do you profess, Dr. Steward?"

"Well," I said, "after investigating a great number of faiths and considering the historical evidence carefully, I was forced to conclude there was only one uninterrupted religion which could be traced back to Jesus, and so about six months ago, I joined the Holy Roman Catholic Church."

The silence was profound. The porch swing stopped squeaking. A mosquito sang above our heads, and only my wicker rocker went noisily on. Finally, the dean spoke. "Interesting," he said, "and I am glad we live in a day when all faiths can commingle."

I got no offer for the fall term.

"Why in the world did you have to tell them that?" Parke scolded me angrily.

I shrugged. "Despite your very pleasant company," I said, "a year in Elkins would drive me completely mad."

When I returned to Columbus, there was word from the placement agency of an opening in a small college in Helena, Montana. It sounded awful—$100 a month, room and board, a small Catholic college called Carroll—but it would cut the umbilical cord that had until then bound me to my aunts and family for all the years of my life. At that moment, there was nothing I could have desired more.

And the West! The glamorous unspoiled West! Cowboys! The gold rush! Chaps! Ghost towns! Cowboys! Silver and gold mines! Cowboys! Ah, I would like the West!

I did not, particularly. Trying to teach cowboys and the sons of cowboys about semicolons is not a rewarding pastime. The college was a dormitory college, and my room was barren and austere, painted green halfway up the wall and dirty beige above. There was absolutely nothing to do in the Helena evenings except play chess with the science professor, Edward Neuman, and look at the Rocky Mountains, twenty miles away, blue, serene, and cloud-capped.

My father's name was Samuel Vernon Steward, and before I left for the

Wild West, he had told me to look up Samuel Vernon Stewart, who lived in Helena and who had been a former governor of the state. It would seem that when my father and the governor were born, back near Jerusalem, Ohio, the two mothers — each carrying her child — had agreed that if it were a male it would be named Samuel Vernon — Steward and Stewart.

And so by this curious coincidence, I felt that after all I had not completely severed connections with my background.

The Stewarts were very good to me, and we went riding a lot in their large black automobile. In Montana, an after-dinner drive on a Sunday afternoon could easily be three hundred miles; no one thought that a great distance at all out there. Under the guidance of "Governor" Stewart, I became acquainted with the landscape — saw my first tumbleweeds and the haystacks that cured green inside. The abundant forests seemed to stand almost childishly straight and placed in rows — evergreen and quaking aspen. I had a faint shudder at first view of the skeletal Hangman's Tree standing stark against the skyline and sunset, with the one low straight-out branch over which the rope used to be flung. We wandered through Marysville, a ghost town, absolutely deserted save for the shreds of one ragged pink blanket flapping forlornly from a line; I wondered how long it had been there, for the empty buildings now were haunted wooden frame houses, weathered to a grey-brown, with rust streaks from all the nails.

It did get cold in Montana. During that winter, we had a two-week period of minus 35-degree weather, warming up in the afternoons to minus 30. To go out, you had to wear a scarf under your hat, swathed around face and neck completely with only a slit open for guidance, and often your kneecaps were frostbitten if you had to be out more than a half hour. We sometimes amused ourselves at the college by opening a third-floor window and spitting out; the spittle would freeze before striking the ground. And a glass of water, if poured slowly in a thin stream, hit the earth with a tinkle of broken icicles.

To my room with its institutionally colored walls I somewhat indiscreetly invited the smartest boys in my English classes to have some sherry before dinner. How civilized, I thought, how like the sherry parties at Oxford and Cambridge when Wilde held forth! Some of them I knew would turn out to be homosexual, and others alcoholics; it was easy to sense. And so Jimmy and Gerry and Juan and Sherman came often. Of the favored four, it was only the hot-blooded Irish-Spanish boy Juan with whom I had anything to do — a curi-

Samuel Vernon Stewart (1872–1939). Progressive Montana politician and governor of the state from 1913 to 1921.

ous young man who washed out his rubbers and used them again. One night, drunk, we went to Ida's whorehouse in Helena—the only one I ever saw with a neon sign: "Ida's. Rooms with Girls." Juan went upstairs whilst I sat and talked with Ida, who as the reigning madam could make or break any new shop which opened in Helena. A floral wreath with a banner saying "From Ida and the Girls" was prominently displayed in those new shop windows which made the grade.

I should have been content with Juan, but late one night—drunk as usual—I crept downstairs and went to the room of a young red-headed butch cowboy I had found sexually exciting named Keith. I never heard any more about it, but I strongly suspect that he confessed the whole episode to Monsignor Riley, the president of the college, and named his partner.

The guilty feeling about Keith, the impoverished state in which the meager salary kept me, the pontifical attitudes of several of the priests attached to the college, my growing alcoholism—all these were not calculated to make me much enjoy the idea of returning to the college for the following year. Secretly, therefore, I pulled a string or two through Governor Stewart and got myself hired as an "information clerk" for the coming summer at Glacier National Park. And working through a teachers' employment agency in Chicago, I also succeeded in landing a job as instructor at Washington State College for the next year.

But the year in Helena was made exciting by at least two things. For three years, I had been corresponding with Gertrude Stein, having written to her about the death of Claire Andrews, who had so often visited her salon. She had responded warmly, and our letter writing continued. When she and Alice made their whirlwind trip through America in 1934–35, lecturing at colleges and clubs, I tried to arrange for her to lecture at Carroll College and to a women's club in Helena. Her fee for universities was only a hundred dollars (a month's salary for me) and for clubs, two hundred and fifty. The two Helena lectures were arranged, with myself guaranteeing the college fee. But Alice Toklas, as business manager, knew that even in 1934 the money was not enough for such a side-trip, and through my efforts she tried to arrange lectures at three state universities—Montana, Oregon, and Washington, at which latter she had studied music thirty-five years before. Alas, nothing happened with the three universities: isolated from what was going on in literature, each of them folded or reneged for one reason or another— and when the telegram came from Alice thanking me for my efforts but announcing the date of their sailing back to France, I broke down and wept. My regret and unhappiness were only slightly tempered by receiving one day a very large matted portrait of Gertrude, one of Carl Van Vechten's studies of her, on the lower margin of which she had written: "For Sam Steward and when we meet we do meet but we do meet as we have met and it always has been and will be a pleasure," with her signature following. It is still a prized possession.

The second somewhat exciting thing was the result of my kicking against the pricks, to use an old Biblical expression that was not originally intended to convey the shades of meaning I put into it. Full of rancor at the shabby treatment afforded a sincere lay teacher—and at the moment, a zealous convert—by the several unfortunately arrogant and dismally uninformed priests on the faculty, I sat down one bitter evening and wrote an article on "The Lay Faculty." I sent it off to *The Commonweal*, a national Catholic magazine, under a scrambled anagram of the letters of my name: "Ward Stames." To my complete surprise, it was accepted and appeared in the issue of April 12, 1935.

Briefly, I wrote a completely negative criticism, asking a number of barbed and touchy questions: Why did not more young Catholic laymen accept jobs in Catholic colleges, and why could these colleges not hold them for more than a year? In my youthful blasting, I railed against the priests who thought that the laying on of hands also imparted to them the wisdom to teach mathematics or sociology and complained bitterly that the insults and humiliations visited upon the lay teacher had the result of turning him

Carl Van Vechten (1880–1964). Influential critic of the arts, patron of writers of the Harlem Renaissance, photographer, and longtime friend of Gertrude Stein, who appointed him her literary executor.

kicking against the pricks. Cf. Acts 9:5, where a "prick" is a pointed stick for driving cattle; the phrase thus means resisting being prodded. Steward uses the term in its twentieth-century slang meaning: "a stupid, contemptible, or annoying person" (*OED*).

the insults . . . visited upon the lay teacher. In a sentence whose periodic structure creates a rising sense of injustice, Steward catalogued some of the indignities he experienced "at a small college in the West": "When announcements posted on the faculty bulletin board and consistently addressed to 'Faculty Members' were discovered to be meant only for the priests and excluded without the suggestion of an explanation or apology the lay professors; when these men were not invited to faculty gatherings; when they were compelled on state occasions to leave their usual place in the refectory and sit like trained seals at a small table below their former seats which had been taken over by the priests, and this in full view of the student body; when they discovered they had no voice in running their own department even though they were head of it; when they were never consulted on a question of policy and were invariably omitted from the committees on studies and discipline; when they found their lives and ambitions crumbling under these and a hundred small humiliations—could they avoid saying rather cynically to themselves that they were mere hired hands?" (Ward Stames [Samuel Steward], "The Lay Faculty," *Commonweal*, April 12, 1935, 668).

into a "glorified janitor." Many priest-teachers, I held, acted as dictators over those whose educational qualifications were superior to their own.

All hell, as one might say, broke loose.

The article created a small storm that raged for many weeks in *The Commonweal*'s pages—answers to the article, refutations, amplifications, plus a host of letters either violently agreeing with my thesis or disagreeing. The president of the college read it and did not recognize it as my work. But the discussions that erupted over it in the faculty room were loud, caustic, resentful, and sour. The only other layman in residence was my chess opponent Neuman, the chemistry/physics/biology/zoology/all-sciences teacher. It was he who finally solved the puzzle by the simple device of putting together "STB degree," which was mentioned in the same sentence as "little Caesar," our private nickname for Father Weber.

"You wrote it," he said accusingly.

"Don't tell Riley until I leave for the summer," I said. He promised he wouldn't.

Then it was off to Glacier Park and to the post of information clerk at Lake McDonald Hotel at the western end of the park.

The surroundings were serene. Now the continental divide was only three miles away and to the east, not the west as it had been in Helena. Mornings and afternoons, you could watch the fantastic play of light on the mountain range called the Garden Wall and as evening came, see it blaze with scarlet light and then change to darkest purple and at last fade into the black of night. The spectacular sunsets made you think that the sky, released from the tedium of maintaining its blinding azure all day long, had at last decided to enjoy itself in lovely orgies of wildest magenta, topaz, and garnet. On days when there was no sun, the Garden Wall turned grey and silver, and its reflection shimmered in the green-black waters of Lake McDonald.

"Information clerk" was a misnomer. My real duties—only in the evening, every evening—were putting on a suit and trying to sell saddle-horse trips at outrageous fees to the dude tourists, pack trips into the wilderness, complete with authentic cowboy guide. You developed quite a line as you learned more about the work and talked to the dudes—low and sexy to the gals, man-to-man to the guys—about the wonders of solitude, of sleeping under the million stars, of coffee brewed over an open fire and steaks sizzling. You never said anything about the mosquitoes, the ever-present wood

STB degree. Bachelor of Sacred Theology.
Lake McDonald Hotel. Built in 1913 in a dramatic Swiss-chalet style; designated a National Historic Landmark in 1987.

Steward on horseback at Sperry Glacier in Glacier National Park,
July 30, 1935. (Courtesy of the Estate of Samuel M. Steward)

ticks, and the dangers of spotted fever and snakes, and you soft-pedaled the extraordinary price of the tours.

For this small restriction of your freedom, you were paid a few bucks a week. You ate in the main dining room, slept in a small cabin, and in general enjoyed your paid vacation. You were free to take a saddle-horse ride when you didn't have to work or to go fishing in the noisy streams in the afternoon. In the chalet, the fire burned every evening in a fireplace large enough to sit inside on rough log benches. And for fun, there was always trying to make Bull, a tall, grey-eyed butch bellboy.

I got along fine with the dudes, being as poetic and persuasive as I could be, and really enjoying the work. I had only a minimal private scorn for the Great American Tourist who came in shorts and knobby knees or slacks stretched over wobbling pear-shaped fat behinds. All of them were seeking some rest and relaxation and perhaps a small flirtation with the leathery cowboy guides, as brave a bunch of unprincipled bandits as you would ever wish to see.

It was all my own little kingdom for a while after my superior left and before brash young handsome Clayton burst into this idyllic summer like a small whirlwind. From the first, there was a personality clash. He was loud and bossy. The two of us did not get along together at all, and the rest of the summer was filled with scores and draws—a hundred incidents and annoyances, the battle between us becoming a kind of deadly game. I remembered Blake's poem "A Poison Tree" and tried to find the apple with which to do him in—maintaining a false and sunny simplicity while I stabbed him in the back. And he did the same to me but less cleverly. By the end of his first four weeks there, everyone was aware of the feud between us, and most of them blamed him for it. People saw through his clumsy tricks and ended by siding with me. I let them.

My search for the ultimate stratagem was complicated by the fact that we had to room together in a very small log cabin. But I had one advantage: I did not drink on duty—and he did. Moreover, he could not hold his liquor well, had blackouts, and was several times caught by Mrs. Barley, the hotel manager. And there was one other complication. Despite my dislike of his dirty tricks, his brashness and arrogance and all the rest, I found him extremely attractive physically—a heavy sexual aura, extremely handsome with black curly hair and a body with excellently defined musculature. Watching him undress from my lower bunk bed created both temptation and desire in me.

One night he was put off the dance floor during the square dance, drunk, and that was the night that I ministered unto him. I was in bed when he came to the cabin and had to help him get undressed. It was too much for me. He could not climb up into his own bunk, so he slept in mine—and so did I, moving to the upper one in the early dawn. Put another card into my Stud File.

Unfortunately, he did not have the memory blackout that night which he should have had, and the next day he told Mrs. Barley, who sent for me.

"I'll get right to the point," the ancient white-haired little lady said; there was no nonsense about her. "Clayton said that after the dance last night you made homosexual advances to him." It rocked me to hear her use the word;

Blake's poem "A Poison Tree." Poem (1794) by eccentric English poet William Blake (1757–1827) in which the speaker nurtures the anger he feels toward his enemy ("And I sunned it with smiles, / And with soft deceitful wiles" [lines 7–8]) and celebrates his ultimate vengeance.

she looked so sweet and grandmotherly that you wouldn't have believed it to be in her vocabulary.

I sputtered with histrionic outrage. She silenced me with her hand.

"It's nonsense, I know," she said. "Anyone who has watched you two squabble all summer would know that homosexual advances would be the last thing you would make. Clayton was drunk and obnoxious, and I have already asked him to leave. He can pack and take the six-thirty bus to the station. If I were you, I would arrange to have someone in your cabin while he packs." She looked at me. "Why don't you ask Bull to be there? You seem to get along with him very well."

I did—and Clayton left, furious. Bull moved into the vacant bunk in my cabin, and the rest of the summer was very interesting indeed.

With my escape from Carroll College came also my escape from the Catholic Church. Besides my disillusion with its western priests, the materialism instilled in me at Ohio State was too ingrained to allow me to continue. My allegiance lasted a year and a half, and then the boyhood indoctrination against the Whore of Babylon won out. I had been attracted by the Catholic liturgy and by Huysmans—and long ago, perhaps in the course of a grim Methodist Sabbath, I had dreamed of an altar before which I could prostrate myself in adoration. The symbols of the Catholic Church met the needs of my imagination and the hungers of my heart, all massed on the borders of my imagination. And I thought I had found a creed elastic enough to allow for my pagan love of life—but the basic honesty infused into me by my early training made me realize that I could never make a perfect act of contrition. I could not swear "not to sin again" because I knew very well that I would, over and over—and I could not endure being such a hypocrite as to return countless times with the same promise, knowing that I might break it before the day was out. And celibacy was not for me. Good luck to the movement of homosexual Catholics called Dignity, but the basic truth remains: as long as Church doctrine remains as it is, no one with honesty can be both a Catholic and a homosexual.

act of contrition. Prayer of penance in Catholic and other Christian practice in which one asks God for forgiveness and promises not to sin again.
Dignity. Founded in 1970, Dignity USA is an organization offering fellowship, support, and worship opportunities for LGBTQ Catholics. In 1986, seven years after Steward wrote, the Vatican ordered American bishops to ban the organization from using church property for meetings or weekly Mass.

When fall arrived, I went on to the State College of Washington at Pullman. I liked the ambience — the rolling green hills intensely emerald from the abundant rain and snowfall, a real Grant Wood landscape. And I also liked the idea of teaching in a state school, away from the religiosity of places like Carroll and Davis and Elkins. For a time, all was very pleasant indeed. But Washington, alas, was not as free and intellectual as one might think. The narrow ideas of the other places were still there — differently and subtly rearranged. Consider, for instance, the question of alcohol. In the state of Washington at that time, you had to purchase a permit to buy liquor — a cheap-enough permit, perhaps two dollars, but without it you could buy nothing. And the president of the college, E. O. Holland, as fanatic a man as the president of Davis and Elkins, did not approve of liquor. He tried during that year to compel the state licensing board to reveal the names of those faculty members who had purchased permits — because, as he threatened, he would fire all those of his faculty who were imbibing the Demon Rum. He did not get the list, or I would have been out before I started.

My position as lowly instructor did not give me much variety in teaching. It was mostly freshman English, with lots of weekly themes to grade and no possibility of an assistant. The freshman program was presided over by a strange nervous bald-headed old maid named Paul Kies. He demanded that we keep our graded to-be-returned themes in certain pigeonhole locations — and from thence he would frequently extract and survey, to see if his freshman teachers were grading too high. They might thus ruin the "grade curve" by which he — as a man trained in a college of education somewhere — lived and moved and had his being. One of the large annoyances falling to me was a class in remedial spelling, administered to all sorts of football players and athletes who had failed freshman English. They had to take the spelling course without credit, and there they sat squirming, the great handsome hulks, while I amused myself by occasionally giving out shock words contained in illustrative sentences to see who would react, and how. For an example: "Spell the word 'queer,' as in the sentence 'All English teachers are a

---

Grant Wood (1891–1942). American painter of rural landscapes, best known for his iconic American Gothic (1930).

E. O. Holland (1874–1950). President of the State College of Washington (later Washington State University) from 1916 to 1944.

Paul Kies. Though Steward mocks his pedagogy as typical of schools of education, Paul Philemon Kies (1891–1971) actually held undergraduate and MA degrees in German and music and had completed a PhD in English at the University of Chicago in 1928.

lived and moved and had his being. Cf. Acts 17:28.

little queer.'" That got reaction, all right—raised eyebrows all over the room and a couple of very pleasant evenings.

Teaching had not yet dulled for me. In fact, I seemed to enjoy it a great deal—the control of your class's emotions, dropping innuendoes now and then, the Andrews archness, the sly poke at authority, the "testing" of the students with remarks inserted without emphasis—as, for example, in speaking of the origins and changes in words, you might casually say, "Oh, yes, you can have more fun with words than anything else in the language." Some would look puzzled, others would write it in their notebooks, and the few who instantly chuckled were always sure to get an A at the end of the course.

And life outside the classroom was enjoyable, too. As in every small town where the native residents are overwhelmed by the student population, there was an abundance of faculty parties. Some drinking went on, but not much. And even though the intellectual qualifications of many of the professors were not great, they were better than those in Montana. Professor Frank Potter was a classics teacher, and his wife Irene the great quidnunc of the town; she knew all the gossip and who was bedding whom even as it was happening the first time. Horace Nunemaker, head of the French department, was well traveled and cultured. And Josephine somebody (everybody called her Horseface behind her back) was agreeable enough. She was also the president's snitch, although we did not know it at the time; we only knew that for some reason she had Holland's ear. Consequently, we were a bit reserved around her. But she drank along with us, and we knew she could not therefore expose *that* secret.

There was plenty of time that year to fall in love a hundred times, and I was almost constantly enamored of the fine upstanding heterosexual male students. With heaving sighs, I tumbled for one after another of those western youths, who all seemed to be taller and straighter and leaner and handsomer than midwesterners, and perhaps they actually were. In the manner of A. E. Housman, I wrote scores of melancholy poems about handsome young men I couldn't have, thinking that if a don of Cambridge could get away with it, so could I. They were certainly not very good poems, and samples are appended here just to prove that I cannot write verse.

'Tis only right you look to wed
    Now you are grown and gone.

A. E. Housman (1859–1936). Distinguished scholar of classical literature and author of an enduringly popular collection of poetry, *A Shropshire Lad* (1895), in which he encoded his homosexuality in themes of male comradeship, transience, loss, death, and the grave.

And I may comfort me to think
   The lads come on and on.

But oh the pain to hear that you
   Had told this to the rest
And never sent a message to
   The one who loved you best.

Not facile, not distinguished—just a simple dingdong rhythm containing the record of a "pain." In certain others of those wintry poems there may
have been a catchy line or two:

A man who's lean and strong and tall
   And with a virgin quick.
But almost slow enough with me
   To be love's heretic.

Or a final sad one:

Then I call you, come and be
   The heavy-bodied groom.
That you may lie calmly when
   You are inside the tomb.

It was a streak of extravagant masochism in me, I suppose, that made
me "fall in love" time after time, be rejected, and therefore suffer—so that
loving and suffering always seemed to go together. I felt I didn't deserve to
be loved by any of the godlike idols I worshiped, and on the rare occasions
when one stepped down from his pedestal to give even the slightest token
of affection in return, I fled from such encounters startled and confused in
alarm and dismay. This did not keep me, however, from having a considerable number of sexual releases with handsome young animals who were not
gods but men.

Things were thus not unpleasant overall, and in March I was told by
the English department head—a roly-poly little popinjay named Murray
Bundy—and by Dean Clare Chrisman Todd of Sciences and Arts—a skeletal

I fled . . . startled and confused in alarm. Cf. "Swept with confused alarms of struggle and
flight," line 36 of "Dover Beach" (1867), by Matthew Arnold (1822–88).

Ichabod Crane—that my contract would be renewed for the following year. Everything seemed settled for me: another year in the Pacific Northwest.

The spring term was made still more pleasant by reading the proof of a novel I had written in the summer of 1933 as a relief from the drudgery of composing my doctoral dissertation. I had called the novel *Angels on the Bough*, taking the title from William Blake, who in one of his letters had written, "I was walking through the fields one day and saw a tree full of angels sitting on the bough." It was just another novel—taking a group of about ten persons, weaving their lives together, and seeing how each affected the other. In essence, I suppose it was close to Wilder's *The Bridge of San Luis Rey*, for it gently presented the question of whether things happen by accident or design, and just as wisely as Thornton had done, it failed to give the reader any definite answer. You were left just where you started. Into the novel I had put a Babbitt—entirely created; two spinsters—based on my two aunts; a man dominated by intellect and reason—Harlan Hatcher; a little blonde streetwalker—another Bobby Creighton; a half-mad mother-stricken crypto-homosexual—based on Jon Gillespie; a wise beauty—Tee Walley; and a great huge lesbian—Marie Anderson. I myself appeared as Thomas Cave, a young intellectual bothered about his spiritual decay. These lives were intertwined, both on and off campus, in a town that quite evidently was Columbus, Ohio.

There is nothing quite like the thrill of proofreading one's first book. I had not done this with *Pan and the Fire-bird*; Ben Musser had accomplished it, together with Henry Harrison. But with *Angels* there was the excitement of galleys and learning the proofreader's marks, and then the waiting for the finished product to arrive—almost like the anticipatory stages of orgasm in the nearly physical pleasure which the whole task brought with it. The book was scheduled for appearance in May.

But in April something else happened. For some time, there had been campus rumblings and rumors about a new set of "rules" of campus conduct

Angels on the Bough. The famous story of Blake's early vision of angels was first told by Alexander Gilchrist in his 1863 biography (*The Life of William Blake*, ed. W. Graham Robertson [London: John Lane, 1907], 7).

Wilder's The Bridge of San Luis Rey. Pulitzer Prize–winning novel (1927) by American novelist and playwright Thornton Wilder (1897–1975) that explores the differing circumstances that brought five people together on a bridge in Lima, Peru, at the moment it collapsed in 1714.

Babbitt. A person preoccupied with conforming to conventional middle-class behavior, from the central character in the novel *Babbitt* (1922), by Sinclair Lewis (1885–1951).

to be released by the deans of men and women. They were finally made public, and the uproar began, for the rules were insulting to the students, presupposing evil sexual intent on everyone's part. Samples: No pillows to be allowed on picnics. No alcoholic beverages of any kind to be permitted in fraternity or sorority houses. Any student possessing a contraceptive device to be dismissed immediately. All girls to be in their residences no later than ten on weeknights and eleven on weekends. If in an auto a girl rides on a boy's lap, four thicknesses of blanket to be between them.

This was too much for the students even in 1936, and we were witness to one of the first student strikes ever held in the United States. The young people refused to go to classes — massing in the gymnasium for pep talks, gathering outside classroom buildings to hold up their fingers in a gesture that Winston Churchill was to make famous — a V for victory.

I was delighted with their actions and said so to the many student friends who kept tramping up and down my stairs to ask my advice on this or that. My sympathies were entirely with them, and yet, aware of Holland's spy network, I was careful to couch my advice in cautionary terms. Only to a few treasured ones did I say, "Go ahead and strike, damnit! It's time for some common sense around here."

The strike did not last long — about two days, I think. And then the two deans caved in, issuing a much revised, more sensible and adult list of guidelines, dropping the words "Rules and Regulations." The students went back to class victorious, and no one bothered to ask the deans of men and women how they felt.

In May, I received my six copies of my novel from the Caxton Printers and gave one to Professor Bundy to read. Someone — possibly Josephine Horse-face — alerted the campus bookstore, which ordered about ten copies.

Within a few days, Bundy called me into his office.

"Dr. Steward," he said, "I am distressed by the inclusion among the *dramatis personae* in your novel of a common prostitute. Such things should really not be written about by a member of the faculty of the State College of Washington."

I was aghast. "But my treatment of her is not prurient," I said, "and she does pay the penalty for her sins."

"In what way?" demanded Bundy.

"She gets syphilis," I said.

"It is not so spelled out," Bundy said, "and even if it were, that is one of those things not discussed in polite society."

Not only aghast this time, but speechless.

"I understand that the campus bookstore has copies on hand," he went on. "I would strongly advise you to communicate with them and ask them to withdraw your book from sale."

Worse than Davis and Elkins, I thought. "I'll do that," I said, swallowing hard.

This little contretemps with Bundy did not remain secret. I told the Potters and—alas!—Josephine Horseface. A few days after Bundy's statement, both Dean Todd and he informed me that in view of my withdrawing the book and canceling any publicity about it, they were inclined to drop the subject and carry it no further, adding that my job would not be jeopardized.

I was badly shaken by the whole episode. But it was not over.

Commencement was on June 7, a Sunday. I was packed and ready to leave on June 8 when a call came from the President's Office, ordering me to attend a conference at two that afternoon. Greatly dismayed, I went to the administration building. Josephine Horseface was there, Dean Todd and Professor Bundy, both looking grim. And of course, President E. O. Holland.

"Sit down, Steward," the president ordered. "I'll get right to the point. I understand, although I have not read it, that you have written a racy novel with a streetwalker in it."

My mouth fell open. I glanced at Josephine Horseface. Her head was lowered, but I could see her face flaming scarlet.

"Such a thing brings discredit to the college and to all its faculty," the craggy old sonofabitch went on. "And we cannot have that. Accordingly, your connection with this institution is terminated and your contract for the coming year is hereby declared null and void."

I know that I turned white. I was utterly confused. "B-but I was assured by Dean Todd and Professor Bundy—" I began.

"I don't care what they said. They have nothing to do with it," said the old autocrat. "I say that you are terminated, and that is final. You may now all leave."

We filed out. Bundy attempted to pat my shoulder.

"Don't touch me, you damned hypocrite," I said. "Both you and Todd are milksops!"

I fled out of the building, as shaken as I had ever been in my life.

After that, I spent the day repacking completely—for I had planned to leave many of my possessions in Pullman for the summer. Now it all had to go. On June 9, I went to Spokane, and in a two-hour layover I called a reporter from the Spokane paper and gave him the whole story. It never appeared in print in Spokane, but somehow it reached the AP wires, and when I got to Columbus by train a few days later, a reporter was on hand with a photographer. It gave me a great chance to say a few pointed things about freedom of the press and narrow parochial attitudes.

Luckily, while at Carroll College I had joined the American Association of University Professors and attended a few meetings at the Washington State chapter—which then had about twenty-five members. Full of anger, I reported my dismissal to Harlan Hatcher, who in turn told Carl Wittke of Ohio State, head of the association's Committee A on academic freedom and tenure.

To shorten a long and complicated tale: the AAUP in January 1937 published a report condemning Washington State College's administration—and specifically President Holland—for "tending to make barren college and university departments of English," holding that a teacher who is a creative writer should have complete freedom of expression so long as what he says does not conflict with postal or other laws.

The membership of the AAUP in Pullman jumped to over four hundred by the time school opened that fall.

Meanwhile, an opening was announced at Loyola University in Chicago. I hardly wanted to go back into religious teaching, but I sent a copy of my novel to the dean there, explaining all. He found it innocuous, and I was hired, to teach in an English department under the direction of Morton Dauwen Zabel, one of the most feared and respected scholars in the field.

So, finally, I would be in a city large enough to absorb me, hide me, challenge me, and keep me happy—City of the Big Shoulders. I looked forward to the experience with eagerness and a very great excitement.

Sources: *Chapters*, 31–40; Manuscript, 155–81.

---

postal or other laws. A reference to the Comstock Law's prohibition of sending anything judged "obscene" through the US mail (see note on page 63).

Morton Dauwen Zabel (1902–64). Distinguished critic, editor, and scholar in the field of twentieth-century literature who chaired the English department at Loyola University Chicago from 1929 to 1946.

City of the Big Shoulders. Line 5 from the well-known poem "Chicago" (1916), by Carl Sandburg (1878–1967).

Chapter Four

CHICAGO AND FRIENDS

1936–65

Learning to love Chicago was a task, like learning to like martinis or getting used to pineapple and cottage cheese as a "salad." There were many things about it that had to be forgotten or overlooked before love could develop.

When I first arrived, I hated it—the dirty papers flying loosely on the streets, the sprawling quality of it, the "mary-ann" backs of the apartment houses you saw from the elevated tracks as the trains groaned and screeched on their way to the Loop. I loathed the dirty clothes hanging on the wooden back porches, the unbelievable squalor and filth of the South Side tenements, the naked babies playing in the mud of backyards—all in contrast with the incredible hypocrisy of the bright and gleaming shops on Michigan Avenue.

And the paradox of State Street astounded me—beginning in nothingness at the river, running down through the proud stores . . . into what? Once you crossed Van Buren Street going south, what happened? Tattoo joints, burlesque houses, prostitutes, and ten-cents-a-shot saloons—a shot of wine, of course. Westward, the stumblebums of Madison Street, the dives on Clark Street—only a mile or so from the stately tower of the Tribune, and less than

---

through the proud stores. The "proud stores" of Chicago's main shopping district in the 1930s included Marshall Field's (in a building designed by Daniel Burnham) and Carson Pirie Scott (in one designed by Louis Sullivan).

Once you crossed Van Buren. State Street south of Van Buren Avenue was Chicago's Skid Row in the 1930s, a seedy, crime-ridden stretch of the street just a few blocks south of the city's most fashionable department stores. Steward operated his Chicago tattoo business there from 1954 to 1963.

stately tower of the Tribune. The Tribune Tower (1925), a neo-Gothic skyscraper that was the home of the *Chicago Tribune*.

that from the elegant hotels of the Gold Coast. Walk a block west from them and you would be in one of the most unsavory sections of the city, if indeed you could get there without being mugged.

At first, the city was terrifying. Ben Hecht's *1001 Afternoons in Chicago* had been my reading since I was old enough to know what Ellis and Freud were saying. He wrote fascinating vignettes—but of course such things could never happen to people. They were the mad dreams of the man who wrote *Fantazius Mallare*. Or were they?

It was only very slowly that the quality of the city grew on me. I found that it broke itself into little neighborhoods, each with a distinct personality, falling apart into scores of small communities, north, south, and west—no east side: that's the lake. The Poles and Italians lived on the west, the blacks south and the Germans elsewhere, the Jews and Catholics on the north side—and yet the whole city fitted together, differently colored pieces in a jigsaw puzzle two hundred and fifteen square miles large.

I spent time wandering. It took me six months to discover how to ride the elevated and find my way around. Policemen growled at me when I asked directions, mumbling something that only a native could understand. I walked along the river and watched the lights of the tall buildings around Wacker Drive break and glitter in the dirty water. I walked along Oak Street beach at night, with the thunderous rush of the water washing against my eardrums, when the lake was white with a nor'easter howling. The lake at midnight was sometimes wild and blowing, with the air full of King Lear. I would stand on an embankment overlooking darkness and see no line between sky and water, but only a sullen noisy void with whiteness fretting and circling at my feet and a dashing black film of water sweeping over a sanded beach, ending finally in a thin and crisping edge of foam with the winds loud and roaring in my ears—and at such moments I believed that I could do anything at all in the world.

Gradually I learned the city. In winter, I handed myself along the ropes

---

Ben Hecht's 1001 *Afternoons in Chicago*. Hecht's column of Chicago sketches, "Around the Town: One Thousand and One Afternoons in Chicago," appeared in the *Chicago Daily News* between June 1921 and October 1922. Steward refers to the book of the collected sketches that was first published in 1922. See also note on *Fantazius Mallare*, page 57.

Oak Street beach. A mile-long sand beach along Lake Michigan at the north end of North Michigan Avenue. In the 1930s and 1940s, it was a popular gathering place for gay men (Chad Heap, "Gays and Lesbians," in *The Encyclopedia of Chicago*, ed. James R. Grossman, et al. [Chicago: University of Chicago Press, 2004], 331).

stretched on windy corners to keep myself on my feet. In spring I prowled the dark alleys of the Loop, watched a street fight, made a pickup on a corner, and got drunker than hell at a half buck a shot. In summer, I tangled with miscellaneous arms and legs on Foster Beach and fell asleep in the sun, drunk, so that I had to spend a week in bed. And as much as I swore at Lake Michigan — its tantrums, its unpredictability, its hot and cold — I knew very well that it belonged to me, and I to it, and that its green and grey and blue and brown were there when I wanted to see them. Faintly remembered, there was the line from my second-rate poet laureate of New Jersey: "I cannot live away from water." I was discovering Chicago and learning that something other than a human being could have life in it. A city could, and for me that city was Chicago.

And when did I become a native Chicagoan?

With my first holdup, of course. Mine occurred one evening long ago when the old Stratosphere Club atop the Pure Oil Building was still in existence. In those days, the building wore a little blue neon Juliet cap, and beneath it was the fantastic expensive club. From its windows, you looked down on the misty abyss that was the cavern of the city. I came down from it and walked westward. From an alley across La Salle Street, a guy emerged with a gun. He took my watch and wallet and told me not to move for five minutes. I sat on the curb until the cops came thirty-five minutes later. I wouldn't even have been able to move if I had had crutches; my knees would have collapsed under me. After that, I considered myself a True Native Chicagoan.

Certainly the city was cultural enough — and the treasures that I found in the Art Institute, the sculptures of man by Malvina Hoffman, the orchestra

I prowled the dark alleys. Steward's search for sexual partners frequently led him into the alleys of the city and more than once resulted in his being robbed or beaten up (Spring, 58–60).

"I cannot live away from water." See note on page 66.

Stratosphere Club. Nightclub located at the top of the Pure Oil Building's forty-one-story central tower in the 1930s. The club's blue-and-silver matchbooks were inscribed with the slogan "There is atmosphere in the Stratosphere."

Pure Oil Building. Office building (1926) at 35 East Wacker, commonly called the Jewelers Building.

Malvina Hoffman (1887–1966). New York–born sculptor commissioned by the Field Museum of Natural History in 1930 to create more than a hundred bronze, marble, and stone sculptures of people from a wide range of ethnicities and cultures, based on models from her own extensive travels around the world. The complete set of works — life-size sculptures, busts, and heads — was originally displayed in the museum's Hall of Man.

and the band shell, the opera house and the old Auditorium were enough—
but what really mattered was that I felt Chicago had a soul. Paris had one, but
London—no. New York had a metronome for a heart, Los Angeles a woman's
wristwatch ticking. But Chicago—all the way, man!

I thought of Chicago as a man-city, healthy, sweaty, and sensual. It was
Gargantua on the lakefront—his head in Evanston, his feet in Gary; and he
lay relaxed and smoldering along the lake. The trees of Lincoln Park were the
curling man-hair of his chest, the trees of Jackson Park the foliage upon his
legs, the tall buildings of the Loop his sturdy upstanding phallus—the whole
anatomy of the city his outstretched body.

I had thought Columbus great, but it was nothing compared with Chicago. For the first time in my life, I really loved the place in which I lived.

And once again, I began to like teaching—although those first years in Chicago nearly exhausted me. Sitting at the head of the English department was
one of the important critical scholars of that time—a gifted man with a razor
mind under his youthfully bald pate, the archetypal egghead with glasses, a
soft yet carrying voice which could cut like a blade of Toledo steel if necessary,
an important Jamesian scholar with many essays and a volume to his credit
on that novelist. This was Morton Dauwen Zabel, perhaps the most closeted
queen of the entire city. He lived with his mother, whom he adored, and when
she died his grief overwhelmed him. This quiet man threw himself upon her
coffin, sobbing, and had to be restrained from jumping into her grave.

In a way, Zabel at the helm was a wonderful protection for all of us in the
department. Although he was a taskmaster, everyone was comparatively free
under him. The school was run by Jesuits, and their reputation for worldly
wisdom and tolerance was well known. Zabel made full use of it. Did the
schedule call for a course to be taught in the modern novel? *All right—Dr.
Steward, will you teach it?* Delighted—but what modern novelists in this religious school? *Please forget about that—the modern novel is the modern novel, of
course.* Will they not expect me to teach people like Hilaire Belloc and G. K.
Chesterton? *Of course not; include anyone you want.* May I teach Dreiser?
Hemingway? Anderson? Lewis? Gide? Mann? *Certainly—they are modern
novelists, aren't they?*

the old Auditorium. Landmark building (1889) designed by Dankmar Adler and Louis Sullivan that contained offices, a hotel, and a theater with 4,300 seats.
Hilaire Belloc (1870–1953) and G. K. Chesterton (1874–1936). Writers whose literary works
were strongly influenced by their orthodox Catholic thinking.

Part of the shaking-down tactics I experienced as I was getting used to my new job was a visit to the president of the university, a smilingly benign red-faced white-haired gentleman named Wilson, who bade me sit, offered me a glass of sherry (just as smilingly declined), and talked to me for about thirty minutes, asking me how I liked the university, how I liked Chicago, how I was getting on, did I have a satisfactory apartment, and all the rest. I felt quite at ease with him.

He asked me about my feelings regarding the State College of Washington and my experience with them. How did I feel about President Holland?

"Well, to tell the truth, Father Wilson," I said, "I am not exactly well disposed at the moment."

"Do you know," he said in a kindly tone of voice, "I have had similar experiences in my life, and in each case I have held a grudge for a very long time—twenty years at least, until I got the chance to stick a knife in someone's back, and believe me then I did—and twisted it!"

I was never sure why he said that—whether he was testing me to see my reaction, or whether he actually meant it. But he was still smiling and beaming, and I suppose I smiled at him. What I said, how I reacted, I do not remember. But I do know that I left his elegant dark office—with its broad windows looking out on Lake Michigan—in a decided sweat and turmoil. Part of the reaction came from the shock to my convert's zeal, for I could not imagine a Christian saying such a thing and still pretending to be a Christian, and a priest moreover . . . but could it be that the Jesuits were a special breed and could rationalize such an attitude away quite easily? Or perhaps they were covered by a special bull—papal, of course.

Then an internal gyroscope stabilized me: after all, it kept whirring, what difference does it make to you? If you were hypocrite enough to accept a job in a religious institution after having lost your religion, why should you expect perfection in anyone else? I tucked the whole problem away, drank a few more martinis, and did not bring it up again. But Father Wilson's remark made a lovely thing to tell my pagan friends in Chicago.

The university made full use of its teachers. Zabel kept me running back and forth between the uptown campus—which was a day school for males only—and the downtown "campus," an old ramshackle building on North Franklin, where evening and graduate students attended. In the first two years of teaching, I prepared about twenty-five or thirty new courses, and the wonder of it is that I managed to accomplish these, what with my drinking and my new sexual liberty. Besides the usual run of freshman English and

bull—papal. A formal papal decree authenticated by a "bulla," or lead seal.

sophomore survey courses in literature, I was handed courses in modern literature—the drama and the novel, in literary criticism, romantic poetry and prose of the nineteenth century, Shakespeare, the Jacobean dramatists, Pope and Blake and the forerunners of romanticism—all these and more, plus a host of rare and exotic graduate courses in such subjects as Anglo-Saxon grammar and literature (*Beowulf* in the original, of course); Middle English—grammar and literature; bibliography; linguistics and semantics and the diabolic technique of *explication de texte*. If I accomplished nothing else in those first two years, it was to become *teres atque rotundus*—complete and well-rounded—in the field of English literature and its allied topics.

Zabel turned me into a better scholar than I had ever been as a PhD candidate. A perfectionist himself, he expected it in others—and although I never reached his degree of acumen and profundity, I did learn much from him and come to respect him as a talented and meticulous savant with an encyclopedic mind, a giant of learning. And I came to also sympathize with him and the tumult that his sexual nature must have caused him. How that small religious institution kept him, how with his erudition he continued to be devout, I could never really understand, unless it was a case of being contentedly a large frog in a small puddle. And religious because his mother was—for he would not have wanted to hurt her. He could have been welcome anywhere with his knowledge and background—and indeed, in the last years of his life he did leave the university and went to the University of Chicago, where he belonged all along.

When I first moved to Chicago, I had no idea that I would be there for the next twenty-nine years, nor that it would come to be considered more my hometown than any other place. In the gradual process of establishing myself, I sent out small rootlets and tested to see if they would take hold and grow into stable and enduring relationships. By the end of two years there, friendships were created that would last for several years.

The first of these came about as a result of my visit to Gertrude Stein and Alice Toklas in the summer of 1937. Gertrude said: "When you go back you must look up Wendell Wilcox, he writes and he writes to me a lot, and we met him in Chicago when we were there, and here is his address and I hope you like each other."

---

explication de texte. A kind of literary analysis, popular in mid-twentieth-century America, that derives the meaning of a work by focusing exclusively on its language and form.
Wendell Wilcox (1906–81). Novelist, short-story writer, and protégé of Gertrude Stein.

The Wilcoxes—Wendell and Esther—lived on the South Side and belonged to one of the many intellectual circles revolving around the University of Chicago. Theirs included such figures as Gertrude Abercrombie and Charles Sebree, Thornton Wilder, and Katharine Dunham and her white male lover. Esther worked in the Chicago public library system and supported Wendell. Many times during the first years of our acquaintance, I was called on to defend this arrangement of theirs, since in those days the feeling was strong that the husband should always support the wife. But I continued to assert that Wendell, being a genius, was outside the realm of ordinary morality and mores and that since Esther firmly believed in his writing abilities and was willing to keep him alive for that reason, it was certainly not up to us lesser mortals to criticise such a way of life.

We knew and enjoyed each other for many years. The Wilcoxes were two of the few persons who continued to know me both as a lush and after I grew sober; they faithfully endured my drunkenness, although they must have been tempted to leave me forever on many occasions. I remember how white-faced they once were as I climbed out of one of my windows and back in the adjoining one while I was drunk—and there was a six-floor drop below me. Periodically they would come to my house for dinner, and then I would go to theirs, these arrangements spaced about two or three weeks apart. They left Chicago before I did and moved to Chapel Hill, where Esther died of cancer in 1972 and where Wendell still lives. His characteristic dilettantism matched my own in many ways; he and Esther were both confidants and friends for a long time.

The second major alliance formed in the first few years in Chicago was with Richie Tucker. We met in a bar, and although he was always one for putting on a great show of heterosexuality, he was primarily the same as I. During the years from 1938 to 1946, I note that Richie and I had 204 "romantic encounters," as they say on the telly (I have always been a record

Gertrude Abercrombie (1909–77). Chicago painter who hosted a salon in the manner of Gertrude Stein for writers, artists, and jazz musicians at her Hyde Park home.

Charles Sebree (1914–85). African American painter, theater set and costume designer, and later playwright who was active in the Chicago black arts movement in the 1930s.

Thornton Wilder (1897–1975). See note on page 86.

Katharine Dunham (1909–2006). Chicago-born African American dancer, choreographer, and dance company director whose style and teaching profoundly influenced modern dance.

her white male lover. Canadian John Thomas Pratt (1905–86), who became Dunham's artistic collaborator in the late 1930s and thereafter designed all of her costumes and sets. They married in 1941.

keeper). Alas, he was not one who survived my career as a lush, and I lost him through some drunken idiocy of mine shortly before I joined AA.

He was slender and appeared straight. His mouth turned down at the corners when he smiled, giving him a kind of cynical appearance—and he hated "old farts" as he called them, those who were continually after him. He was two years older than I—and Richie, if you're still around somewhere, how do you feel now about being an old fart yourself?

He was a good drinking companion, an excellent bed partner—and he loathed all things swish and nelly. But he enlisted in the navy during World War II, and that worked a remarkable change in him. When he came home, he was no longer cynical and sardonic, but talked long and earnestly about what it was like in the navy, of the deep enduring friendships you formed, of the bond of comradeship "which you civilians could never understand," and on and on until he began to sound like an untalented Whitman with an endlessly repeated one-line chorus.

Moreover, he did something I could never understand: he took his severance pay, put it with what he had saved up, and purchased a flower shop near Belmont Avenue and the Outer Drive. I was speechless. I could no more understand or visualize the macho jock of the pre-navy days involving himself with floral arrangements than I could see myself as a lumberjack. I tried several times to renew our acquaintance—and even wrote him the AA letter of apology ("Make direct amends to such people as you have harmed"). But I never received an answer. I must have indeed upset him a great deal, for all I remember of our parting was his final statement as he went out the door with a friend he had brought to meet me (was I triggered into some horrendous reaction by jealousy?): "I don't have to put up with all this shit."

The third major tie that was formed in Chicago came about in a strange fashion. I had not been in Chicago long—a few months, perhaps—when I was propositioned on the elevated platform at Sheridan and Broadway by a white-faced, heavily beard-marked flabby sort of gentleman in his midforties (I was then about twenty-seven) who asked if he could "see" me. I did not find him attractive—he was even repulsive to me—and I was not interested. I told him that I was on my way downtown on some errands and at his request gave him my telephone number—with one number transposed, a devious trick which would furnish me with an excuse if I should be embarrassed by him again.

Well, I was. For several mornings, he waited on the same El platform for me and finally caught me a week later.

"You gave me the wrong number," he said accusingly.

"What do you have?" I said innocently.

"It's Longbeach–2078."

"Ah ha!" I said. "You took it down wrong; it's 2087."

He rode downtown with me. "You must come over to Paulina Street with me some evening for dinner," he said. "I am staying with a charming woman and her mother, and you would like them very much."

After several telephone calls, I finally succumbed. And that was the way Harry Winthrop introduced me to Emmy Dax Curtis and her very German mother Augusta Dax, an elderly woman we always called "Mutter Dax." Emmy was to have a profound effect on my Chicago life, and I on hers, although Mutter Dax did not live to see it.

At the beginning, I exercised my usual casual attitude toward women with her; she seemed no threat to me, for she was obviously in love with Harry. She was eighteen years older than I and had been widowed after a marriage of only three or four months to a handsome soldier of World War I named Howard Curtis. He died really before she had done more than taste the fruits of "romantic encounters"—and anyway, judging from his pictures and from what she told me from time to time, Howard must have been a club member himself.

Emmy taught French at Roosevelt High School—having learned a very pure kind in Switzerland—and when I first knew her, indeed looked like the stereotype of the old-maid school teacher: greying brown hair parted in the middle and combed severely down over the ears and into a small bun low on the neck; thin-lipped and seeming to be easily shocked. In a few years, both her appearance and attitudes were greatly changed.

Harry was playing Emmy and her mother for all they were worth. He lived on a meager pension of some kind—also from the first war—and was always broke. He freeloaded on them, staying in their apartment for a month-long stopover on his journey from the summer months in Wisconsin—his home—to winter in Florida, eating their food, sleeping in their spare bedroom—and cruising everything on the North Side. He borrowed large sums from them and never repaid them, always leading Emmy to think that he would marry her "as soon as my ship comes in." Mutter Dax was also taken in with this not-so-charming scoundrel, who two or three times got into serious trouble with his cruising and had to be bailed out by Emmy—always with some outlandish cover story which she believed. But Harry told me the truth, which often was ghastly.

As my fondness for Emmy and her mother developed over the years, I

Emmy was to have a profound effect. Besides her steady and unquestioning friendship, Curtis offered Steward a safe place to store his expanding collection of erotica, the possession of which was illegal (Spring, 222, 233).

grew more and more irritated with the double game Winthrop played and felt that I had to interfere. Accordingly, one evening after Harry had safely gone to Florida and I had fortified myself with several old-fashioneds, I let fly.

"Do you know, m'dear," I said, "that Harry Winthrop is queer?"

"He certainly does have a lot of strange traits," Emmy said, laughing.

"I guess I'll have to make myself clear," I said. "I meant—Harry is a homosexual. He likes other men. Not women. If you are thinking he'll marry you, better get over it. He's just using you and your place here and your hospitality as a convenient stopover."

Having gone that far, and bedeviled by my own conscience and the Methodist honesty instilled by my aunts, I knew that I had to continue. "It would not be fair," I said, "to tell you this without saying that I also am homosexual. Harry 'cruised' me on an El platform, and that's the way we got acquainted. I will also tell you that we have never had any sexual encounters."

I was not looking directly at her while I said these things—and I felt somewhat like a Judas. When I looked at her again, she had lowered her face and was weeping soundlessly into a small square of handkerchief. Her pain was contagious; my own eyes filled.

"I'm sorry to tell you this," I said, "but I can't stand to see you and Mutter Dax made fools of, nor you to go on vainly hoping one day to be married to him or expecting a sort of happiness that can never exist."

After a little while she stopped crying and looked at me. "I've been an idiot," she said. "I should have suspected something was wrong a long time ago—especially on the occasions when he would seem to be in trouble and beg me not to answer the phone or ask me to deny that he was here or that I knew anyone by the name of Winthrop."

I consoled her, and our relationship went on—plenty of old-fashioneds (the only drink she could make) and a chicken dinner at her place about once a week—prepared by Mutter Dax, for Emmy was no cook. She approached a stove with the feelings of a virgin for the wedding bed.

Yet before long I noticed a change—subtle but marked—in her attitude toward me. It was the familiar "rebound" or "transference" reaction so beloved by psychiatrists. She sliced Winthrop out of her life and fell in love with me—and in my peculiar way, I loved her. About 1943 we began to go to bed together and continued this for about six years (211 times), until Kinsey said after our interview, "Why don't you stop?" And I, of course, was not

---

continued this for about six years (211 times). Steward's sexual encounters with Emmy Curtis are also documented in his Stud File index.
Kinsey. See chapter 11.

heterosexual. I bought her a wedding ring as a common-law wife, both of us having fulfilled the legal aspects by announcing it to three people. We did not want to get married; it was as much her reluctance as mine, for she would have lost her husband's pension as a war widow.

Emmy—dear faithful friend! She was one of the three who stuck by me through the most repulsive and revolting stages of my alcoholism (in a fit of rage, I once seized her finger and broke it).

She went with me once to Paris in 1950 and met Alice B. Toklas. And it was in Paris that the first signs of the mysterious ailment which took her life began to appear: at a restaurant, I was horrified to see this gentle proper grey-haired woman try to eat peas with her knife. It was the beginning of polycythemia, in which the red blood cells grow thick, the capillaries are clogged, and the brain begins to malfunction. I joked with her as much as possible—called her Lady Macbeth (who cried "Make thick my blood!") and went with her when she had to drink radioactive phosphorus to control the raging enemy within her veins, asking if her urine now glowed in the dark. And as the disease grew steadily worse for ten years and could no longer be controlled, I acted as her court-appointed conservator, seeing her into a nursing home, watching her waste away until her hands were mere claws at the end of scrawny flesh-covered bones, weaving and weaving in the air, calling for me. And with the tears flowing, holding her fingers (befouled as this once-elegant woman would never have permitted herself to be), I listened to the long-damned stream of ugly words issue from her proper lips.

Oh, yes—I thought of it, of course. I even prepared a capsule of amphetamines, enough to kill her—but never tried to give it to her. She could by then swallow only with difficulty, and it would have stuck in her throat. And from this nest of stink and foulness, her spirit was luckily released all of itself, and the struggle was over.

Then the vultures descended, the distant relatives who had abandoned her in her illness, tearing her apartment to pieces, looking for silverware, diamonds, antiques, no matter what. Emmy was gone irrevocably, and with her the last vestige of sexual attraction that I ever felt for a woman.

Sources: *Chapters*, 40–43; Manuscript, 182–99.
Steward based portions of the first part of this chapter
on his earlier *IDJ* essay "On Chicago" (August 1946).

---

polycythemia. A disorder in which the body produces an excess of red blood cells, slowing circulation and increasing the risk of stroke.
"Make thick my blood!" Shakespeare, *Macbeth*, I.v.43.

Chapter Five

THE MAGIC SUMMER

1937

Sometimes, looking back over the succession of years in a life, it is possible to pick out a watershed, a continental divide — and the summer of 1937 was that for me.

By the time I reached high school — where I had a "mentor," Gertrude Korner, who encouraged me in my intellectual tastes — I was in love with authors and writing. "Lo, with a little rod I did but touch the honey of romance" — but the rod this time was a pen, and the romance was the living authors who were all around me in the 1920s, a decade in which I am glad to have existed. Perhaps it was Miss Korner who planted the idea in me, or perhaps it arose spontaneously: I began to write fan letters to those whom I most admired, just a few weak attempts, handwritten tributes in a youthfully awkward script.

And the first? Sherwood Anderson. With what trembling recognition I had read through the stories in his *Winesburg, Ohio*, a copy of which had somehow found its way into the public library. The story called "Hands" in that volume, the tale of Adolf Meyers, alias Wing Biddlebaum, set the hairs on my neck alert and furnished me with perhaps the first literary treatment of a condition which I was already recognizing in myself.

On my very best stationery, then, and with a good pen, I composed a letter to Sherwood Anderson, telling him how much I had admired his book of

"Hands." Story in *Winesburg, Ohio* (1919) by Sherwood Anderson (1876–1941) about a man isolated from others by his secret desire to touch and embrace other men.

stories and ending with a request for him to autograph the enclosed small white card and return it to me. It never occurred to me to send a stamped envelope — but anyway, the postage was only two cents in those days.

In a little while, the card was returned bearing his signature — just that and nothing more. But the elation! The success! Wildly enthusiastic, I showed it to Miss Korner, who beamed on me and encouraged me to write again.

Then came Carl Sandburg, whose "Chicago" and other poems of the "City of the Big Shoulders" we had been reading in class. And he responded. So did John Erskine, Ernest Hemingway, and Eugene O'Neill, who even wrote "Sincerely" above his signature. But though I tried several times to snare George Bernard Shaw, he never responded — save for a dubious signature on a pink postal return receipt which I sent in final desperation.

Autograph hunting then became for a few years a passion with me. I had a high-school autograph book, bound in soft brown suede with pages of vari-colored paper, and from 1926 to 1929, I dragged it with me everywhere. I did not brag much about the signatures to my contemporaries. Instead, I was more likely to savor them in secret — to turn the pages of the rubbed suede book over and over, remembering how each of the persons had reacted: How Mae Murray, in a filmy gown of many layers of tulle and netting, had shrieked at me in the dressing room of the RKO Palace theatre because I had a lighted cigarette in my hand, and she was afraid her skirt might catch fire. How I brazenly entered the dining room off the lobby of the Deshler-Wallick Hotel to interrupt Fatty Arbuckle at dinner (this was following the Virginia Rappe scandal, as his star went down), and how annoyed he looked. How gracious Galli-Curci was ("and I haf to zing tonight when I have zis — apple in my t'roat" — a cold, or laryngitis) and Rachmaninoff with his skull-like face. How surprised Thornton Wilder was eight years later, when I knew him in Zurich, to be told he had first given me his autograph in 1929!

By the time I reached the university, I had graduated from being a mere autograph hunter. Although that particular obsession continued, it was

---

high-school autograph book. Steward's autograph book is in the Yale Steward Papers.

Mae Murray (1885–1965). Silent film and early talkies star who was at the peak of her fame when Steward encountered her.

Fatty Arbuckle. Roscoe "Fatty" Arbuckle (1887–1933), comic star of silent films whose career declined under the shadow of his trial for rape and manslaughter following the death of film star Virginia Rappe (1895–1921) at a party in his suite in the St. Francis Hotel in San Francisco. Arbuckle was eventually acquitted.

Galli-Curci. Amelita Galli-Curci (1882–1963), Italian-born coloratura soprano and international star of opera productions until her retirement in 1930.

supplemented and refined by a new device: writing to an author I admired in wording as skillfully devised as I could make it, I intelligently analyzed what it was that appealed to me about his or her work. The trick to getting a response, I found, was never to ask any questions nor to ask for anything in my letters, not even a reply. It was remarkably successful, and in those days there were indeed great authors to whom one could write. By the time my autograph-letter collection was more or less ended in 1946, it contained letters either in typescript or holograph from Somerset Maugham, Thomas Mann (6), Julien Green (6), Carl Van Vechten, Alfred Lord Douglas (4), Paul Cadmus (3), James Branch Cabell (3), Sigrid Undset, Christopher Morley, James Stephens, Havelock Ellis, John Erskine, Helen Hayes, Sigmund Freud, A. E. Housman, Paul Morand, William Butler Yeats, André Gide, Vita Sackville-West, Virginia Woolf, Prince Felix Youssoupoff (who killed Rasputin), Romain Rolland, Thornton Wilder (24), Benedetto Croce, Sir Francis Rose (about 30 items), Glenway Wescott, Padraic Colum, and Eleanor Roosevelt. In addition, there were signed volumes from many of these, plus volumes with signatures of James Joyce, Dylan Thomas, Jacques Maritain, George Moore, Alexander Woollcott, Dorothy Parker, George Platt Lynes (50 photographs, a dozen letters), John Masefield, Theodore Dreiser, Jean Cocteau, and a few lesser lights such as Charles du Bos and Henri Daniel-Rops.

Naturally, whenever a literary figure came to the university campus to lecture, we were all there en masse—to hear John Cowper Powys declaim like thunder and James Stephens read Keats in a murmurous whisper—and in 1934 to listen to Hamlin Garland, who wrote *A Son of the Middle Border*, give us the October reminiscences of his long career. He was a pleasant silver-haired giant, by then somewhat diminished in reputation and obscured by men like Hemingway and Dreiser and Sinclair Lewis. But during the course of his lecture, he mentioned that he had known Whitman, and that electrified me.

Afterward I went up on the stage to speak to him. "Did you really know Whitman?" I asked in awe.

John Cowper Powys (1872–1963). British novelist, poet, and popular lecturer.

James Stephens (1880–1950). Irish poet and fiction writer known for his fables and tales rooted in Irish folklore.

Hamlin Garland (1860–1940). Wisconsin-born writer whose boyhood spent on midwestern farms provided settings and themes for his novels and stories later in life. *A Son of the Middle Border* (1917) is his autobiography.

"Yes," said the patriarch. "I was very young, but he shook my hand and laid his hand on top of my head."

"Well, Mr. Garland," I said with the rash bravado of youth, "I've shaken your hand, but may I put my hand where Whitman laid his?"

He was somewhat taken aback, but he smiled.

"I want to be linked in with Whitman," I stammered, feeling my face grow red.

"Of course," he said, and bowed his head slightly. I put my left hand on his silver mane. Someone giggled, and I escaped sweating into the auditorium.

That was the genesis of the idea.

The next day I wrote to Lord Alfred Douglas, finding his address in *Who's Who*. And in due time, a letter from him arrived, chatty and somewhat avuncular, asking who I was and telling me about his latest book, *The True History of Shakespeare's Sonnets*. I answered, saying that I was a student working on my doctorate and that I would try to find a copy of his book somewhere in the States. He replied that he would be glad to send me a copy, but he would have to charge me for it, since all his author's copies had been given out. I sent him a draft for two pounds sterling and waited.

The book arrived. It contained a "dedication" of a full page in his handwriting, with the statement that he had corrected two misprints.

It soon became obvious from his inquiries in letters that followed, inquiries that were at first veiled and then direct, that what Lord Alfred was really looking for was someone who could help him find an American publisher for *The True History*, and I had to confess to him that I had no ties or any influence in the publishing world. And at that point, our correspondence dwindled and died . . .

. . . until three years later, 1937, when I made my first trip to Europe as a literary pilgrim, to visit Gertrude Stein at her invitation, and Thomas Mann and André Gide, all of whom seemed a little curious about me. And after a little side trip to Trinity College at Cambridge University to visit Whewell's Court and Great Court B2 where A. E. Housman had lived for twenty-five years (to stand silently weeping, with chills along my spine), I wrote again to

Lord Alfred Douglas (1870–1945). Oscar Wilde's friend and lover, whose father accused Wilde of sodomy in 1894, setting in motion a series of trials that eventually led to Wilde's conviction and imprisonment for "gross indecency" in 1895. After Wilde's death in 1900, Douglas converted to Catholicism and publicly renounced him. *The True History of Shakespeare's Sonnets* (1933) is more valued for its link to Douglas than for its content.

Lord Alfred and received a short note from him, asking me to come down to Hove to call on him should I find the time during my London stay.

I must honestly admit that I had no interest whatsoever in Lord Alfred Douglas as a person or as a writer, but only in the fact that he and Oscar Wilde had been lovers and that back in those shrouded days, the name of Wilde had a magic all its own for us who had to live without the benefits of liberation or exposure of our wicked lives. Besides, I was in my twenties and Lord Alfred was by then sixty-seven, and in anyone's book that's *old*. To go to bed with him was hardly the most attractive prospect in the world—it was terrifying, even repulsive. But if I wanted to link myself to Oscar Wilde more directly than I was linked to Whitman, there was no other way.

Even so, the possibility seemed remote. After Wilde's death, Lord Alfred had been extremely outspoken in print in his defense of Wilde—and then suddenly changed. He had married in 1902 and become a Roman Catholic in 1911 and thus put behind him all such childish things as fellatio, mutual masturbation, sodomy, and so on.

After returning to London from Cambridge, I established myself in a small hotel in Suffolk Place called Garland's (which seemed a curious omen to me after the Hamlin Garland experience) and from there telephoned Lord Alfred in Hove.

His voice was high-pitched and tinny over the phone. He seemed cordial enough and invited me down to tea on an afternoon two days hence. I found my way to the great blackened ugly skeleton of Victoria Station and took the train to Brighton in Sussex, which was next door to Hove, where he lived, connected in those days (and perhaps still) by a kind of boardwalk along the seafront.

My nervousness increased on the way down. He was a lord of the realm, descended from the Marquess of Queensberry. I must remember not to mention the names of Robert Ross, Frank Harris, André Gide—and a host of others who had been involved in controversy with him—nor even that

Robert Ross (1869–1918). Canadian journalist, early sexual partner of Oscar Wilde, and Wilde's lasting friend and literary executor. For Ross's faithfulness to Wilde, Douglas relentlessly sought to have him arrested on grounds of sodomy.
Frank Harris (1855–1931). Irish-born journalist, novelist, and friend of Wilde who ran afoul of Douglas when he attempted to publish his sympathetic biography, *Oscar Wilde: His Life and Confessions* (1916), in England.
André Gide (1869–1951). Gay French author and winner of the Nobel Prize for literature in 1947, who wrote unflatteringly about Douglas (see note on "the passages in *Si le grain ne meurt*," page 117).

of Winston Churchill, who had sued Lord Alfred for libel and won, with
Lord Alfred spending six months in the prison of Wormwood Scrubs as a
penalty—all this while continuing as editor of *Plain Speech*. And I must not
talk about the Jews or mention Gertrude Stein, for he was often very obviously anti-Semitic, even in print. He was the originator of the quatrain

How odd
Of God
To choose
The Jews

What, in heaven's name, could we talk about at all?

I found out when we met. The only safe topic was Lord Alfred Douglas
himself.

His address gave me no trouble—St. Ann's Court, Nizell's Avenue. The
stationmaster said that it was not far, a fifteen-minute walk from Brighton
past the flimsy pavilions, dingy from the sea air. I turned a corner and found
myself facing a block of flats, perhaps in Regency architecture, little plots
and gates and short sidewalk entrances. It was hardly Coleridge's countryside "enfolding sunny spots of greenery," nor Wordsworth's "pastoral farms
green to the very door," but it was pleasant and British and the sort of dwelling I was used to seeing in British movies.

He opened the door himself—a man of medium height with hairline receding on the right side where it was parted and the somewhat lacklus-
ter straight mousy hair falling down toward his left eyebrow. His nose was
very large and bulbous. The red rose-leaf lips beloved by Wilde had long

Winston Churchill (1874–1965). In a 1923 court case, Douglas was convicted of libel by
alleging in his journal *Plain English* that Churchill, as First Lord of the Admiralty, had been
paid to make a false report of British defeat in the naval Battle of Jutland (1916) in order to
destabilize world markets and benefit wealthy Jewish investors. Besides being an example
of preposterous anti-Semitism, the charge overlooked the fact that Churchill had left his
government post in 1915.

Plain Speech. One of two anti-Semitic journals (along with *Plain English*) that Douglas published in the early 1920s.

"enfolding sunny spots of greenery." Line 11 in the poem "Kubla Khan" (1816), by Samuel
Taylor Coleridge (1772–1834).

"pastoral farms / green to the very door." Cf. lines 16–17 in the poem "Tintern Abbey"
(1798), by William Wordsworth (1770–1850).

red rose-leaf lips. Phrase in a letter from Wilde to Douglas in January 1893 that was read
aloud at his trial.

since vanished; the mouth was compressed and thin, pursed somewhat, and the corners turned slightly downward. I looked in vain for a hint, even the barest suggestion, of the fair and dreamy youth of the early photographs with Wilde. None was visible. The skin of his face had not suffered the dreadful slackening of the flesh that goes with age; it seemed rather to be of the type that grows old by stretching more tautly over the bones, until—at the end—a skull-like face results. Yet the skin was not stretched tightly enough to pull out the fine network of tiny wrinkles that entirely covered his face and neck.

"Do come in," he said, but then instead of standing aside to let me precede him, he turned and walked ahead of me into the flat, leaving me to shut the door. He looked at me closely and then waved to a chair. "Do sit down," he said.

It was a pleasant room with three or four chairs, rather grimy white curtains at the windows, and a general air of crowding everywhere.

I had been in England just long enough to perceive that most British conversation was all form and no content, a kind of boneless thing, a sort of ping-pong game played without balls. There were no awkward gaps; it ran on and on, pegged to the flimsiest topics—the scenery, the weather of today and yesterday and tomorrow.

Perhaps to put me at ease but more likely to sound me out, Lord Alfred launched into that kind of talk, with a literary flavor. Hemingway was a prurient cad, and Dos Passos a proletarian, probably a Communist (like all left-wingers). Americans do not get enough exercise, and skyscrapers are too too utterly dreadful. Marriage is a mockery in America. If there is another war, the only decent thing for America to do will be to come to Britain's aid immediately; we waited too long in the war of 1914–18—and of course, as Rudyard Kipling pointed out (had I read his poem about that, "The Vineyard," the one that began "At the eleventh hour they came"?), America then took all the credit for winning.

On and on . . . I received a detailed account of the ten or eleven lawsuits he had been involved in, the trouble he had had over the money of his inheritance, his youthful passions for horse racing and gambling, his poetry (how much of it had I read, rilly?)—thank you for saying it: yes, he *was* probably England's greatest living poet. Masefield was a poetaster, a hack who had sold his birthright, who had never written a good line after 1930, when he was made poet laureate; George Russell ("A. E.") wrote mystical trash . . . and of course Yeats and the other Irish ones—well, you couldn't really call them British poets, now, could you?

The pale blue eyes were never still, nor were his hands, nor his feet—for he was continually crossing and recrossing his ankles or tapping his shoe against a nearby chair leg.

"I suppose," he said suddenly, "you want to hear all about Oscar Wilde and myself!"

By then I think I had analyzed him enough to know that I must disclaim all interest. "Not necessarily," I said with a rather wan smile. "I've read everything that you have written on the subject, and the work of several others . . ."

"Including, I suppose," he said in a fierce voice, "the vile canards and lies of persons like Robbie Ross and Frank Harris and that unspeakable sod André Gide."

"Well, yes . . . ," I said lamely.

"Lies, all lies," he said hoarsely and rose to pace around the room. Had he lived later, doctors would have called him hyperkinetic. He gestured toward the untidy desk. "I am doing a final book on it," he said. "I think I will call it 'Without Apology.'"

Suddenly he sat down again, the storm having passed.

"Shall we have a spot of tea?" he asked.

"That would be nice."

I took milk in my tea, largely because it was there and it helped to disguise the taste of the brew, which I hated. With the tea, he served a small plateful of pink cakes, disastrously sweet, with small silver pellets sprinkled on top, possibly silver-plated buckshot, to judge from the internal content.

He never stopped talking—a long monologue in which "As a poet, I . . ." and "As an artist, I . . ." recurred again and again. He seemed not ever to realize the extent to which he revealed his violent prejudices and hates, nor the immaturity of his view of himself. It became obvious before very long that he had never really grown up. He remained psychologically (and in his own eyes perhaps physically) still the radiant and brilliant adolescent beloved by the gods. He was a man of vast essential egotism yet burdened with a well-concealed inferiority, aggressively insistent on his social position, glossing over his repeated failures in business, and furious with Lord Beaverbrook ("essentially a commoner, donchaknow") for turning down the publication of his poems in the *Evening Standard*, grudge-holding for real and fancied slights, damning White's Club for closing its doors to him.

Lord Beaverbrook. William Maxwell Aitken, 1st Baron Beaverbrook (1879–1964), Canadian-born British politician and newspaper magnate who acquired the fabled *Evening Standard* in 1923.

White's Club. Exclusive London men's club, founded in 1693, from which Douglas was barred after suffering bankruptcy in 1913.

As for homosexual leanings and entanglements—that had all been given up when he became a Catholic—oh yes. He still got hundreds of letters from curiosity seekers and homosexuals, and he could have his pick of any of them (my ears and armpits flamed), but that was all finished. Sins of the flesh were obnoxious and uninteresting. I did not know at the time of his liaison with "D. E."—a young person with whom he was infatuated after his wife left him—and all this after he had become a Catholic! These initials were those used by André Gide in telling me, later that summer in Paris, that Lord Alfred had become enamored of "une personne" (feminine gender, but referring in French to either a male or a female) and had been to bed with him/her. There were actually two recorded liaisons: the first with an American girl in 1913, who with jewels and money offered to help Lord Alfred in one of his many litigations and with whom in his *Autobiography* he admits to "a loss of innocence." The second was a male, a young man sent down from Oxford for low grades, who always introduced himself as the reincarnation of Dorian Gray and whose camping and good looks and "butterfly devotion" delighted Lord Alfred for over a year in 1925. It was to this young man that Lord Alfred addressed a poem: "To ——— With an Ivory Hand Mirror."

The more he talked, the more I saw the possibility of linking in with Oscar Wilde fading along with the afternoon sun. Yet I did not give up. It was inconceivable to me that any man who had spent approximately the first forty years of his life in homosexual activity could have lost those leanings completely on joining the Catholic Church. I knew from my own experience. It still seemed to me, as we said in the Midwest: "Once one, always one."

And then, since this was still in my drinking days, a happy thought:

In vino veritas.

"Perhaps you will accompany me," I said, "to a nearby pub so that I may buy a round of drinks for us."

He waved his hand. "Hardly necessary, m'boy," he said. "All we need is here. Scotch? Gin and bitters? Sherry?"

"Gin and bitters, please." I had learned to drink it without ice.

And that did it. Within an hour and a half, we were in bed, the Church renounced, conscience vanquished, inhibitions overcome, revulsion con-

an American girl. See *The Autobiography of Lord Alfred Douglas* (London: Martin Secker, 1929), 256–60.

"butterfly devotion." Steward's account of Douglas's relationship with this boy (Ivor Goring) seems to come from Rupert Croft-Cooke, *Bosie: The Story of Lord Alfred Douglas, His Friends and Enemies* (London: W. H. Allen, 1963), 330–31. See also Douglas Murray, *Bosie: The Biography of Lord Alfred Douglas* (London: Hodder and Stoughton, 2000), 266–69.

quered, pledges and vows and British laws all forgotten. Head down, my lips where Oscar's had been, I knew that I had won.

After I finished my ministrations and settled back, his hand stole down to clamp itself around me. It began to move gently. Still moving it up and down, shafering me, he spoke: "You really needn't have gone to all that trouble, since this is almost all Oscar and I ever did with each other."

Genuinely astonished, I stammered: "B-b-but . . . the poems, and all . . ."

"We used to get boys for each other," he said. "I could always get the workers he liked, and he could get the intellectual ones I preferred. We kissed a lot, but not much more."

I got to Brighton for the ten o'clock train that night. Lord Alfred never wrote to me again, nor I to him. He died in 1945.

In these days, it may be of no great interest to those who have graced and honored my bed since 1937 to know that they are directly linked in with Oscar Wilde. But on the other hand, if they have a sense of history, they may welcome the information.

From London during that magic summer of 1937 it was on to Paris, and even today, recalling the excitement of that first visit to the heartland of art and literature, the feeling remains hard to define. It was like a slight trembling of the fringe around one's soul, a vague and not unpleasant quivering of the secret marrow deep in the bones, a prickling in the skin that made one restless and yet content.

Come April or October in Paris, it is all the same—the golden hazy afternoons, the life of the cafés, the sweet grey spirit of the old city. And when you breathe and look and listen—no matter whether you have seen one or a score of springs or summers in Paris—you know that this is the very best season Paris ever had.

Paris had always been the holy city of artists, writers, and composers, and in the year I arrived, the subtle ghosts of the great were still strolling the boulevards and drinking in the cafés. I was young and romantic and laid open to all the city's charms. When I had tasted as many of them as I could, I remembered that André Gide had also invited me to come to see him whenever I arrived in Paris.

His name is nearly forgotten today for some reason—but he was one of the first writers of the twentieth century who dared openly to confess his homosexuality in print. He produced two classics of homosexual literature—*The Counterfeiters* and *The Immoralist*—as well as a very early Platonic dialogue on the subject—*Corydon*—in 1911. Unabashed, he could write—

and be accepted for writing—a haunting sentence about the Arab boys whom he loved: "More precisely, I was attracted to them by what remained of the sun on their brown skins"—and could in 1920 say in print: "In the name of what God or what ideal do you forbid me to live according to my nature? . . . My normal is your abnormal, and your normal is my abnormal." These were strong statements indeed for those early years, especially when it is remembered that despite France's reputation for tolerance, the basic tradition in that country was heterosexual, that of a man for his wife and mistress. Homosexuality, when it occasionally reached the public press, was referred to as an "outrage of manners/taste" (*outrage des moeurs*), later modified to "*une affaire rose.*"

In my callow literary judgment of the time, Gide did not measure up to such other "greats" as Thomas Mann and Romain Rolland, but he was nonetheless important to me, because his brave and brilliant stand for homosexuality was like a lighthouse in those dark and stormy days of the 1930s. His writing lacked the realism of today, of course, but it had skill, comprehension, talent, and understanding of the human heart. To many, Gide's writing was thin, but to me in my twenties, he was one of the first knights of Camelot.

It is difficult to say what was in my mind that muggy Parisian afternoon in August when I sought out his address on the rue Vaneau, climbed a flight of stairs, and very timidly rapped at the door. I was quite nervous and a little frightened.

Neither Gide nor a maid answered my knock. Instead it was an eighteen-year-old Arab boy. He was like a very handsome young Roman, dark and bronzelike with splendidly chiseled nose and mouth, and (to borrow a phrase from a letter of Wilde's) the tents of midnight were folded in his eyes; moons

---

"**More precisely, I was attracted to them.**" English translation (apparently by Steward) of a line from Gide's autobiography, *Si le grain ne meurt*. The passage is given a more poetic rendering in the standard English translation by Gide's friend and translator Dorothy Bussy (*If It Die* . . . [New York: Modern Library, 1935], 273).

"**In the name of what God.**" *If It Die* . . . , 254. The French first edition of twelve copies was published in 1920.

Romain Rolland (1866–1944). French playwright and novelist, and winner of the Nobel Prize for literature in 1915.

the tents of midnight. Wilde to Reginald Turner, January 3, 1899 (*The Complete Letters of Oscar Wilde*, ed. Rupert Hart-Davis [New York: Holt, 2000], 1117). Steward's entire sentence is taken from Wilde's letter; his source in 1978 would presumably have been Hart-Davis's 1962 edition of Wilde's letters or Rupert Croft-Cooke, *The Unrecorded Life of Oscar Wilde* (London: W. H. Allen, 1972), 268.

hid in their curtains. His face rose like a classic sculpture above the straight lines of his white burnoose, and on his head was a tasseled red *chéchia*, a fez.

"I am expected by Monsieur Gide," I gulped in French.

"De la part de qui?" His teeth gleamed in a curve of white. "Who is it?"

I was so overwhelmed by his beauty that all French momentarily deserted me, but it soon came back. I gave him my name, and he asked me to wait in the study. I sat down, dumbstruck by his beauty, and he disappeared.

It was a very untidy room with piles of books here and there—stacked on the floor and filling many shelves. A decrepit old typewriter stood on the scarred desk, and the windows were closed with louvered shutters. A moment's panic rose in me, for what reason I did not know, a feeling, a subcurrent of something almost evil and mysterious. Perhaps it was the heat, or the claustrophobic sensation induced by the shuttered room.

And then André Gide entered. He was a tall, slightly stooped man in his late sixties, wearing a shabby old unbuttoned brown cardigan sweater that sagged from somewhat narrow shoulders. His shirt had no collar but was secured at the neck below his mobile Adam's apple by a brass collar stud. The face was sensitive and thin-lipped, and he was nearly bald save at the back of his head. His cheekbones were high and hollowed underneath—the sort of face in which Lombroso would have seen Gide's troublesome puritan-Protestantism reflected.

"Monsieur," he said, shaking hands with the usual short sharp French snap. "I am enchanted to meet you." And then he looked around the room. "This is not an inviting place to talk. Let us go to another room which may be more comfortable."

It was one of those characteristic long French "railroad" apartments with rooms opening on each side of a central corridor. In one of them with an open door sat the young Arab who had let me in, nearly naked and cross-legged on a bed, sewing a fine seam in his burnoose which he had removed and laid across one knee.

"What an extraordinarily handsome young man," I murmured to Gide.

"Yes," he said in English. "He is one of the most beautiful creatures I have ever seen." He smiled. "I speak a little the English. If he hears a compliment one cannot live with him . . . the rest of the day." Then he switched to French again. "In here," he said, opening another door at the end of the hall.

It was an amazing room. It had a huge circular bed draped with a pink

---

Lombroso. Cesare Lombroso (1835–1909), Italian criminologist who theorized a connection between criminal behavior and physical features, especially cranial and facial oddities.

satin coverlet, and a frilly canopy at one end. Circular beds were very rare indeed in 1937.

Gide sat down in a noisy wicker chair with his back toward the windows. "I hope the monsieur will excuse me," he said. "The light is very painful to my eyes."

He had the habit of a small cough which constantly interrupted his speech—not exactly asthmatic, but dry and a little rasping. "It is a great pleasure to meet Americans. My books seem to be more popular in your country than in mine. And I thank you for your letters. They have been most moving . . . most flattering."

"Thank you very much," I said. "Yes, your work is very popular in the States," adding that in a course in the modern novel, I included his *The Counterfeiters* and much admired its experimental structure.

He smiled. "I wanted to call the translation *The Coiners*, but Madame Knopf said that such a term would not be as well understood."

"We have just finished reading your *Return from the USSR*," I said.

"And that too," he said. "I thought 'Back from' would be more forceful than 'Return,' but once again Madame Knopf said no. Women are strong in America. One wonders whether she or her husband is the publisher."

"You were gravely disappointed with Russia," I said.

"Ah!" he said, striking his forehead with the palm of his hand. "That is hardly the word. I was profoundly disillusioned. So much there, so wonderful, so fascinating. I went there expecting to find the new race, the handsome young men, the workers . . . and all I found was a state headed for the worst kind of dictatorship of the few, those high in the party. And no freedom at all in sexual matters, except marriage and divorce. It has gone the way of all great centralized powers." He smiled again. "I apologize, but your country must be included. Have you been to the Exposition yet?"

I nodded.

"Then you have seen the two pavilions—the Russian with the hammer and sickle on its facade, confronting the German eagle and the swastika directly across the way. I find that extremely symbolic. And it will be all too

Madame Knopf. Blanche Wolf Knopf (1894–1966), president and cofounder (with her husband, Alfred Knopf) of the publishing house of Alfred A. Knopf, Inc.

the Exposition. L'Exposition Internationale des Arts et Techniques dans la Vie Moderne, held May–November 1937 in Paris. The opposing siting of the gigantic Soviet and German pavilions, the latter designed by Nazi architect Albert Speer (1905–81), suggested the political antagonism that would turn to war four years later.

short a time, I fear, until Germany and Russia really do confront each other. It will be Armageddon; we will all be destroyed."

I thought that perhaps it would be wise to try to turn him to another topic. "What do you think of American writers?"

"I like many of them," he said. "There is Steinbeck—such simplicity and understanding. And empathy with his characters. His *Cannery Row* is beautiful."

"And *The Grapes of Wrath*?"

"I did not like that too much. It was very painful."

"*The Immoralist* was a painful book too," I said, "at least for some of us. You had the courage to speak out about 'the problem' here in France when few others dared touch the subject. What do you think of Hemingway?" I went on, like a reporter.

The Gallic hand vibrated in front of his face. "No, no," he said forcefully. "He is too . . . too physical. One can see through the hairy chest. He is a poseur. He pretends to be a man but all the time struggles against what he really is—else why the overwhelming male friendships in all his works?"

I wanted to get the word out of him. "Do you mean you think him homosexual?"

Gide smiled and shrugged. "It is not for me to say."

"What other writers do you like?"

"Faulkner. He did a splendid piece of work in *Sanctuary*, but nothing since. And Dos Passos is interesting. Some critics claim he is a disciple of mine. And Michael Gold—such feeling, such pity for the Jews."

"Gold has been bitter against homosexuals," I said, thinking of Wilder. "Do you like Dreiser?"

"I can't read him. He is too . . . lumpy. Too ungrammatical."

I smiled to hear the current titan of American letters so easily cast aside. "A lot of critics feel that the floral period of the American novel was the 1920s," I said. "Wharton, Wilder, Hemingway, Willa Cather. . . ."

"Who is Cather? I have not heard of him."

Michael Gold. Pen name of Jewish-American writer Itzok Isaac Granich (1894–1967), ardent communist, author of proletarian literature, and often scathing critic. Here and below, Steward refers to Gold's attack on Wilder in the October 22, 1930, issue of the *New Republic*. Gold not only mocked Wilder as "the poet of the gentle bourgeoisie" and called his novels a "historic junkshop" with no "usefulness to the world"; he also derided the "homosexual bouquet" in Wilder's work and called his conception of religion "a daydream of homosexual figures in graceful gowns moving archaically among the lilies."

I explained gently that she was a woman and then asked, "Have you ever thought of coming to America?"

"I am afraid of New York," he said.

"A lot of persons are," I said. "But they would be very kind to you."

"Ah, yes . . . perhaps too kind. I would like to go incognito, but that is not possible. Even in Russia I was recognized. I do not think I would be physically able to stand your great country."

Shifting topics a bit, I told him that I had seen Lord Alfred Douglas in England. His eyebrows went up. "A dreadful man," he said. "A shocking man."

"Will you ever write any more about Wilde and Lord Alfred?" I asked.

"I think not," he said. "There is my little book on Oscar Wilde that pleased Robert Ross so much, and the passages in *Si le grain ne meurt*. I have said most of what I wanted to say."

It was a short interview, but I did not want to tire him. "Your *chef d'oeuvre*," I said, holding out a copy of the French edition of *The Counterfeiters*. "Would you be kind enough to sign it for me?"

"Delighted," he said. "It is always flattering." He took the book and inscribed an elegantly phrased sentiment, pausing to make sure of the exact spelling of my name. At the door, he said "Au revoir" and then delivered himself of a short speech deploring the lack of an exact American equivalent for the expression. "I hope that you will come to see me again when I am recovered from my recent travels."

I assured him that I would. He took down my address at the Hôtel Récamier and promised to give me a *coup de téléphone* soon.

I thanked him, not expecting to hear from him again. But about ten days later, the patronne at the hotel, much impressed, told me that Monsieur Gide had phoned and left a message which said: "Can you come this evening at nine o'clock?" Of course.

Gide himself met me at the door. "I have a little surprise for you," he said, handing me an inscribed copy of his novel, *Les Caves du Vatican*.

"I am overwhelmed," I said.

"Ah, but that is not really the surprise," he said. "Come with me."

Once again, we went down the long corridor toward the room with the

---

"my little book on Oscar Wilde." *Oscar Wilde* (Paris: Mercure de France, 1910), translated by Bernard Frechtman (New York: Philosophical Library, 1949).

"the passages in *Si le grain ne meurt."* See pages 293–316 of the Bussy translation, where Gide presents the young Douglas as erratic and petulant, observing that "nothing ever satisfied him; he always wanted to go one better" (300).

circular bed. He half-opened the door, and I went in, and then to my amazement he closed the door again with himself on the outside.

Lighted only by the frilly little pink tulip lamp on the bed table, the young Arab who had opened the door for me on my first visit sensually stretched his naked limbs on the bed and smiled and held out his arms in invitation.

"I am Ali," he said.

Small wonder that I have never forgotten the works of Gide.

I was in Zurich from September 11 to 17 and sought out Thornton Wilder. My feelings about him in 1937 were different from those of the first time we had met. I was eight years older and considered myself much more knowledgeable—the levels of sophistication change every decade. Another thing marking a shift in my opinions about Thornton was Michael Gold's attack on him in *The New Republic* in 1930. Echoes of that vicious slashing assault had never left my mind, and phrases still hung in the valleys, for Gold had called Wilder a prophet of the genteel Christ, the Emily Post of culture, producer of a chambermaid literature peopled with daydreams of homosexual figures in graceful gowns. Gold was simply following the Communist party line of attack, but I was not astute enough at the time to recognize it.

The criticism had affected me so much that I had almost lost interest in Wilder. I had not read anything of his since our first meeting except *Heaven's My Destination*, which I found totally unlike his previous writing. In fact, I liked it a great deal—a picaresque accounting of the adventures of a "pure fool." But in the ladder of my ranking of literary favorites, Thornton had slipped considerably. Still, Gertrude had said, "Meet him"—so meet him I did.

Our week began with a whirlwind of talk—eager, lively, and fascinating to me—in the bar of the Carlton Elite, where he was staying. I liked him immediately. The richness of his mind reminded me of that of Oscar Wilde, and I wondered if Thornton—like Wilde—exhausted his resources in talk instead of writing, the urge to put things on paper diminished by the audience for his conversation. He excused himself somewhat by saying that he

sought out Thornton Wilder. When Stein heard that Steward was going to Zurich for a prearranged lunch with Thomas Mann, she wrote him a note of introduction to Wilder and suggested they meet while he was there (Manuscript, 150).
Carlton Elite. Famous Zurich hotel frequently patronized in the 1930s by James Joyce, who had in fact stayed there in the previous week (Roger Norburn, *A James Joyce Chronology* [New York: Palgrave Macmillan, 2004], 179).

had spoken nothing but German for so long that he was delighted now to return to English.

I recognized that many of his ideas had come from Gertrude Stein—and he was frank to admit it. "But I really can't understand her writing," he said. "Try as I may, there are clouds and darkness over the land, so much of it."

"But you've done the introductions to *Narration* and *The Geographical History*—" I protested.

"Largely based on our conversations together," he said. "Our exchanges of ideas. She is very clear to me when she speaks about writing and thinking. And in much of her writing, I feel the authority of what she says, even though it may not be at all clear to me."

We had progressed from the bar of the Carlton Elite to the dining room, still talking furiously, he doing most of it and myself listening. And of what? Of Japanese warlords, of Siegfried's lime leaf, the meaning of the Greek word *olisbos*, the death of tattooing, the superiority of drama over the novel, of Druid rites and curses and runes and Stonehenge and the nature of the Eleusinian mysteries as Sir James Frazer described them. I discovered that he had scores of little set speeches, and these issued forth automatically when properly triggered; such reactions are usual in schoolmasters (of whom I was one) who talk so much they forget what they have said to whom.

At meal end, we got started on religion, and I found myself denigrating the Catholic Church and telling him of the various sad experiences with western priests in Montana.

Thornton listened for a while and then suddenly slapped his hand down flat on the tablecloth. A large orange, perched precariously on top of a *corbeille* of fruits on our table, rolled off and across the floor. A waiter, scowling, picked it up and restored it to its place. Thornton never paused in his talking.

Narration. Published version of four lectures Stein delivered at the University of Chicago in March 1935, near the end of her American speaking tour.

The Geographical History. *The Geographical History of America, Or, The Relation of Human Nature to the Human Mind* (1936), a wide-ranging philosophical meditation in Stein's characteristically difficult prose style.

Siegfried's lime leaf. In the late twelfth-century epic poem *Das Nibelungenlied*, the prince Siegfried bathes in dragon's blood to become invulnerable, but a tree leaf falls on his back and leaves him with one unprotected spot. Steward and Wilder may have been discussing the 1924 film version of the story, directed by Fritz Lang (1890–1976).

olisbos. A dildo (*OED*).

Sir James Frazer (1854–1941). Scottish scholar and author of *The Golden Bough* (1890), a pioneering study of the intersections of myth and religion. The Eleusinian mysteries were secret initiation rites in an ancient Greek cult.

"Don't say those things!" he exclaimed. "Because, suppose—just suppose—the Catholic Church may be the right answer to all we are looking for!" And then he went on, tracing the line of authority through the New Testament down to the Reformation until I was quite wearied with the bottle I had uncorked. He was religion-haunted all his life, repeatedly asking the unanswerable question and ever waiting for a sign.

Then he returned to talking about Gertrude, full of stories and anecdotes.

"I can praise her to men but not to women," he said, looking intently and somewhat owlishly at me through his glasses. "Women don't want to hear about her. She seems to be the only woman today who is seriously trying to develop a metaphysical mind, and that impulse overwhelms the feminine in her. I myself have never 'come clear' to her, I think. She eyes me constantly—"

"As she did me," I said, fiddling with the brandy glass. "I frequently caught her at it."

"She does that when she doesn't understand a person. She's writing the second volume of her autobiography—"

"Yes, she let me read it," I said.

"You were singularly honored to be permitted to read it. It's a fascinating volume—it will go—but I don't like the 'ballet' ending. Seemed awfully gabby to me. Still, I wouldn't dare criticize anything she did."

"Oh my," I said. "I did, once or twice."

"It's a wonder she didn't throw you out," he chuckled. "As her literary executor, I often find myself worried silly about what may happen after she dies. What Alice may say and do. Alice can be difficult."

"Alice may die first," I said.

During those days in Zurich we saw each other every afternoon and evening; his mornings were devoted to writing, or attempting it, for he confessed that he was blocked at the end of the second act of the play he was composing. As Boswell reported of Goldsmith when he was around Dr. Johnson, Thornton seemed to have a great desire to "shine" for my benefit. Or perhaps it was just that he had not had an American to talk to—not with—for a number of days.

Of the six or seven afternoons and evenings with Thornton in Zurich, there was one extraordinary night when it started to rain while we were

"the second volume of her autobiography." Everybody's Autobiography (1937).
"As her literary executor." Before her death, Stein changed her mind and appointed her longtime friend Carl Van Vechten as executor instead of Wilder.
As Boswell reported of Goldsmith. See the account of dinner on July 6, 1763, in The Life of Samuel Johnson (1791), by James Boswell (1740–95).

walking around the town—not hard, mostly a drizzle. He had been telling me about the establishment of milk bars in Switzerland to combat the growing incidence of alcoholism among the young (with perhaps a slanting reference to my own drinking in those days) and talking about his visit with Freud and how Freud had rather obliquely suggested that Thornton and Freud's daughter Anna would make a good match. Then he somehow got started about the historical Zurich and the writers it had harbored over the years.

And so in the light rain, a kind of lengthy literary pilgrimage began. I kept getting drunker and drunker, hardly able to pass a bar without getting another cognac ("to ward off a cold," I said) while he steered me to the Café Odeon to see the spot where Tristan Tzara read laundry lists into poetry and invented Dada to shock the intellectual complacency of Europe.

And all the time we were getting wetter and wetter—while I kept hollering for an umbrella or wishing loudly and repeatedly that I had a pair of rubbers and wanting more brandy. Thornton continued effervescent and euphoric, as if he were the one getting drunk—and then we had to search out the house where Nietzsche "in great loneliness" wrote *Also Sprach Zarathustra*.

I still called for an umbrella, but we had to stay up until dawn so that we could "hear the bells of Zurich, as Max Beerbohm described them"; and then finally, soaked through and thoroughly soused, I was steered back to my hotel by Thornton, where I fell into bed and slept until late that afternoon.

would make a good match. Freud made the suggestion when he met Wilder for the first time in Vienna on October 13, 1935 (Penelope Niven, *Thornton Wilder: A Life* [New York: HarperCollins, 2012], 408–9). He seems to have misread not only Wilder's sexuality but his daughter's: Anna Freud (1895–1982) never married but lived for more than fifty years with Dorothy Burlingham (1891–1979), the heir to the Tiffany fortune.

Tristan Tzara (1896–1963). Romanian-born writer and performance artist and a key figure in the Dada movement, a nihilistic rejection of contemporary culture and aesthetics whose founding coincided with the outbreak of World War I. The Café Odeon, opened in 1911 and still operating, was an early Dadaist gathering spot.

the house where Nietzsche . . . wrote Also Sprach Zarathustra. In a frequently cited account, Nieztsche's sister noted that he wrote preliminary notes for the first part of *Zarathustra* in September 1884 while in Zurich (Elizabeth Förster-Nietzsche, "Introduction," *Thus Spake Zarathustra*, trans. Thomas Common [n.p.: Floating Press, 2009], 25).

Max Beerbohm. Henry Maximilian Beerbohm (1872–1956), English essayist and theater critic known also for his pencil and ink caricatures. Switzerland is famous for the number and volume of its church bells, many of which begin ringing at 7:00 a.m., but Wilder seems to be thinking of Beerbohm's statement "I was born within sound of Bow Bells" (that is, near St. Mary-le-Bow church in London) in his radio broadcast "London Revisited" on December 29, 1935.

He, meanwhile, went to his hotel to work on the last act of his play. When I met him the next evening for dinner at the Baur-au-Lac, he announced triumphantly that he had finished. It was not until I first saw *Our Town* that I connected the umbrellas at the opening of that act with my yelling for one that wet night in Zurich. He had, as Gertrude told me later, "struck a match on me."

Thornton was only twelve years older than myself, but it seemed more like thirty; he was a little too sweet and old-maidish for my contemporary "slickness." During those several days he lectured me about my homosexuality—which he had got me to confess early on—telling me how to handle it in a kind of four-way treatment (which was, perhaps, Thornton's own advice to himself): Think how to run your classes most easily without draining yourself; write some essays (why, in heaven's name?); consider your childhood and youth thoroughly, seeking out and examining all the disgusting things regarding sex until they are no longer repulsive; and study the lives and careers of the great homosexuals from the beginning down to the present day—Leonardo and Michelangelo to Whitman and beyond.

After this wordy intellectual preparation, sort of like tenderizing a tough cube steak, we climbed into bed together, myself half-drunk as I had to be in those days to have an encounter.

Thornton went about sex almost as if he were looking the other way, doing something else, and nothing happened that could be prosecuted anywhere, unless frottage can be called a crime. There was never even any kissing. On top of me, and after ninety seconds and a dozen strokes against my belly, he ejaculated. At this he sprang from our bed of roses and exclaimed in his rapid way: "Didntyoucome? Didntyoucome?"

No, I didn't.

Thus began the casual acquaintance with Thornton Wilder that lasted through the war years and beyond, ending sometime in 1948. I became his Chicago piece, possibly his only physical contact in the city. If there were others, I knew nothing of them, for there was a double lock on the door of the closet in which he lived. Later in our acquaintance, he let me understand by various oblique hints that he had sometimes been emotionally involved, but nothing was said directly. He could never forthrightly discuss anything sexual; for him the act itself was quite literally unspeakable. His puritan reluctance was inhibiting to me as well; I could not talk about such matters while I was with him, for he made such discussion seem somehow indecent,

Baur-au-Lac. Legendary luxury hotel in Zurich.

in bad taste. It was once, while saying how good-looking he thought Mont-gomery Clift to be, that he caught me regarding him rather quizzically. More for the satisfaction of my own curiosity than for knowing about Thornton, I wanted to ask about Clift, who was also an attractive person to me.

"Have you—?" I began tentatively, and then stopped.

There was a brief silence. Then Thornton said, looking off into an upper corner of the room, "I am afraid—" and he chuckled nervously, "that in all of my male friendships there is always a touch of Eros."

He could not bring himself to say any more. But the sentence itself was revelatory; it opened speculation on many horizons and many landscapes with figures.

Every time Thornton came to Chicago, I would receive in advance a phone call or one of his chatty postcards containing about two hundred words in his minuscule handwriting, and I would go down to the Stevens Hotel (now the Conrad Hilton) to spend the appointed night in Room 1000. On such nights, he might show me his elaborately annotated copy of *Finnegans Wake*, the margins so black with his innumerable notes that there was hardly any white to be seen; or he would draw a score of Palestrina from his suitcase and tell me how he spent hours alone in hotel rooms "reading" the music to himself, enjoying it as much as if he were hearing it. And it kept him from cruising.

Occasionally he would come out to my North Side apartment. Once he left his wristwatch on the night table beside the bed and sent me a telegram the next day asking me to forward the watch to him in Arizona or else bring it to the hotel. The telegram was possibly one of the few bits of evidence he might have left that would have exposed his dread secret.

In 1945, my good friend Wendell Wilcox had a novel published, *Everything Is Quite All Right*, and planned to write a new novel about his great passion, the Latin poet Catullus. But Wendell made the mistake of detailing his care-fully researched plot to Thornton, and sometime later, Thornton's *The Ides of March* appeared. Therein, alas! Wendell found his plot. After that, Thornton discovered that many of his friends in Chicago disappeared or grew cool as

Montgomery Clift (1920–66). Handsome stage and film actor whose homosexuality was not widely known until after his death.

Conrad Hilton. Now known as the Hilton Chicago.

Finnegans Wake. Final novel (1939) by James Joyce (1882–1941), known primarily for its radically unconventional diction and style.

Palestrina. Giovanni Pierluigi da Palestrina (1525–94), prolific Italian composer of eccle-siastical music.

the story about Catullus gained wider circulation. I was one of the friends who vanished.

One night in Paris in 1939 he had been to the theatre, and we met afterward at the Café de la Paix. He said that he would walk me home to the Hôtel Récamier.

And so he did. As we went down the Avenue de l'Opéra, a female prostitute on the street side plucked at his arm, importuning him to come with her and falling into step beside us. He pulled his arm away and went on busily talking to me as if he had not seen or heard her. Not to be put off, the girl continued to pull at him. Finally, he disengaged his arm, turning to her as if he had just then become aware of her existence.

"Not tonight, not tonight," he said, with an inflection suggesting that on any other night in the twentieth century he would have said yes. The girl went away, and Thornton continued his euphoric monologue as if she had never been there at all.

And so he went through life, bright-eyed and eager, interested in everything, talking, talking, looking away from the specter of sex that walked beside him, always hoping that it would disappear. But it never did.

And there was never, never, never a kiss.

Lunch had long been planned with Thomas Mann, who was then living in a small suburb of Zurich. On a day when Thornton was busy with something else, I consulted the interurban train schedules and went to Küsnacht. It was a delightful ride along the Zürichsee beside blue water and tall greenery. But I was very ill at ease. The prospect of lunch with Thomas Mann, the grandeur of him, the Nobel Prize—these things made me uncomfortable, so that, arriving early, I sat for many minutes in the waiting room at the station getting my courage together until the exact moment came.

I need not have worried. Herr Mann—and his lively wife Katia, beautiful Erika, and quiet Klaus—all seemed bent on putting me at ease. Even the dog, which was about four feet high at the shoulder, seemed friendly. They were more than hospitable, and Frau Mann was spritely in her conversation. She spoke English very well.

"There was that time when Thomas and I went to the States," she said, "and Alfred Knopf gave a party for us, a cocktail party it was, and they served something that tasted very sweet and good. You know, it was unusual for us; we do not have cocktails in Europe. And I liked it so much that I had two of

Thomas Mann. See note on page 47.

them, and then—and then—I got dark in the head!" She laughed merrily, and Erika added, "When we got back home, Mother insisted that we have them every night before dinner."

The conversation at lunch consisted mainly of their asking me questions about life in the States; it was not until Herr Mann and I retired to his upstairs room, his study, that we spoke of literary things . . . in French, since I knew only little German, and he little English.

"Do you," I asked naively, "think that you will ever write a sequel to *The Magic Mountain*?"

"No," he said smiling. "I said everything I had to say about such things in *Der Zauberberg*."

"What do you think," I asked, "will be the topic of the greatest twentieth-century novel? That is, unless you have already written it in *The Magic Mountain*."

He thought for several moments. Then he said, "I believe the theme will be the desire of every man for solitude, versus his need for companionship, and the need of every man for solitude, versus his desire for companionship."

"The affection of Hans Castorp for his cousin Joachim and also your *Death in Venice* suggest that you have a favorable attitude toward love between men."

He smiled at me and quoted a Latin phrase: "Nihil humani a me alienum puto."

There was an aura of greatness about him, his tall spare frame, his close-cropped mustache, his gentle way. Truly, the Latin phrase was right: nothing that is human is strange to me.

"You have written what is possibly the greatest paean of love to the human body that has ever been put on paper," I said. "The passage which is left in French even in the English version, the love song of Hans Castorp to Claudia Chauchat."

He smiled. "You praise me too much," he said. "By writing it in French, I let Hans Castorp say things which he would find difficult to say in his own language. The French allowed him to take one step away from his own modesty."

"That is an extremely wise observation," I said. "But I am curious about one thing."

"What is that?"

"I suppose you are above such things as wordplays," I said. "But did you

---

Death in Venice. See note on page 58. As Steward seems to surmise but could not have known in 1937, Mann's diaries, available after his death, suggest that he was in fact bisexual.

realize that 'Chauchat' is almost a translation of 'hot cat'? That it lacks only the 'd'?"

The grey eyebrows went up. "I had never thought of that," he said. "The sound is indeed the same. It is very perceptive of you to notice it."

We talked at length of the differing philosophies of Herr Naphta and Herr Settembrini and the worldviews they represented, of the little essays — ruminations, really — on the subject of time which were scattered through the book, and of the "heightening" which occurred in Hans, raising him from the simple-minded "flat-lander" to a person of real intelligence by the time the book was ended. We discussed the book as an important one in the "quester" tradition, not only in German but universal literature.

"It is the only novel I have ever read," I said, "which keeps coming closer instead of diminishing, going farther away as time goes on."

And then, seeing that Herr Mann grew tired of speaking French (as indeed I did myself), I thanked him and began to make my departure.

"It is through persons like you," he said, "that I hope to keep on living." And with that he put his arm around my shoulders.

It was not an erotic manifestation in the least but a friendly one. And of all the remembered gestures in my life, that one is perhaps the most treasured.

Sources: *Chapters*, 44–58, 70–77; Manuscript, 138–42, 150–54, 200–218.

Herr Naphta and Herr Settembrini. Jesuit (Naphta) and atheist (Settembrini), characters in *The Magic Mountain* whose discussions offer the young Hans Castorp alternative ideologies and perspectives on the world.

Chapter Six

GERTRUDE AND ALICE

1937–67

Two weeks of that magic summer of 1937 were spent at Bilignin in southern France as the guest of Gertrude Stein and Alice B. Toklas, two weeks of
a golden romp with them, afternoons of excursions over the lovely French
countryside, evenings of delicious meals prepared by Alice, and days of feeling that life was wonderful and exciting. Such a flood of happy recollections
rushes to the screen of memory in recalling those days at Bilignin that it is
hard to enfold them in a capsule of time and space, especially since the two
weeks were repeated two years later, and the two visits happily mingled in
mind and memory.

When Claire Andrews died in 1932, I knew Gertrude might never hear of
it. I summoned my courage, found her address in *Who's Who*, and wrote to
inform her. She answered pleasantly enough and asked me to continue writing; thus began a friendship and correspondence lasting until her death in
1946 and continued by Alice B. Toklas until 1967.

Bilignin. The French village not far from Geneva where Stein and Toklas rented a summer
home. When the Germans occupied and divided France in World War II, Stein and Toklas
closed up their Paris home and moved permanently to Bilignin in order to be in the un-
occupied zone. They spent the last part of the war in nearby Culoz before returning to Paris.
the two visits happily mingled. In this chapter, the chronology is slightly confused by the fact
that Steward conflates details from his two visits with Stein and Toklas, in 1937 and 1939.
I summoned my courage . . . and wrote to inform her. Steward's first, very formal, letter to
Stein is dated November 19, 1933, almost a year after Andrews's death. Stein responded,
and a regular exchange of letters ensued, the correspondence becoming increasingly in-
formal and personal as Steward advanced from graduate student to professor to published
novelist between 1933 and 1936. Remarkably, Stein saved these early letters of adulation
from a mere graduate student.

At the moment in 1937, however, a highly nervous youngish man of twenty-eight—suffering from a Pernod hangover that should have ended forever all the love I had for alcohol—descended from the train at Culoz and looked around an empty station. Anise was reeking from every pore; I walked enveloped in a cloud of scent from the wicked greenish liqueur. The train had gone puffing on toward Marseille—and the globe of silence it had left behind was profound, so deep that within it I heard the small singing of the blood in my ears.

There was no sign of Gertrude and Alice. I heard, then, some locusts somewhere and the far-off tinkle of a cowbell. A cart moved nearby over cobblestones. Within the station, one could almost hear the paint peeling from the walls, a faded brown and beige. There was a sudden crash, as of a box being dropped, and I went inside in search of the noise.

A station attendant—blue coveralls, a sweat-stained red handkerchief knotted at his neck, complete with dusty beret and walrus mustache—was upending another box from a baggage cart. In my then halting French I asked him if he knew the two American ladies from Belley or Bilignin.

"Ah," he said, "but certainly, monsieur."

"Have you seen them today?"

In a torrent of rapid French, I heard that they often came to shop in Culoz, but that he had not seen them for more than two weeks, and certainly not on this day, but perhaps monsieur would like to telephone them at Bilignin. He collected some francs from me and showed me the station telephone.

I was dismayed but brave. French telephones frightened me. I had to make the operator understand what I wanted, spelling out "Stein," and when I finally reached the house at Bilignin, it was to speak with Madame Roux, the housekeeper, and she spoke a patois beyond me.

I did manage to understand that they were not there, that they had gone to Culoz to meet "un jeune américain." Yes, I said; I was the one. I hung up, checked my suitcase, and set out to try to find them.

An hour of walking passed. I could not know that as I was going down one narrow street, they were going up another. They had decided to do some shopping before the train arrived and had consequently not been at the station when it did. Gradually many of the townspeople of Culoz were out looking for us, trying to bring us together, for half the village had seen one or the other of us wandering around. At that time, I had not yet heard Gertrude say, "I hate meeting trains and saying goodbye to them and meeting people and seeing them go away," or I would have been even more upset than I was.

At last I returned to the station and unchecked my baggage and sat down on it to wait—a thing I should have done in the first place. Within five minutes, Gertrude and Alice appeared at the top of a street leading down.

"Jesus," I said to myself, starting toward them.

"Damnation!" Gertrude shouted. "There he is, the lost is found, it's Sammy himself!"

We spent the next half hour alternately swearing and explaining, while they looked at me and I looked at them.

Gertrude was in a pink silk brocaded vest with a pale-yellow crêpe de Chine blouse. Her skirt was monk's cloth, a sort of homespun burlap, and she wore flat-heeled shoes. Alice's hat was wild with fruits and flowers, yellow and red; her dress was black, and triple loops of purple beads swung down to her waist. I forced myself not to stare at her faint mustache nor even at Gertrude's short-cut grey hair circling in a fascinating whorl at the back of her head. Her craggy face was like the profile on a Roman coin.

We climbed into the Matford and set off, with Gertrude driving and Alice sitting sidewise on the back seat, filing her nails.

The first evening was memorable. They lived in a seventeenth-century chateau which they rented every summer, with a mansard roof and a small formal garden behind it. "Tumbledown," Gertrude called it, but to me it seemed charming and in good repair. It was lovely and old, with gleaming hardwood floors and a stone stairway to the second floor. The garden had plots of trimmed box hedges with dark lustrous leaves, and Gertrude pointed out to me the broad beautiful valley sloping casually down to the Ain River and rising again to a circle of misty blue unforgettable hills, with the barely visible peak of Mont Blanc far in the distance, rosy and golden in the setting sun.

Then Gertrude showed me my room and the bathroom—of which she was very proud. She turned on the hot water in the washbowl, and it came out with a great gush of steam. "There, what do you think of that," she said. "We just had it put in. All that water as soon as a hotel and hotter too."

Evenings, we sat in the drawing room, happy after the wonderful meals that Alice prepared. In the blue paper-thin china cups the after-dinner infusions of verveine cooled. There was a great squeaking rocking chair which was Gertrude's alone, and its gentle noise, the happy squeaking song, remains the all-pervasive sound of Bilignin that has fastened itself in memory. By the tempo of its sound, sometimes slow as old Time and sometimes,

Matford. Automobile produced in France by Ford Motor Company between 1934 and 1940.
infusions of verveine. Tea made with leaves of the verbena plant.

under the pressure of Gertrude's excitement, rapid and allegro, punctuating her sentences like the commas she disdained, you could judge just how well or how poorly the evening's talk was going. It was Gertrude's chair, and Alice never sat in it, nor any guest. She rocked against the background of white woodwork and painted trompe l'oeil panels of corbels and hunting horns and musical instruments in tones of grey, brown, soft yellow, and faded purple. The smoke of cigarettes drifted lazily out into the burst of rose and gold that fell upon the garden. And we talked of everything under the sun—of the ballet, of Wally Simpson and her duke, of gardens, scenery, Mussolini, politics, teaching, salads and herbs and dressings, gasoline and spiders and cuckoos. The timbre of Gertrude's voice was rich and deep, and her great laugh—booming out over the valley—was the throat-filling laughter of the Valkyries.

Mornings, Gertrude did not come down until late, and we generally took a walk before lunch, as well as another before dinner—either the "upper turn" through green and brown vineyards with the grapes fragrant upon the vines, or the "lower turn" down toward the river, among the cool of the trees, walking on a cushion of leaves and moss and loam. And always the talk—of how the mutter of threatening summer storms made the farmers fear for their grapes, of the painting of Sir Francis Rose, of literature and her theories, of dipsomania and the authors who fell into it, of Roman roads in France.

In the afternoons, there were usually automobile trips here and there. Gertrude and Alice delighted in showing the quiet French countryside to their friends. Sometimes it was a flying trip to the Chambéry markets for meat and vegetables, or to Belley for rice and olive oil. Sometimes it was a party for the colony of *surréalistes* under André Breton, meeting Matta and

Wally Simpson and her duke. Having abdicated the English throne in December 1936, Edward, Duke of Windsor (1894–1972), married Wallis Simpson (1896–1986) in June 1937 in France, just before Steward's first visit with Stein and Toklas.
the Valkyries. Powerful female spirits who decide human destinies—especially who shall triumph in battle and who shall be defeated.
Sir Francis Rose (1909–79). English painter in the circle of French avant-garde artists whom Stein met in 1931 and whose work she championed. Steward first met him at Bilignin in August 1939 when they were both guests of Stein and Toklas. Gay, hapless, and sexually indiscreet, he became a (nonsexual) friend of Steward, who drew on Rose's life as the basis of his 1984 novel *Parisian Lives* (Spring, 70–72; *Dear Sammy*, 71–80).
André Breton (1896–1966). French writer, art collector, sometime communist and later anarchist, known for his founding role in the surrealist movement.
Matta. Roberto Antonio Sebastián Matta Echaurren (1911–2002), Chilean-born architect turned surrealist painter.

Photograph of Gertrude Stein taken by Steward during an outing to Aix-les-Bains, summer 1937. (BANC PIC 1972.017:47 — PIC. Courtesy of the Bancroft Library, University of California, Berkeley.)

Yves Tanguy, or a trip to the Abbey of Hautecombe for an hour with their Benedictine friends. Once we went on a journey to Geneva to see the Spanish paintings from the Prado that had been sent to Switzerland for safekeeping during the Spanish Civil War, with a pause for luncheon in a field, eating a delicious chicken that Alice had steamed over white wine and herbs. Again, it was a lively discussion with Henry and Clare Boothe Luce at Aix-les-Bains about a proposed collaboration on a play. Now it was a trip to Virieu-le-

Yves Tanguy. Raymond Georges Yves Tanguy (1900–1955), French surrealist painter mentored by Breton.

Abbey of Hautecombe. Reconstructed twelfth-century Cistercian monastery in the environs of Stein and Toklas's summer home. When Steward visited with them, it was occupied by the Benedictine order of monks.

Spanish paintings from the Prado. Paintings from Madrid's Prado Museum that had been shipped to Switzerland for safekeeping during the Spanish Civil War were exhibited in Geneva in the summer of 1939.

Henry and Clare Boothe Luce. Henry Robinson Luce (1898–1967) was the influential founder and publisher of *Time, Life,* and *Fortune* magazines. His second wife, Ann Clare Boothe (1903–87), was an author, playwright, and until 1934 managing editor of *Vanity Fair* magazine. In the 1940s, she was elected to the House of Representatives and later served in the Eisenhower administration as the ambassador to Italy, becoming the first American woman appointed to an ambassadorial post.

Grand and a small agricultural fair, with butter in molds shaped like small sheep, nine-inch mushrooms, and Gertrude firing at the whirling tin grouse in a shooting gallery. Or it was a ride in the cool dusk, the fragrant twilight, to Artemare, to eat *terrine* of duck, tomatoes in oil, partridge and thin crusted potatoes, with tiny wild strawberries which Madame Bérrard's son had picked in the hills that afternoon.

I was not old enough then—nor indeed was anyone wise enough at that time—to evaluate accurately her place in literature; and certainly, it was hard to be conscious of it while one was near her. Often I was overwhelmed by her presence—while we were walking or talking—and by the fact that I had been permitted the rare privilege and pleasure of visiting her. I remember her as a great and very human woman, an intricate yet simple and earthy personality, tremendously alive. I think of her on a rainy day in a small garage, down on hands and knees on the oily floor discussing the axle of her car with a young mechanic. I remember how we worked together in her garden, both bent over hoes as we weeded the tomatoes. I see her walking along the dusty roadways, switching her dog leash at the ragweed as she talked, and now and then shouting to Pépé, the little Mexican Chihuahua that Picabia had given her, to stop chasing chickens. I see her turn quickly away from the sight of a helpless calf with its legs tied for market, saying, "Let us not look at that." I hear her hearty laugh as she showed me how, with one quick movement, she had mastered the French peasant's trick of catching a napkin under both arms at once.

On one odd afternoon when only Gertrude and I were in the car, the mood slowly changed and became strangely intimate. Alice had been left behind by her own choice, while Gertrude and I were sent on an errand to Belley for milk and oil. We had been talking of my projected trip to Algiers, the dangers of being alone in the Casbah—and then the topics had shifted, so that she was asking me questions about my parents and about the two maiden aunts who had brought me up.

Suddenly, while still driving, she grabbed my kneecap and squeezed it hard. "Sammy," she said, "do you think Alice and I are lesbians?"

I was startled. A curl of flame ran up my spine. "It's no one's business one way or another," I said.

"Do you care whether we are?" she asked.

"Not in the least," I said, suddenly dripping wet.

Madame Bérrard's son. Steward refers to a dinner with Stein and Toklas at the Hôtel Bérrard in Artemare during his first visit in 1937 (*Dear Sammy*, 15–16).
Picabia. Francis Picabia (1879–1953), French avant-garde painter and close friend of Stein's.

"Are *you* queer or gay or different or 'of it' as the French say or whatever they are calling it nowadays?" she said, still driving as fast as always. She had let go my knee.

I waggled my hand. "I'm currently both," I said. "I think," I added. "I don't see why I should go limping on one leg through life just to satisfy a so-called norm."

There was not very much more to the conversation. She said that she and Alice had always been surrounded by homosexuals, that they both liked all people who produced—"and what they do in bed is their own business, and what we do is not theirs." She had denigrated male homosexuals to Hemingway to see if he would squirm because he was a secret one. And then, after those shattering few moments that day, she never referred to the matter again. She and Alice were very private persons, really Victorian—completely monogamous, abstemious, and on the surface more than a little reserved.

On another extraordinary afternoon, Gertrude sat in her rocking chair, her feet on the crossbar between the two rocker ends while she read aloud to me her recently completed book for children, *The World Is Round*. Her voice was mellow and pitched somewhere between alto and baritone—yet it could rise higher if the reading demanded it, and then it would take on a husky, almost whispery, quality. But usually it lived in the lower range—deeply resonant as if there were an extra secret chamber within her which gave depth and body to her tones. And when that wonderful instrument exploded in laughter, as it so frequently did, there was an infectious quality to it which compelled everyone to join in—a deep booming laughter that carried over the whole of their small domain and spilled down the garden wall into the valley. So she read to me in that voice, its cadences timed by the counterpoint of the wicker chair rocking, weaving its high reedy voice around hers, filling the interstices and underlining the human quality of her tones. There was no way at that early time to capture the golden rotundities of her voice, save to carve it deeply into my conscious memory, for tape recorders then—using wire—were as cumbersome and unwieldy as a suitcase.

It was not possible for the visits to Gertrude and Alice to be oil-smooth all of the time. It seemed to me that I was responsible for an unconscionable number of gaffes. One of the mildest occurred when the three of us were riding to Chambéry one afternoon to do some shopping. I wanted a cigarette,

---

"Are you queer or gay." Stein's short story "Miss Furr and Miss Skeene," first published in her *Geography and Plays* in 1922 and reprinted in *Vanity Fair* in 1923, is widely regarded as the first use in print of the word *gay* in the sense of "homosexual."

The World Is Round. Children's book (1939) by Stein with illustrations by Clement Hurd.

and since I was in the front seat I pushed in the electric lighter on the dashboard. Then with my mind on something Gertrude was saying, I very casually tossed the lighter out the open window.

It had no sooner left my hand than I howled with the realization. Gertrude's foot went down heavily on the brake, and Alice was dislodged from her Madame Récamier position in the back seat.

"What's the matter, my god, what's the matter, Sammy?" Gertrude asked.

I told them what I had done. Gertrude laughed and backed up a hundred yards. "Calm down," she said to me, for I was trembling. "We'll find it."

And she did, spotting it almost at once by the roadside.

I was still shaken. In Chambéry, Alice, to quiet me, bought me a serrated tomato-slicing knife, a beautiful small thing exactly like the one she had at Bilignin. And that night I slipped downstairs to her sacred kitchen, found her knife in the drawer, and substituted the new one for her old one . . . a more personal remembrance than the shiny new blade. I often wondered if her sharp eye caught the difference, and presumed that it had.

On another occasion, while I was in the garden reading one of the manuscript volumes of *Everybody's Autobiography* which Gertrude was in the process of writing, Alice called to me to go with them, again to shop. I put the volume upside down on the low garden wall, where it remained overnight. The next morning, I was scolded by Alice — but soon forgiven when she saw how intense my chagrin was.

"There, there — no harm done," she said, "and I won't tell Gertrude. But it was lucky, really. Suppose it had rained — where would the manuscript be?"

But by far the most awful of the episodes happened as I was packing my things to leave on a trip to Algiers. Gertrude and Alice had retired and shut their bedroom door, which angled with the bathroom door. I was in the bathroom, stuffing my toiletries into their case. The light was on and I had left the door open. I was being as quiet as I could, thinking they might already be asleep.

Suddenly I heard their bedroom door open and looked up, startled. There at the bathroom entrance stood Gertrude, completely naked. She covered her pubis quickly with both hands, said "Whoops!" in a loud voice, and vanished back into her bedroom, slamming the door so hard the bathroom mirror rattled. I had only the barest quickest glimpse of her, but my shocked

---

her Madame Récamier position. That is, reclining, after the favorite position of French socialite Jeanne-Françoise Julie Adélaïde Récamier (1777–1849).

Everybody's Autobiography. A continuation (1937) of Stein's first widely popular book, *The Autobiography of Alice B. Toklas* (1933).

eyes noted the glistening hollow pink scar that remained from the excision of part of her left breast. As I stuttered something like "I was just packing—" she was at the same time saying, "I thought you'd left the light on in the bathroom—."

Upset and trembling, I made it back to my room—for aside from the doctors who had delivered her and operated on her (if they were men), I was convinced that I was the only male who had ever seen her naked. With shaking hands, I poured myself a large drink of my "emergency" cognac and went to sleep with nightmares. But the next morning, bland as Buddha, Gertrude said nothing about it at all.

Because some other guests were to arrive at Gertrude's in August, I headed for Algiers and my first view of a foreign culture, to return to Bilignin toward the end of the month.

I do not know what it was that drew me to northern Africa in that summer, but it was powerful. In each of us there is a certain "call," an attraction or a feeling of spiritual kinship with one or two spots in the world. We feel that we must go there, that perhaps we lived there in some former time, and that we must somehow get back before we die. Perhaps I had been reading too much of the strange and exotic travels of André Gide in Algeria and Tunisia, accounts filled with descriptions of tawny, long-limbed young men, darkly handsome, and was attracted to them as Gide was "by what remained of the sun on their brown skins." Or perhaps it was just that I had recently seen the movie *Algiers* and was half-hoping to find Hedy Lamarr or Charles Boyer still lurking in the dark wet twisting alleys of the Casbah.

At any rate, I went to Algiers. The city itself, seen from the cobalt-blue sea, was breathtaking—built on a high hill, with buildings a rich cream in color; under the morning sun it exploded in a dazzling burst of white radiance that sent reflected golden spikes of light into the purple sky. My hotel was halfway up the hill and looked down over the switchback streets that climbed up to it among the creamy buildings. The Bay of Algiers glittered in the distance.

In a new place, one always feels a little lost at first, and in August, the climate of Algiers also makes one lazy. I wandered over to a little park that had

strange and exotic travels. Steward seems to refer to Part II of *Si le grain ne meurt*, in which Gide describes his awakening homosexuality during his travels in Tunisia and Algeria in his early twenties.
"what remained of the sun on their brown skins." See note on "More precisely, I was attracted to them," page 113.
Algiers. 1938 film starring Charles Boyer and Hedy Lamarr and directed by John Cromwell.

a fountain and sat on a bench to watch the people—the men in burnoose and scarlet chéchia, the veiled women with curious blue jewels of tattoos upon their foreheads or heels, the porters carrying bundles—even a sofa—on their heads.

It was there Mohammed Zenouhin found me and picked me to be his employer during my stay in Algiers. I had absolutely nothing to say about it—he saw me, and I was his thereafter. How he did it I will never know, but those children of the East have a psychological know-how that makes the most sophisticated Western expert in human relationships look and feel like a two-year-old. By this kindness, that suggestion, this wish for my amusement or comfort, he had woven me into his subtle silken net before the evening was over. He was an attractive eighteen-year-old, wearing a European coat and trousers with an open shirt; his only Arabian article was an old red fez with a black tassel, worn cockily angled on his sleek black hair. His handsome skin had the sun in it beneath the surface, and his black eyes were keen and laughing.

Looking back on that visit now, I do not know how I would ever have got along without Mohammed. I had planned to stay only a few days, but under his gay and teasing guidance, the stay stretched to two weeks, then three. The twenty francs—then about sixty cents—that I gave him every evening seemed little enough, but it was evidently a huge and satisfying sum to him.

Mohammed's French was not very good, but we understood each other. His Arabic, of course, was evidently superb, judging from the rows he could stir up with it. One day before he came to pick me up, I made the hideous mistake of giving five francs to a gamin bootblack for shining my shoes at the sidewalk café. By the time Mohammed got there, I was surrounded by half the little Arabs of Algiers, all clamoring for money. With a few excellently chosen words, Mohammed chased them off. What he told them I'll never know, but they used to run from me after that when they recognized me.

It was Mohammed who first guided me down the Rue N'Fissa in the Casbah, protecting me from beggars and helping me dodge the slops thrown out of the upper windows, keeping me out of the way of the panniered donkeys that plodded slowly up the stairway streets. With him I went to the huge church of Notre Dame d'Afrique, high on a bluff overlooking the Mediterranean, to see the famous Black Virgin's statue, whom sailors in danger im-

Rue N'Fissa in the Casbah. Famously narrow, hilly, and picturesque street in the old city of Algiers.
Notre Dame d'Afrique. Our Lady of Africa, Catholic basilica dedicated in 1872 and sited on a cliff overlooking the Bay of Algiers.

plore—but he, a good Moslem, tactfully excused himself from going inside. Together we went to the Jardin d'Essai to see the rare and exotic blooms of Africa and curious animals I had never even heard of. With him I smoked my first tiny pipeful of *kif*, which he seemed to enjoy very much but which left me with a dreadful headache and a dry, brackish mouth. And one day, putting our shoes back on after leaving a mosque, he gave me something to think about for a long time. He looked thoughtful and finally came out with his philosophy: "The beggar who lies in the street, the worker, the tired woman—all those who believe in *le bon Dieu* receive force from Him, force which makes them live when they have nothing to eat and nowhere to go except the gutter. I myself believe in this force."

"Do you go regularly to the mosque?" I asked.

"Yes," he said. "Yes. We and *le bon Dieu* are all comrades here."

It was a tug to leave, but a card came from Gertrude warning me to hurry back because of the danger of war.

There were only two letters from Mohammed for a number of years, written for him by a professional scribe (in very poor French) whom I pictured sitting cross-legged in one of the narrow streets. Mohammed was well and happy—and could I send him a few dollars? I did.

Then silence, until several years after the war, when I got a letter in not-very-good English from a Polish law student who was later to become my best friend in Paris—Pick, who had been attached to Mohammed Zenouhin the way I had been. Here it is in part:

> It was some time ago he comes to me one day and said he feel very sad and fed-up because his father ask him to come home spend the holiday with family. He cries! So what happened? I told him, you go and you will be back in few days in Algiers (his family was near Constantine in Djidjelli). "I suppose," he said, "I will never see you again nor anybody in the world . . . I will never be able to come here . . . My father want I get married with Arabian girl. I can't. I will refuse. . . ."
>
> In family he was oldest. As you know, it is habit with Arab people, the oldest son must be married first if he wish to keep his father's fortune and to take that of his future wife. Mohammed doesn't like girls at all. He refuse to his father's proposals. One evening his father gave him during the supper a poison in the meal.

Pick. Steward eventually met Witold Pick during his trip to Paris in 1950 (Spring, 124).
the way I had been. Steward's Stud File card for Mohammed indicates that they had two sexual encounters (see also Spring, 69).

The next day Mohammed died. . . .

In his latest minutes before death — his mouth and face have turn blue — he gasp to cousin to write tell me what happen, and to tell you also goodbye.

When I returned to Bilignin from three weeks in Algiers, war was in the air. Sir Francis Rose and Cecil Beaton had my former room, so I slept in another. Everyone was tense and frightened, and we all hovered around a small radio Francis had. Tiring finally of the same bulletins endlessly repeated, I wandered out into the rose garden. Cecil Beaton was there reclining in a canvas chair. He wore a thin jacket over a light summer sweater with broad red and white horizontal stripes, and one of Gertrude's high-crowned Korean straw hats. He had on a pair of khaki walking shorts and was fiddling with a rose in one hand while he seemed to be sketching the Ain Valley with the other.

"Why aren't you listening to the war broadcasts?" I asked.

"Ch-chamberlain . . . has ar . . . arranged things," he said. "'ll be no war." His slurred speech indicated he was completely drunk.

I beckoned Francis out of the living room. "You know Gertrude's rules about alcohol," I said. "Cecil is smashed."

The remark galvanized Francis. "My God," he said. We went out toward the chair. It was empty, save for the sketch pad and straw hat. Cecil had vanished.

So began a wild afternoon. Francis and I went looking for him on the road to Belley, but he was nowhere to be found. Meanwhile the sky had clouded over, and later in the afternoon, a drizzle began. It grew darker.

"You'll have to tell Gertrude," I said.

"You do it," Francis said. "I'm really afraid to."

"Not I," I said. "You march right in and tell her."

He did. There was a loud bellow from the house, and soon Gertrude came out wearing a kind of droopy Garbo raincoat. Francis was behind her.

The next few hours were a mad mixture of phone calls, instructions from Gertrude to tell the mayor, to call out the troops from the caserne. ("With all

Cecil Beaton (1904–80). British-born photographer known for his work for *Vogue* and *Vanity Fair* in the 1930s and later for his photographs of World War II and of the British royal family. When Steward met him in Bilignin in 1939, he had recently been fired by *Vogue* for inserting tiny anti-Semitic phrases into an illustration that had been published before anyone noticed. As Stein explained to Steward, "Cecil is anti-Semitic and I know that but he doesn't know I do, so maybe when you come back from Algiers something may boil up and be delightful" (*Dear Sammy,* 71).

due respect to Mademoiselle Stein," shrugged one gendarme, "war is near, and after all it is only one man. He will be found when dawn comes.")

At one point I was left in Belley to check the bistros. Cecil was in none of them. I consoled myself with a drink at a café. And finally, the auto came around the corner from Bilignin, Gertrude at the wheel, Alice and Francis in back, and between them a very wet and bedraggled Cecil.

"Where on earth —?" I asked.

They told me that Cecil had been at the caserne all afternoon, drinking and learning Senegalese songs from the huge black Senegalese quartered in the barracks there ("and heaven knows what else was going on," said Francis *sotto voce* to me), and that two six-foot-four Senegalese soldiers had been walking him home, all fairly snockered and singing "L'Alouette" at the top of their lungs.

Francis said, "I told him to behave while he was here, but you know Cecil. Show him a. . . ." He broke off and looked straight ahead.

"Well, all is quiet now," I said. "The lost sheep is found."

Cecil struggled upward from his collapsed position but Alice pushed him back down; ". . . no sheep," he muttered.

That night — although we did not need it — Gertrude warned us all to leave before the military commandeered all the trains, and we departed the next morning, finding our way home as best we could. Gertrude and Alice stayed behind. When I got back to America after strenuous vexations, I sent them a Mixmaster — which delighted them both and was the subject of several playful letters from Gertrude.

---

finding our way home. Steward left Bilignin for Le Havre on August 29, 1939, with plans to board the *Normandie*, scheduled to depart for New York on September 6. Once in Le Havre, he discovered to his shock that the *Normandie* was still in New York, but he managed to book passage on the crowded SS *President Harding* (Steward to Stein, ALS, September 15, 1939, Steward Letters).

I sent them a Mixmaster. The Sunbeam Mixmaster electric mixer, first manufactured in 1930, debuted in August 1939 as the Model 5, which came with either milk-white or jadeite-green glass bowls ("Sunbeam ID," http://www.decodan.com/Sunbeam-ID). Steward chose the latter, had the wiring and plug adapted for use in Europe, and in late November 1939 shipped it to Stein and Toklas in a wooden crate (Steward to Stein, TLS, January 26, 1940, Steward Letters). It arrived on Easter Sunday, March 24, and sparked a series of effusive letters of thanks from Stein: "Oh so beautiful is the Mix Master, so beautiful and the literature [directions for use] so beautiful, and the shoe button potatoes that same day so beautiful and everything so beautiful" (Stein to Steward, ALS, March 25, 1940, Stein Letters). In July, Toklas accidentally dropped the jadeite mixing bowl, which "fell into little pieces on the kitchen floor, such lovely green little pieces," and Stein wrote to ask if Steward could send

I did not see her again. On July 27, 1946, the newspapers carried the word to the world of her death. On that evening, there were many empty hearts in the world, and many lonely people remembered her. I walked long along the lakefront in Chicago, almost as sadly lost as the young Tennyson who—hearing of the death of Byron—crawled out upon a finger of land jutting into the sea and carved upon a rock the words: "Byron is dead." With him an age came to an end, and so, too, was a door closed with the death of Gertrude Stein.

It was not possible for me to get to Paris again until 1950 to see Alice. But the letters from her began at once after Gertrude died, and her strong and vital personality emerged from the shadow in which she had deliberately kept it during Gertrude's lifetime. They were often voluminous, done with the thinnest nib in the delicate spiderwork that was her handwriting, which Mercedes de Acosta said was done with the "eyelash of a fly." She wrote on both sides of translucent paper, so that one side confused the other. The letters were filled with humor and tidbits of gossip, sharp and often hilarious, witty and sometimes sentimental.

Alice had gone on living at 5 rue Christine, where all the paintings were. The maid ushered me into the salon—with its walls covered with the work of Picasso, Matisse, Juan Grist, Picabia, and others. I sat down on the shabby old horsehair sofa on which Gertrude used to curl up, directing the chatter of the salon, talking in that warm golden voice which would not ever again call me her "silly, bashful boy."

There were red roses in a white china vase on the table; I laid my bouquet beside them. It was quiet; the clatter of Paris was stilled. A huge ornamented silver tray with tea things was on the table in front of the sofa. Through the ceiling-high French windows, I looked out upon the chimney pots in the quiet enclosure formed by the tight-pressed houses—and the flat roof on

---

a replacement (Stein to Steward, ALS, July 8, 1940, Stein Letters), repeating the request in subsequent letters: "You see you can use other bowls but they do not twirl around in that lovely green mix master way and when they do not twirl then they instead of staying down rise up and spill and therefor [sic] the mix master will have to be a mix master still" (Stein to Steward, ALS, November 18, 1940, Stein Letters).

the young Tennyson. The story's source is Frederick Locker-Lampson, whose daughter married Tennyson's son Lionel; it is repeated, among other places, in Hallam Tennyson's biography of his father (*Alfred Lord Tennyson: A Memoir by His Son* [1897; Cambridge: Cambridge University Press, 2012], 2:69).

Mercedes de Acosta (1893–1968). American playwright, poet, and novelist better known for her lesbian relationships with stage and film celebrities.

Steward on the terrace of 5 rue Christine with Alice Toklas and
Basket II, Paris, April 1952. (BANC PIC 1972.017:60 — PIC.
Courtesy of the Bancroft Library, University of California, Berkeley.)

which the aging deaf and blind old Basket went to do his little duties and
from which he had fallen fifteen feet at midnight.

And Alice? She was the same — a little more bent, more drawn, frail,
tiny, and wispy. Somehow, however, the essence had not changed. After
Gertrude's death, there had to be someone tending the altar of the dead, and
she fulfilled the role. In my seventeen visits to her from 1950 until her death
in 1967, I was conscious of the way she kept the flame alive, insisting on the
genius, perpetuating the legend and *la gloire*.

I grew equally fond of Alice, perhaps even more than of Gertrude because it was my privilege to know her longer. Often we roamed the Paris

Basket. More precisely, Basket II, the white standard poodle that Stein and Toklas acquired
after the first Basket died in 1937.

streets together while she could still walk, went shopping or to lunch or on happy errands to the houses of friends. They were years of both happiness and pain for us. She supported me when I finally abandoned the grape entirely; and I was amazed when she joined the Catholic Church, brought to it by a priest who assured her that in the afterlife she would see Gertrude again. When we were together at the Christmas season, we gossiped like old ladies over a back fence. I was able to tell her all the details ("I eat 'em with a spoon," she used to say cheerfully) about how Sir Francis Rose had unwittingly hired his illegitimate son as his "valet de chambre" and screwed him for four months before learning his true identity. To her question about how I knew all of it, I could answer that I was the one who had first pointed out the young man to Francis and sent him waddling after him. And I met her in Rome for some hilarious adventures among the seven hills. There were painful moments such as the one when — returning from a winter spent in a convent at Rome — she found her apartment stripped bare of all the paintings, confiscated by the greedy widow of Gertrude's nephew on the ground that left alone, the paintings were "a national treasure left unprotected." I knew her plight, her poverty; I suffered silently with her and did what I could. Alice's last years were spent under the financial protection of friends, of whom Donald Sutherland and Thornton Wilder were the leading contributors, the others of the group giving only dribbles.

The most emotional moment with her occurred one day in Paris while we were lunching at La Méditerranée, a restaurant frequented in the old days by Gertrude and Alice and many of their friends — Pablo, Bébé, Gerald, Cecil, and Francis. We sat with our jugged hare at a table near some workmen who were enlarging the restaurant with an additional room. Just as we started to eat, the foreman of the workers approached Alice with beret in hand and started to speak in French.

"Mademoiselle," he was saying, and with that she extended her left hand for him to kiss lightly, "Mademoiselle, I am only a humble worker but I have seen you here many times and at the opera and elsewhere, and I hope that

found her apartment stripped bare. Toklas spent the winter of 1960–61 in Rome, returning to discover that in her absence, Roubina Stein, the widow of Gertrude's nephew Allan, had successfully sued to have the valuable painting collection removed from the apartment for safekeeping (Linda Simon, *The Biography of Alice B. Toklas* [1977; Lincoln: University of Nebraska Press, 1991], 306–10).

Donald Sutherland (1915–78). Classics professor at the University of Colorado who first met Stein as an undergraduate at Princeton University in November 1934 when she visited the campus on her American speaking tour.

you will permit me to thank you for bringing to our city the luster that you and Mademoiselle Stein have brought for so many years. And we thank you for living among us." He bowed his head over her hand again and was gone.

"Wh-what was that?" I stuttered.

"Ah," said Alice, "he was remembering the old days."

Then the full meaning of the gesture hit me, and I reacted with great emotion, blinded by a sudden flood of tears as I realized the historic importance of Gertrude and Alice. I tried to eat and at the same time hide my weeping heart from her, but could not succeed at either. She closed her hand over mine and said, "Now Sammy, stop it this instant. We who are left behind can only wait." And the wait was long for her—twenty-one years.

Gertrude's tombstone in the cemetery of Père Lachaise has graven on its reverse side the facts of Alice's life—name, birthplace, and dates. And when she died, they opened Gertrude's grave and placed her smaller coffin beside the larger one. The inscription around the tomb of Héloïse and Abelard—down the hill in the same cemetery—might well have been reworded for this double grave:

> Here at long last the ashes of
> Gertrude and Alice are reunited.

Sources: *Chapters*, 58–70; *Manuscript*, 142–50, 221–24. Steward based portions of this chapter on his earlier *IDJ* essay "On Gertrude Stein" (February 1947), on his 115-page introductory memoir in *Dear Sammy*, and on his untitled *IDJ* essay on Mohammed Zenouhin (October 1948).

Père Lachaise. Large Parisian cemetery laid out in 1804.

Héloïse and Abelard. Héloïse d'Argenteuil (1101–64), a renowned classical scholar, and Peter Abelard (1079–1142), a brilliant French theologian, whose love affair ended in tragedy but produced a celebrated exchange of letters between the two. In 1817, their remains were reputedly moved to a crypt in Père Lachaise that remains one of the cemetery's most famous monuments.

Chapter Seven

THE ALLERGY YEARS

1932–49

For about seventeen years, I suffered from an ailment brand new to medicine, one which was to become very fashionable. Before that time, it used to be that when Grandpa sneezed, Grandma told him to move out of the draft. But from about 1930 onward, she might be more likely to say, "Ah ha! Been eatin' tomatoes again, hey?" Ten to one he had been. Allergy, a commonplace malady today, was a strange and wonderful thing in these years, a newfangled disorder that took the country by storm.

It all began in the year when I was working on my master's degree. I felt that something was dreadfully wrong with my digestion, since I continually had to take antacids and laxatives—yet at the same time was occasionally wracked by intense diarrhea.

"Maybe you've got an ulcer," Aunt Bebe quavered, since one of the family had been once so troubled.

"I thought you got those from worrying," I said.

"Aren't you a worrier?" she asked.

"No, I'm a fretter. There's a difference." But I went to the family doctor

---

a strange and wonderful thing. The modern study of food's role in illness began in 1905 with the publication of *The Food Factor in Disease* (London: Longman's, 1905) by the Australian physician Francis Hare (1857–1928). In a landmark paper published the next year, Clemens von Pirquet (1874–1929), an Austrian physician and pioneer in the field of immunology, coined the word *allergy* to describe an organism's hypersensitivity to such stimuli as pollen, bee stings, and foods such as strawberries and shellfish (Thomas M. Daniel, *Pioneers of Medicine and Their Impact on Tuberculosis* [Rochester: University of Rochester Press, 2000], 141–42).

anyway. He thumped me desultorily, cocked an ear, allowed as how something was wrong, and put me on a diet of *milk and eggs!*

For three weeks, I lived on egg milk shakes and flabby custards—and went steadily down the tube. In that time, I lost eleven pounds. The doctor was perplexed but had sense enough to send me to a specialist in something new—allergy.

Dr. Jonathan Forman was the first in the Columbus area in that field. He asked me a great many questions about family history that seemed silly— such as was my mother that way about dahlias. When he heard about my father's hay fever, his eyes narrowed.

"Once it was enough," he said, smiling, "if your parents led a clean moral life, but we are beginning to learn that flitting through a garden may visit its sins unto the third and fourth generation."

He put me on the medical conveyor belt and gave me all the tests, took gun and camera through the alimentary canal, making a lot of reconnaissance photographs, checking oil and gas.

Nothing.

So the skin tests were next, up one arm, across the back, and down the other. And that did it. He discovered the four major substances to which I was sensitive and put me on a barren diet, with a folded Turkish towel for a pillow.

The effect was as magical as if I had rubbed Aladdin's lamp. Within three days, all the symptoms had disappeared, and for seventeen years I kept faithfully to the diet—so long, indeed, that I forgot the taste of potatoes, coffee, eggs, and cake. Long before the rationing of World War II set in, I had nothing left but a vague and elusive memory of butter. For all these years, I ate a breakfast of bananas, cornflakes—and water to moisten; prepared that way, they tasted faintly like plaster and shavings. Aunt Bebe rediscovered cornmeal mush for me as a variation—fried in corn oil, with Karo on it. But I morosely watched people devour the elemental potatoes and the universal bread, while I tried desperately to conceive a passion for turnips, unseasoned peas—and carrots. Carrots! God help me, they always tasted like carrots no matter what was done to them. The idiosyncrasy even extended itself to my

---

Dr. Jonathan Forman (1887–1974). A pioneer in the study of food allergy who would go on to publish widely in this still-nascent field (Paul Metzger, "Jonathan Forman, MD: A Visionary of the Last Century," *House Call* [Medical Heritage Center of The Ohio State University] 5.2 [Winter 2002]: 1, 3).

visit its sins. Cf. Numbers 14:18.

drinking—beer made me sneeze, and there was a secret something in gin that gave me hives.

Prodded by necessity, I had to invent some dishes for myself. I could eat rice and St. John's bread. Out of a thick paste of split peas mixed with chopped onion, I spooned little dollops onto a cookie sheet and baked them crisp. Into a casserole, I put small peeled whole white onions, covered them with tomato catsup and honey, and baked them; it sounds horrible, but it turned out to be delicious. Or I cooked a leg of lamb, ground it up with salt and chopped onions and other herbs, and molded it into a meat loaf. One had to be ingenious.

But naturally there were drawbacks. I could not travel easily; it became a kind of game. I became friendly—nay, even intimate!—with dining-car stewards and hotel chefs. I seduced dozens of cooks in several lands and languages into fixing my food properly and cajoled hostesses in ten states into serving my broccoli butterless. New environments were challenges to be met—and an allergic sufferer frequently had to become a master diplomat. But eating in restaurants grew to be such a chore that for many years I had to stay at home and cook for myself.

I suppose that the most unforgivable demands connected with my allergy were made during the two visits of more than two weeks each to the chateau of Gertrude Stein and Alice Toklas at Bilignin. Alice Toklas was already well known among the members of their circle as a chef of uncommon abilities— but she was really somewhat set back when she heard of the restrictions that had been put on me.

"But how on earth do you manage in restaurants?" she wanted to know. (I remember her best in two positions, either filing her nails as she sat sidewise on the backseat of the old Matford or bending, slightly stooped, over a pot with a tasting spoon halfway to her lips and a gleam in her eye. When she asked that question, she was bending over the stove in the kitchen at Bilignin.)

"It takes some doing," I admitted.

Alice rose to the occasion like the great innovative chef she was. I have never seen rice prepared in so many ways. I do not know whether she invented most of the recipes or whether they came from Brillat-Savarin (for

---

St. John's bread. More commonly known as the chocolate substitute carob.

Brillat-Savarin. Jean Anthelme Brillat-Savarin (1755–1826), celebrated gastronome who was born in the Ain district town of Belley, less than two miles from Stein and Toklas's summer home. Steward alludes to recipes in his major work, *The Physiology of Taste* (1825).

Ain was his department) or Escoffier. But she made Cuban rice and Span-ish rice, saffron rice (in balls and croquettes), rice à la Dreux (without the eggs), cream of rice, rice Greek style, rice Impératrice, India rice, Maltese rice, rice pilaf (both plain and Turkish), and rice pudding (sometimes plain, sometimes with lemon or other flavorings).

"You know," Gertrude said during our last meal together, just before I left in 1937, "since you've been here and we've all been eating this Chinese food I've lost seven pounds and I feel just fine, and maybe from now on, yes cer-tainly from now on if Alice agrees we'll eat more rice and thank Sammy for making us make it so much, so thank you very much."

"More than welcome," I said.

Gertrude was certainly an illustration of Tennyson's line about Ulysses: "I am a part of all that I have met." I had read enough of her to realize the intensely personal and autobiographical nature of even her sealed and her-metic writing and to know that everything that happened to her was stored away and thought about. Eventually, most of it appeared in the process so well described by John Livingston Lowes in *The Road to Xanadu* when he writes about Coleridge and the "deep well of the imagination." Thus it did not surprise me many years later to find that in her posthumously published *To Do: Alphabets and Birthdays*, she included a long passage under the letter "S" about "poor dear Sammy" and his Aunt Fanny, and how Sammy could not eat bread or potatoes or chocolate or cake or eggs or butter or even a date. If he did, he fainted away. And what could Sammy eat? Well, a lemonade per-haps or a beefsteak or a plate but dear me no not ice cream. . . . And Aunt Fanny just went on cooking and eating and Sammy just went on looking and fainting. . . . And then there was a pretty girl named Sally who invited Sammy to her birthday party, where there was a great big cake with frosting and Sammy said he could not eat it but he could eat the candles but Sally wouldn't let him do that—and so on, ending with "Poor dear Sammy."

Escoffier. Georges Auguste Escoffier (1846–1935), legendary French chef who promoted French cuisine and whose books remain standard texts on French food preparation.

"I am a part of all that I have met." Line 18 of the poem "Ulysses" (1833), by Alfred Tenny-son (1809–92), a dramatic monologue spoken by the central figure in Homer's *Odyssey* at the end of his life.

John Livingston Lowes (1867–1945). Lowes's *The Road to Xanadu: A Study in the Ways of the Imagination* (1927) examines the creative processes of Samuel Taylor Coleridge (1772–1834) by tracing the ways that Coleridge's reading surfaces in two of his most famous poems.

To Do: Alphabets and Birthdays. Stein's second book for children, written in 1940 but first published in 1957, after her death, and in its first illustrated edition in 2011.

In 1939, when I visited them a second time, the trauma was not so great for Alice. "I've had two years to prepare you some new recipes," she said — and this time she concentrated on veal, lamb, vegetables, and various salad greens. Each day's dinner was different, and the magic of Alice in the kitchen made the second stay of about three weeks a very great delight. But I fancy that Alice was just as happy with the news that I outgrew my allergy at the age of forty (exactly the number of years it took father to outgrow his hay fever).

My allergies had one profound effect on my life during these seventeen years of their existence.

I was teaching at Loyola University when the United States was drawn into the war in 1941 by Pearl Harbor. Although I was then thirty-two and hardly subject at the moment to the draft, I nonetheless went through all the patriotic seizures that descended on almost every male under thirty-five. Oh, they'll get around to taking you before long, everyone said — but at thirty-two, you're slowing up a bit, and they want the young and active cannon fodder first.

I did two things. I had been interested in cryptography for quite a while and was a member of a Chicago group involved in cryptanalysis. In the second year of the war, then, I wrote to the Army Cryptographic Center at Fort Monmouth, New Jersey, and succeeded in getting enrolled in the army course in cryptanalysis. And during several months, I faithfully did all the lessons they sent me and enjoyed working with all the wonderful devices that arrived by registered mail — enciphering machines and such like.

Meanwhile, I convinced the university it should do its part in the war effort by allowing me to teach a beginner's course in cryptanalysis — and they agreed. So I began it with six students, and by the time it was over in June 1943, each one of them had joined one of the services for cryptographic training. I was left — on the night of final exams — with a set of questions and an empty classroom.

It seemed that everything was beginning to point toward an army commission and a career for me in intelligence. But the army — and even myself — had not reckoned with the Imp of the Perverse, as active as ever in me. For seemingly the most flippant reason, I gave up the army lessons in

---

a beginner's course in cryptanalysis. Steward's *IDJ* essay "On Cryptography" (October 1944) provides a window into the content of his course.

cryptanalysis: I loathed the color of khaki! Blue was better for me — and that meant the navy.

On June 10, 1943, I enlisted in the navy, was sworn in, and sent to Great Lakes Naval Training Station, a few miles north of Chicago. I notified the army; they were immediately furious at wasting time on my cryptographic lessons. Although I was quite aware that I was still highly allergic to all those foods — the very staples of navy chow — I thought with mild war-engendered hysteria that perhaps by an effort of will I could overcome it all and be a sailor brave (Ahoy there, mate!) without any trouble. I had always liked sailors and bell-bottomed trousers. And at no time either in writing or in oral interviews for the navy had anyone ever asked me if I were allergic to certain foods. The closest they came was the question about whether I had asthma, and I could truthfully say I did not.

It was not long before I discovered there was a helluva lot of difference between entering the navy as an apprentice seaman and entering with a commission as ensign or lieutenant j.g. No one seemed to be interested in the fact that I had a considerable background in cryptography, and the PhD stood for nothing. An examiner of some kind looked at me blankly and said, "What's that?"

Toting a full sea-bag was something that nearly did me in, what with the wretched physical condition brought on by my years of drinking, plus the fact that at thirty-two, it was impossible to compete or keep up with eighteen-year-olds. Nightfall of the second day found me with aching back and blistered hands . . .

. . . and worst of all, the most violent return ever of all the physical symptoms of my food allergies! My tongue was white, my eyelids were swollen nearly shut, and giant hives marched in triple-row formation across my back.

By midnight I could hardly breathe. I crawled out of my bunk and staggered toward the swabbie on duty just at the barracks door. He took one look at me.

"Jaysus!" he said. "What's the matter with you?"

With swollen tongue, it took me two or three trials to get the word out. "Allergies," I finally managed to gasp.

Great Lakes Naval Training Station. Major naval installation that opened in 1911 forty miles north of Chicago, processed a million recruits during World War II, and remains a major naval training center (Perry R. Duis, "Great Lakes Naval Training Station," in *The Encyclopedia of Chicago*, ed. James R. Grossman et al. [Chicago: University of Chicago Press, 2004], 362).

He sat me in a chair where I took to shivering, while he called the medics. So, walking between two rumpled and rudely awakened sailors, I was escorted to the hospital, injected with Benadryl or some antihistamine, and then went peacefully to sleep.

In the morning, a doctor came, a navy commander, to take down some information. I was still groggy and somewhat swollen and itchy but sensible enough to realize that I had to answer his questions very, very carefully.

"Did you know that you were allergic to certain foodstuffs when you enlisted?"

I shook my head, batting my eyes. "No, Doctor."

"You must certainly have had some evidence in the past that you were."

I looked vague. "Well, for a number of years I haven't eaten milk products," I said, "but they just gave me indigestion, and I didn't really think much about it. I just didn't eat them anymore."

He made some notes. "Does anyone in your family have hay fever?" he asked.

"Yes, my father does."

"Didn't they ask you about that on your first physical?"

"No, sir," I said politely.

"Damned incompetent draft boards," he muttered, writing some more. Finally, he finished and looked at me. "Son," he said, "we're going to make some tests, but I'm afraid you won't be a sailor after they're done."

"Aw, Doctor—" I began, looking sad. At that point, even the rigors of double classes in the summer session at the university were attractive. But I realized it would take some careful tippy-toeing to get out without being accused of enlisting fraudulently, or under false pretenses, or whatever they were calling it in these days.

"Never mind," he said, looking friendly. "You'll be out with an honorable discharge." He referred to my dossier. "I see you have a PhD in English literature."

"Yes," I said, looking humble.

"Well," he said. "It's commendable, your wanting to enlist—but you didn't realize how severely allergic you were, and trying to make you eat navy chow would do nothing except keep you in the hospital permanently."

"I did so want—" I began.

"Yes, I know," he said. "But never mind. You can just sit this one out. This way, you can stay at home and represent what all the boys are fighting for."

"Thanks, Doctor," I said. But I wasn't thanking him for the discharge; instead, I was grateful to him for furnishing me with a tagline to use for the duration of the war: "I decided to sit this one out, to stay home and represent what you boys are fighting for." Some of the military were annoyed at that sentence.

Getting out of the navy was a lot more complicated than getting in. There were all kinds of tests—including a whole series of scratch tests, which was enough to cause several medics to be called in to observe the wheals—and other investigations: dye in the urine and whatnot.

The most annoying detail was that I was moved away from my "company" and into the holding barracks of those who were about to be discharged. Imagine being cooped up with handsome tough ex-felons (who had concealed their records), boys discharged for obesity, and a whole gaggle of fags—who went screaming around the barracks in the daytime and went visiting the ex-cons' bunks at night. The sounds of the springs squeaking in that barracks were enough to keep the whole roomful awake all night. I was visited a few times and did a little visiting myself—lonely, you understand, and wanting to talk over my troubles with some sympathetic soul.

Then there were interminable interviews with the psychiatrist. I passed— save that he was annoyed at the shortness of my fingernails; but when he examined them closely, he saw that they were not bitten or chewed. Thus he was deprived of the surest sign they had of psychosis in those days—and sometimes the only one they bothered about. The Red Cross field worker seemed to think I was well adjusted. He invited me to walk with him over to the wooded area and the bridge across the ravine that evening. I passed the test with him, too, without any trouble except muddy knees.

Considering everything, I got off lucky. The feelings about affectional orientation in the 1940s were rather narrow. Had I by chance got into the navy cryptographic school—and had it been later discovered that one queer had been set down among all these healthy young mansouls—there might have been a scandal indeed. For were not people like me subject to the worst kind of blackmail, and could anything be worse than the blackmailing of a code-and-cipher man?

So it was that one week later, clutching my discharge in my hand, I boarded the old North Shore electric line for the forty-minute ride to the Loop. For transportation, I received a navy check for $26.40—a magnificent payment for a short ride. The discharge read: "Conduct 4.0. Total net service for pay purposes: -0- years, -0- months, -7- days."

The following day, a Thursday, I showed up bright-eyed and bushy-tailed in class at the university. The only noticeable change was a mere ghost of a mustache, for I had shaved it off at Great Lakes, and it had not grown in yet—but a bit of brown-tinted mustache wax had helped to take care of that. At Great Lakes, lacking the wax, I had tinted the sprouting hairs with a burned match stick, at which some wiseacre called me a fairy but then came crawling into my bunk that night to apologize for his rudeness.

After class was over, a nun who sat in the front row came up to me, shyly smiling, and said, "I somehow knew you'd be back."

"You did, sister?"

"Yes," she said. "I prayed very hard that you wouldn't stay."

Prayed out of the navy? Well, that's one way to do it. Or have it done.

Source: Manuscript, 124–37; omitted from *Chapters*.
Steward based portions of the first half of this chapter on
his earlier *IDJ* essay "On Fifteen Years of Lent" (January 1945).

Chapter Eight

ANOMALIES AND CURIOSITIES

1945–48

Richie Tucker, my bed companion of many years in Chicago, introduced me to an elderly friend of his, an old Greek doctor by the name of Stephen Anthony, who turned out to be my best drinking companion for the bitter years. It was not strange that those of us who knew him always thought of him as Ulysses, a wanderer over the earth, a wise man, a part of all that he had met, counsellor and friend. He had been born in Athens on a little hill opposite the Acropolis, where as a schoolboy on moonlit nights he used to climb up to the Parthenon and there, amid the crumbling fluted columns of the great temple, declaim his favorite passages from the *Iliad* or the *Odyssey*, imagining himself to be in turn Achilles or Agamemnon or Hector or Paris, the great and lordly ghosts whose shadows still were there.

Then there was a period of military conscription, when Greece was trying to annex the island of Crete, and after that, studying chemistry at Heidelberg in Germany. At twenty-two, he arrived in New York wearing a tag to take him to Minneapolis. He spoke French, German, Latin, Italian, and Greek—but no English. But when he eventually learned it, he worked for the government during World War I as a chemist developing synthetic dyes for American use. Then suddenly he quit all that and went to the University of Chicago to study medicine, "because I wanted to be my own boss."

And so he became a doctor. We felt the same urge for freedom. When I

---

a part of all that he had met. Steward also quoted this line from Tennyson in chapter 7 with regard to Gertrude Stein.

the island of Crete. Steward refers to the Greco-Turkish War of 1897, when Greece attempted to wrest Crete from the Ottoman Empire.

first met him, his star had somewhat descended, his ambition dulled. He lived in quarters in the rear of his office, and to his home trooped an unending stream of male friends for advice or counsel, to borrow money or have a drink, to talk, to be prodded into ambitious activity or warned against folly. Or occasionally—to bring pleasure to the old man.

The habit of him grew on me, and since in those days I did not teach until late afternoons and evenings, I found myself in his place almost daily, listening to his fascinating words. He would sit rocking in his easy chair with a glass in hand, occasionally bellowing with a hearty Rabelaisian laugh at something said or done. In the mornings, he generally read, and it was curious to find in him as keen an up-to-the-minute mind on current medical progress as could be found anywhere. He predicted penicillin before Fleming and said that when a cancer cure was found, it would turn out to be a dye of some sort (are you listening, Sloane-Kettering and Battelle?).

What did each of us get from that charming old lush? That is hard to answer—for each one got what he needed. When I first met him, I was a twittering jumpy collection of wild neuroses filled with more than my share of darkness, growl, and venom. And although I did not realize it until later, he expertly diagnosed me and laughed me out of my troubles—yes, *laughed* me out of them until I found myself joining in the bellows that came rumbling straight down from Olympus, filling his tiny rooms and rocking and rolling down the corridor to his office. How he roared when one day I confessed my fear of *siflis*! "Oh ho ho!" And in his heavy accent, "Either you quit worrying or quit fucking—it's as simple as dat." After pondering for a while, I decided to quit only one. After all—there were cures, as I had found out at one time.

Fifteen years after the death of Professor Andrews, old Doc Anthony filled the niche for a while—another model, a father-figure, a person to admire. He helped me over many a hurdle, but there was only one thing wrong. We had lost ourselves in the bottle.

He lived in quarters in the rear of his office. Anthony's storefront medical office was located at 109 West North Avenue in Chicago, in a building slated for demolition in 2017.
Rabelaisian. From François Rabelais (1494–1553), French writer known for his raucous and sometimes coarse humor.
Fleming. Alexander Fleming (1881–1955), Scottish-born bacteriologist who discovered the antibacterial properties of the Penicillium fungus in 1928.
Sloane-Kettering. New York cancer hospital and research center founded in 1884.
Battelle. Battelle Memorial Institute, a wide-ranging scientific research center founded in 1929 in Columbus, Ohio.

On a dreary January afternoon, with the rain falling as dismally as it can only in Chicago, we had been arguing somewhat drunkenly about the relative advantages and disadvantages of being either butch or swish—and of course had reached no conclusion at all. And Doc, his red face turned faintly purple in the light from the pink-shaded lamp beside him, had sighed, "Oh yuth, yuth, yuth, yuth!" and fallen into a short nap. He could not pronounce the ōō sound of "youth" but gave the vowel the short italic sound it has in "circus." I was holding an empty shot glass in one hand and a glass of water chaser in the other.

The next thing I knew, I was on the floor screaming, doubled up in the fetal position with the most intensely sharp pain I had ever known in my life stabbing me in the right testicle. My howl of agony brought Doc Anthony wide awake. "For gossake, whatsamatter?" he said. It was some moments before I could gasp out an answer. The sweat was streaming down my face. He raced to the office in front and came back with his medical bag and with trembling fingers prepared a shot of codeine or morphine—some painkiller. It took effect almost at once; the pain no longer hit so violently at the perineum but subsided to a steady breathtaking ache in the whole groin.

During the next few days, the growth of the right testicle began. The details are relatively unimportant: how Doc Anthony first diagnosed it as a possible hydrocele and unsuccessfully attempted to extract some fluid; how we went to consult with a Dr. Kenny—himself dying of a rare viral lung disease called in those days "mosaic," before the term came to be used almost entirely in genetics. Kenny was in a wheelchair, and upon examination of my ailment, hefted it in his hand and said thoughtfully, "I believe we should let this see the light of day."

Thereupon the two arranged it, after discussing the best surgeon to use for the operation and settling on a Dr. Edward Hess. And a hospital—Alexian Brothers, an all-male hospital using many conscientious objectors as orderlies.

There is no moment of greater loneliness than the one which comes as you are wheeled down the corridor to the operating room, half-stupefied with drugs, conscious of the blinding lights above you once the gurney has

---

hydrocele. Buildup of fluid in the scrotum.

Alexian Brothers. Hospital formerly located at 1200 West Belden Avenue in Chicago, whose patients were exclusively male and whose nursing staff until 1939 consisted entirely of religious brothers trained in the order's nursing school. See Barbra Mann Wall, "Religion and Gender in a Men's Hospital and School of Nursing, 1866–1969," *Nurs Res* (May–June 2009), 158–65.

paused to transfer you to the operating table. And then, of course, blessed unconsciousness, from which if you are lucky you awaken several hours later, bandaged and aching.

The removal of a testicle is an operation called an orchidectomy. The next morning, somewhat groggy from the cyclopropane and unable to smoke without a vast wave of nausea, I opened my eyes—still seeing a bit double— and there was good old faithful Emmy peering around the door to my room.

"May I come in?" she asked.

"Of course."

She had in her hand a small box tied with a frilly lavender ribbon. "For you," she said.

I awkwardly untied it. Inside was a tiny orchid, its end sealed in a small tube of water or nutrient.

"What in the world—?" I began.

"To replace the one you lost," she said.

It hurt to laugh, but I couldn't help it. The word of the joke flashed around the hospital, and a dozen brothers and helpers of all kinds trooped in to see my orchid. Dr. Hess was overcome with amusement, and Doc Anthony laughed so hard that his great belly undulated up and down.

My convalescence was not overlong and was hastened by the demands of the university to return to classes. I really did not want to know everything, I suppose; I presumed it was cancer and that the tumor had been malignant. The radiation therapy which followed—and which temporarily denuded me of all pubic hair—would have been enough to tell me that. I hesitated to ask Dr. Hess—and he never told me, beyond saying something vague about a dermoid cyst. And the word "teratoma" was also used; I studiously avoided looking it up. It was not until about three years later that I got sufficient courage to peek into my dossier at Dr. Hess's office while he was out of the room. Yes: diagnosis—teratoma; remarks—malignant. Contained hair follicles, sweat and sebaceous glands, nerve and teeth elements.

What had happened, there in the mysterious alchemy of the womb? Something had gone greatly awry, of course. And now I began to remember other small things about myself—how my first dentist in Woodsfield, a Dr. Koontz, had remarked on the fact that I had been born with four fewer teeth than usual. And that tiny, almost invisible rudimentary nipple two inches below my right one. There was no getting around it! I had been meant to be

---

cyclopropane. A now-obsolete anesthetic introduced in the 1930s.

dermoid. "Of or belonging to the skin" (*OED*).

teratoma. "A tumour, especially of the gonads" (*OED*).

one of twins. And it had not worked. I cast around through various books, such as *Anomalies and Curiosities of Medicine*, and discovered that my ailment was not all that unusual, that it generally struck one before (or in) the thirty-fifth year, and that the cysts could be located anywhere — back, base of spine, abdomen, tongue (thank God I had been spared the impossible-to-conceal look of a monster!).

Since I was an autosite for a twin, then, other philosophical questions began to arise. I remembered that old wives' tale saying that if you were a twin, you shared one soul with another — so quite possibly I had no more than half a soul. I did not greatly concern myself, however, about the metaphysical aspects of a shared soul. I was more interested in a complete recuperation and a return to the sexuality of my life up until then.

But for more than thirty-four years, I have been burdened with what the physicians call a "c. a. mentality," taking the initials "c. a." from the first and last letters of "carcinoma." What is that, pray tell? It is quite simple. It means that no matter what illness you have from then on — whether a crust on the skin, a pimple at the hairline, a digestive disorder, a wart or naevus — no matter what the ailment, great or small — the spectre returns to haunt you, to distress and disturb. Is it a return of cancer? What shall I do about it?

There is no protection against this insidious neural connection, and physicians suffer from it as well as laymen. Matter of fact, perhaps more.

Following my January operation, I went back to teaching during the summer session. But something strange began to happen.

I was teaching a graduate class in the romantic poets, and in it there was a chinless woman whose last name I have completely forgotten. But she was mad, utterly mad. The first signs of it appeared when I entered the classroom one day and noted the deathly silence, the downcast eyes of all the students — all, save one. Then my eyes touched the blackboard. On it was written in large sprawling letters: "I love Dr. Steward and would do anything to get him in bed with me."

I erased it at once, sure that the back of my neck was flaming. Then I turned to the class and said, "But how do I know that such an experience would be pleasant to me?"

The students laughed uproariously — all, save one; I identified her at

Anomalies and Curiosities of Medicine. Illustrated encyclopedia of rare bodily deformities by George M. Gould and Walter M. Pyle (Philadelphia: Saunders, 1896). Frequently reprinted.

naevus. "A mole or birthmark" (*OED*).

once—the mousy one with husband trouble who sat in the front row. Looking directly at her, I made my second remark: "What are you prepared to pay?"

This was outrageous, and the laughter the second time went on for several minutes. Then I opened my various texts and proceeded as if nothing had happened.

But it did not stop there. The class met every weekday for double periods, since a lot had to be crammed into a summer session. And every day there was one full square of blackboard filled with her writing—most of it rambling and incoherent, but all of it based on the theme first expressed.

I went to the dean about it and even dismissed the class one day, leaving the writing on the blackboard to show to him. "Ah," he said, "she is evidently quite disturbed." But he made no move to expel her from the class nor to discipline her in any way, and the task of erasing the blackboard every day became quite onerous to me.

Then the telephone calls at night began, always after I had gone to bed. Groggy from the first deep sleep, I did not immediately know who it was— but found out soon enough. "Irene," I said to her, "you ought to have help. Have you ever thought of going to a psychiatrist?"

"God will help me," she whispered—and thirty years later, I can still hear that ghostly whisper chilling me over the telephone. "God is my psychiatrist."

I reported the calls to the dean; still nothing was done. After they had gone on for about two weeks, I decided to take matters into my own hands. When the phone rang at 2:00 a.m., her usual hour, I put on my deepest huskiest accent and said:

"This is God speaking."

She let out a shrill little shriek. "Oh, I have *so* wanted to talk with you!" she said. "You see, I am in love with my English teacher."

Still with God's voice, I said, "Have you not a husband?"

"Oh, yes, but he doesn't understand, he wants to put me away."

"Are you a good Catholic, Irene?" I asked huskily.

"Oh, I try to be."

"Then you must do as your husband says," I said, male chauvinist pig and God to the end.

"I can't. He doesn't understand."

After being God for another two weeks, I started to tell her—when she proposed it first—that if she couldn't have Dr. Steward in bed, there was only one thing left to do: kill herself.

Of course, she didn't, and luckily the summer session came to an end. But I never forgave the dean and the administration for making me endure the madness of that woman for an entire summer. What happened to her after the session ended I do not know; someone said that she had finally been put into a sanatorium. One of the nuns in the class commiserated with me: "I don't see how you put up with it so long, Dr. Steward," she said. "I prayed every night that the burden would be lifted from you."

She did not know about the telephone calls, so I said, "It was probably your prayers that gave me the strength to go on, Sister."

"I don't see why the dean didn't remove her," the nun said.

"Neither did I."

And so we went on to the fall quarter, but the sour taste left in me by the dean's inaction had a final effect, which was this:

In one of my downtown classes, there was a thirty-year-old man, pudgy and lacking one eye because of glaucoma. The only thing I remember about him in class was his challenging me one night when I said that the word "News" came from an arrangement of the initial letters of North, East, West, and South. Of course, I was wrong, completely, and even today I am embarrassed to think that I ever said such a thing. But after class one night he approached me and introduced himself (as if I didn't know his name after that horrid error in class!).

"I am Everette Senteman," he said.

"Yes, I know," thinking idly that something must be wrong with him to spell his first name that way—and then criticizing myself for so doing. For had I not as a sophomore spelled my middle name "Morise" just to be different?

"I am assistant managing editor of the *World Book Encyclopedia*," he said, "and I am wondering if you would be interested in rewriting, in simple language, the mythology articles which Padraic Colum has 'authenticated' for us."

"What's the matter with the way he's done them?" I asked.

"They are much too academic," he said. "They sound as if they were written for scholars. We would pay you so much a line." (I have forgotten how much he offered, but it was considerable.)

"Do you think I could do it?" I asked.

"We can give you a trial," he said. "If you can't, there'll be no hard feelings on either side, I hope."

Padraic Colum (1881–1972). Irish poet, novelist, folklorist, and author of award-winning books for children.

I was still smarting from the summer's madwoman. "Agreed," I said, and he promised to bring me a batch the next night.

I must indeed have been tetched in the head when I gave up my pleasant little sinecure to take the job as editor the following February, when the new quarter began. "The articles are splendid," Senteman had said. "I have never read anything so simple and beautiful."

It is very painful to think of those dear departed halcyon academic days when I never had to get up before noon and when the week's work consisted simply of lecturing with a certain ironic and aloof dignity for only sixteen hours a week. It is incredible that I voluntarily committed myself to a madhouse for two full years.

For we rewrote the whole encyclopedia, all nineteen volumes of it, the damnedest best encyclopedia there ever was. It was a hellygolander. It was peachy keen. A gem. For young people from eight to eighteen. For readers from six to sixty. Come one, come all! Over ten thousand pages. Over sixteen thousand pictures! And one thousand contributors! A record of what has been thought, said, and done from the dawn of civilization to the present day. O wondrous, O lovely, O superb!

To accomplish this, four strong young male editors and one strong young female editor (my sister Virginia) sacrificed their all on the altar of knowledge. We were a gallant crew when we first began—all starry-eyed and idealistic, aware of the tremendous power and influence that we had. The managing editor did a wonderful job of selling us on the project. Were we not interested in upgrading the young American mind? Had we no faith in the future of America? Did we not want to make some more money? We all nodded solemnly, feeling like dedicated spirits. And just as innocently as Hansel and Gretel when they walked into the old witch's house in the woods, we entered the fluorescent halls of our prison, over the gate of which should have been written Dante's motto: "All hope abandon, ye who enter here."

Things went rather quietly for the first few weeks. Then the business office

the following February. At the end of the summer term, Steward applied for and received a leave of absence from Loyola to begin in February 1946 (James T. Hussey, SJ, to Samuel Steward, TLS, September 7, 1945 [Yale Steward Papers]). He never returned.

we rewrote the whole encyclopedia. The 1947 edition of the *World Book* was the second complete revision and, at nineteen volumes, the largest edition since its first publication in 1917 ("100 Years of *The World Book Encyclopedia*," https://www.worldbook.com/landing%20pages/Timeline/index.html#firstPage).

Dante's motto. Famous inscription over the gates of hell in *Inferno*, by Dante Alighieri (1265–1321).

Steward (standing, second from right) with the *World Book* editorial staff, 1947. Steward's sister, Virginia, is seated at right. (Courtesy of the Estate of Samuel M. Steward)

got out its Schedule, which is a polite way of saying they strapped us to our desks and put on the thumbscrews. This multivolumed set, they said, must all be done by December 1948 and the first six volumes bound and ready for delivery by January 1947. We will expect you to have them done by that date.

Well, that started things off. We soon discovered that in order to get the work done, we had to stay at our desks in the evenings and on Saturdays, carry a briefcase of copy home to read on Sunday, answer screaming letters from prima-donna contributors, and in general eat, live, and breathe the encyclopedia. Yes, and even sleep it, too, for our dreams were so haunted with our daily work that usually we labored all night in our sleep. The bosses refused to give us overtime pay for that.

We worked under what seemed a foolproof plan. We got all the "big names" of the country, the names of those who were "authorities" in their fields, by going through *Who's Who* and using many devious means. Then we teased those people with the idea of writing for an encyclopedia and so insuring their immortality. We tickled them with the prospect of future generations and an audience in posterity. Oddly enough, most of them responded, for we offered them a great incentive: enduring fame. They sent in their manuscripts at a fairly comfortable fee per thousand words.

The next step was to simplify what they had written. This was first done scientifically (using Rudolf Flesch's method), but later it was done by "feel." We wrote on four grade levels—third, fifth, seventh, and ninth. Exhaustive studies gave us an indication of what subjects were studied in what grades. A third grader would be more interested in "Fairy" and "Circus," a fifth grader in "Dude Ranch," and a ninth grader in "Theory of Relativity." Consequently, "Circus" would be written in simpler language than "Relativity."

At this point the demon contributor stepped in, howling his head off, for you have simplified his copy and returned it to him for final "authentication." You have tampered with his sacred words inscribed on tablets of brass. You have profaned his concepts, perverted his meanings, and insulted his intelligence. "I will not permit my initials to appear beneath this article. It has evidently been edited *by* a nine-year-old instead of *for* a nine-year-old." Or something like the following gem, which leaves no doubt about the writer's meaning: "You have taken my accurate, clear-cut presentation of the subject and, by dint of rehashing and rearrangement, transformed it into an inaccurate, garbled, illogical, unpedagogic collection of arrant nonsense."

The gallant crew became a wild and crazy bunch. Nerves grew jagged and tempers taut. Under the pressures, most of us took to having tee-martoonie lunches, stumbling back to our desks and sometimes working through an opalescent fog all afternoon. Every one of us wrote more than a million words—rewrote more, I should say, since we were working from the manuscripts of the "authorities" who had submitted the new articles.

Part of the requirements for all the editors was that we have dirty minds so that we could extract all the possible *double entendres* from the articles. But after taking out the most obvious ones, sometimes we inserted slyer and more skillful ones of our own. As an example: the word "fairy" fell to me. I began the article: "Fairy is a little imaginary creature which likes to meddle in the affairs of men," which in a way was bad enough. For an ending, I had: "Grown-up people do not very often believe in fairies today. They are too busy making money. But if they knew the right kind of fairies, they would not have to work at all."

Senteman caught that and took out the last two sentences, shaking a cautionary finger at me. He substituted: "But both young and old people can still

Rudolf Flesch (1911–86). Educator and pioneer in readability studies based on quantifiable features of prose. *The Art of Readable Writing* (1949) popularized his famous readability formula.

enjoy reading about them," which in a way was just as packed with meaning as was my statement.

Or the article on Tantalus: ". . . was the son of Zeus (Jupiter) and Plato." That one went through many editions for many years. Blame Robert Graves for that.

It drew to a close eventually. We headed into the red glow of the sunset, and there were only a few months more. Then to a quiet insane asylum and a lifetime among the editors, babbling happily over the set of the encyclopedia which we all hoped the business office would be kind enough to send us.

Well, not a real asylum, of course. The rewriting had lasted nearly two years, and after it came to an end, I was reluctant to return to the university which had left me so much at the mercy of the madwoman. A friend of mine — or so I thought — worked at Marshall Field's department store in the book section, a large hulking fellow named John Scheele. One day he called me.

"Why not come to work the Christmas season with us?" he asked in dulcet tones. "We are always in need of help at that time."

An adventure — so why not? At first I demurred, remembering with a kind of agony how I had been teased into the months with the encyclopedia, an experience that had left me old and weak.

"Oh, come on," he said. "It'll be a new experience for you — a real lark. You like people; you like books. I'll put you in rare books and fine bindings."

That did it, alas! I had always wanted to see myself in a fine binding, so bright one Tuesday, I went downtown. I don't know exactly what I expected. I rather imagined I would go in to my friend, bow from the waist (and perhaps just *suggest* a small genuflection), be handed a sales-check book and

Tantalus. In Greek mythology, Tantalus was the offspring of Zeus and the female deity Pluto, not the male philosopher Plato.

Robert Graves (1895–1985). Author of *The Greek Myths* (1955), a popular if idiosyncratic interpretation of ancient Greek mythology.

Marshall Field's. Founded in 1865, Marshall Field's was the grande dame of Chicago department stores, occupying an entire city block in a lavish building designed by Daniel Burnham in 1907. The third-floor book department in which Steward worked was large and famous, with annual sales of $1.5 million by the early 1950s and regular book signings by celebrity authors like W. Somerset Maugham, G. K. Chesterton, Willa Cather, Aldous Huxley, Edgar Lee Masters, and Carl Sandburg (Lloyd Wendt and Herman Kogan, *Give the Lady What She Wants!* [Chicago: Rand McNally, 1952], 362–63).

see myself in a fine binding. Steward puns on his predilection for sadomasochistic sexual encounters.

given a cash-register drawer, step out on the "floor," and begin to sell. My gracious attitude toward the customers, my wide background in rare books, and my innate charm would all help make me one of the most popular salespersons in the department before the first day was over.

No such stuff. When I showed up, John looked up rather coolly and said, "Oh, you're here"—a statement which was evident. "Well, you'll have to go over to the personnel department and fill out an application blank and go through the regular channels, of course."

I looked dumb and founded for a moment and he saw it. "Merely a matter of routine," he said. "Everyone has to do it."

So I went to the personnel office and stood in line for a long time and got some lengthy and complicated forms to fill out. Then they gave me a number, and then I sat in a chair and waited for an interview with a Mr. Pemberton. When my number was called, I watched Mr. Pemberton and another guy decide to go out for a smoke, so I sat for forty-five minutes until he came back to interview me. Then there was a medical examination with all the thumpings and proddings and indignities that always accompany medical examinations, and I went back to Mr. Pemberton.

"Fine," he said, "you are accepted. And now there is a training class that lasts two days, and you will start yours on next Friday."

"T-t-training class!" I stuttered. "You mean you have to be trained before you start to work at Marshall Field's? To sell books?"

"Merely a matter of routine," he said smugly. "Everyone has to do it, whether you sell books or hairpins."

The "training class" was a fearful and wonderful thing. It consisted mainly of a series of pep talks about courtesy, the-customer-is-right, you'd-rather-have-a-satisfied-customer-than-make-a-sale, and lots more of the same. We saw two films, one a movie called *By Jupiter* and the other a film that was simply a succession of still photographs with a voice-over and a moon face alternately grinning and frowning and leering from the middle of the big clock that hangs at Randolph and State. I began to feel somewhat night-

---

fearful and wonderful thing. Cf. Psalm 139:14.

By Jupiter. A 1946 training film produced by Marshall Field's in which veteran character actor Chick Chandler (1905–88) plays a grumpy businessman who is given the opportunity to relive the events of his day in order to learn that "courtesy is contagious." The full film is available at https://www.youtube.com/watch?v=aDHO-duygG8.

the big clock. One of two massive beaux-arts clocks, iconic Field's images, that hang from corners of the building; the other is on the corner at State and Washington Streets.

marish, as if I were in Dr. Caligari's cabinet and could not find the way out. It was all very unreal.

The largest part of the training was practice in making out sales checks. Many times as a customer, I had stood fretfully beside some dim-witted clerk, tapping my foot or finger, thinking that it was taking an unconscionably long time, and wondering why Field's didn't get more efficient help. But after the training session I understood all. The checks had seven parts— three sheets, three carbons, and a tissue for the auditing department. For two solid days, we practiced making out sales checks—such thrilling and soul-exalting things as Cash Take, Cash Send, Charge-Take (with and without a Charg-a-Plate), Charge Send (again, with and without a Charg-a-Plate), Employee Cash (with 10% or 20% discount), Employee Charge (with discount), C.O.D., Exchange Checks—and five or six more which in my few weeks of working, I never really did learn. There was scarcely a one of the 125 in our class who was not a wild-eyed and dry-mouthed picture of befuddlement by the time the two days had come to an end.

On the first morning of real work, clutching my red sales book in my grubby little paw, I ventured into the book section and out onto the "floor." It was like entering some vast and noisome hell, smelly and hot and crowded. I had advanced barely five feet into the domain of culture and knowledge when I was spotted, and the questions began. Do you have the new Toynbee book? Where are the books on air-conditioning? Who wrote the *Rubaiyat of Omar Khayyam*? Is *Hello, Mrs. Goose* all right for a six-year-old girl? Where is Santa Claus? Where is the men's washroom? Where are the Lutheran religious books? Is this all the Zane Grey you have? Have you got large-print

---

Dr. Caligari's cabinet. *The Cabinet of Dr. Caligari* (1920), German film directed by Robert Wiene about an asylum director who is apparently able to induce a somnambulist to do what he commands.

Charg-a-Plate. A type of metal credit card embossed with the purchaser's name, address, and account number and used to imprint this information on a sales receipt.

Toynbee. Arnold Joseph Toynbee (1889–1975), best-selling British historian in the 1940s. The humor here consists of Steward's juxtaposition of the erudite Toynbee with *Hello, Mrs. Goose* and books on mundane subjects like air-conditioning.

Rubaiyat of Omar Khayyam. The title refers to the nineteenth-century translation by Edward FitzGerald, but the joke is of course that the author is Omar Khayyam.

Hello, Mrs. Goose. The first edition of Miriam Clark Potter's *Hello, Mrs. Goose* was published in 1947 by J. B. Lippincott.

Zane Grey (1872–1939). Enormously popular American writer of stories and novels about American frontier life.

Bibles for old people? Where is the john? Where can I buy elastic thread? Why don't you have a stamp department anymore? Where is the head? Where is Santa Claus? Are these all the books you have on astrology? Can you direct me to the men's washroom?

Ah, Christmas, Christmas! To me that year it was a howling madhouse, a lunatic Sabbath, a frenzied nightmare of females and squalling brats, a time of aching feet and back, of muscles in the ankles and calves that shrieked with pain, of complete nervous and mental and physical exhaustion. In moments of calm — over coffee and doughnut — I wondered if it was the world or I that had gone mad.

Many years ago, when I was in high school, I thought it would be wonderful to know how a milkman felt in the early morning, to know a streetcar motorman's reactions, to experience the emotions of everyone in every kind of profession — not with Walter Mitty dreams of grandeur, but just to see how everything felt.

That, of course, was when I was much younger. By the time Field's was done with me, I was more than done with them and all my childish hungers. And ready to go back into the kind of faculty backbiting I knew so well and in which I was reasonably proficient.

Source: Manuscript, 84–87, 225–43; omitted from *Chapters*. Steward based portions of this chapter on his *IDJ* essays "On Ulysses, Grown Old" (May 1948), "On How to Write an Encyclopedia" (October 1946), and "On Fabulous, Fabulous Field's" (January 1948).

Walter Mitty. Character in a short story by American humorist James Thurber (1894–1961) about a mild-mannered man who imagines himself in a series of larger-than-life roles involving danger or heroism. First published in the *New Yorker* in 1939, "The Secret Life of Walter Mitty" was made into a film in 1947 starring Danny Kaye (1911–87) and directed by Norman Z. McLeod.

Chapter Nine

THE WORST OF ALL DRUGS

1920–47

I suppose that by the time Prohibition was repealed in 1932 — and effectively wiped out in 1933 — I was fairly well on the way to being an alcoholic. The drinking began in high school, with the raids on Clem Rausch's wine cellar — and others — in Woodsfield. When we moved to Columbus, the drinking continued, on more sophisticated levels. We soon found where the speakeasies were — purveying the kind of romance easily available for fifty cents a shot in the days when the businessman could leave his office, walk two blocks down the street to Joe's, whisper the password through the small hole in the door, and find romance in the dusky darkened lights, drinking the bathtub gin and looking with unfocused eyes on the beauties of the trollops lounging against the bar . . . available for two bucks if you wanted one. I didn't.

You bought bathtub gin at about four or five dollars a gallon, or you bought plain alcohol from 80 to 150 proof and added some juniper-berry juice to it; the flavorings could be bought in many places. There were even bourbon and scotch essences — but they did not taste much like the real thing. The rotgut burned the throat and stung the nostrils — it was like the French *marc*, green to the taste and packing a mighty wallop. Sandusky reputedly produced the best for our region — and we all bought it as soon as the word was passed around that a new shipment had arrived.

A lot of drinking was done at private parties. I remember that when I was about twenty-one in 1930 and my sister sixteen, we spent nearly every Saturday night at the home of two friends — Bob and Bubbles Hagan — where the

marc. Coarse alcoholic drink made by fermenting the residue after grapes have been pressed.

liquor flowed freely. You were supposed to bring a bottle whenever you could find or afford one. My sister and I held contests with each other to see which one could swallow a shot glass full of the raw stuff without having the throat muscles contract involuntarily in a second or third or fourth swallowing motion. And if there were nothing available on a particular Saturday night save plain alcohol, we filled large gelatin capsules (size 000) with a medicine dropper, quickly popped the top of the capsule on, and swallowed the thing with water. In that way, the throat did not get scorched, and in about a half hour, you were so definitely plastered that you could barely walk.

And there was much drinking also at the apartments of Merle Dean or Browne Pavey, near the public library in Columbus — where those of our own persuasion gathered, with no women around. Or we drank red wine at the apartment of Professor Frierson, sitting on the floor and listening to *Le Sacré du Printemps*, just recorded, and trying to comprehend it.

Before Chicago there was Helena, Montana, where the loneliness and isolation — physical, intellectual, aesthetic — were equally as horrid as they had been in Ohio. And so it was at Carroll College in 1934–35 that the drinking grew. Almost every evening, before we went downstairs to a community dinner, I would be tanked on sherry or often something stronger, for my life as an alcoholic was by now well under way. The president of the college, Emmet Riley, and I used to get soused together, whereupon he would don mufti and we would drive past Wood Street in the town's center to watch the town's whores go yawningly to breakfast at 5:00 p.m.

By the time I reached Chicago and started teaching there in the autumn of 1936, I was fairly established as a secret drunk. Things grew steadily worse for the next ten years, until I was consuming — at home in my apartment — a quart a day, to which must be added the shots I had en route to and from class. These were the vacant years, the empty years, when the blackouts steadily increased — until sometimes I had to take to marking the calendar with crosses, the way a convict might in prison, so that I could remember what day it was — and whether I had to teach at that time. It was a period filled with dreadful scenes, the gradual loss of friend after friend, the deterio-

Professor Frierson. William C. Frierson, assistant professor of English at Ohio State from 1929 to 1937.

Le Sacré du Printemps. "The Rite of Spring," composed by Igor Stravinsky (1882–1971) in 1913 for the Ballets Russes. The first recordings of the work were made in 1929 and 1930.

don mufti. A monsignor in the Catholic Church, Riley put on street clothes rather than clerical attire before driving through the town.

ration of my health and sleep patterns, the inexorably growing loss of memory, and the slow ruin of my potency and my body. I somehow usually made it back to my apartment, though in what condition of befuddlement and befouling I hate to recall. But I never landed in jail for drunkenness, nor did I miss classes, nor did I lose my position — even though I strongly suspect that I was perhaps the only professor who ever fell asleep in class while he was lecturing. And though it was a nap of perhaps only three or four seconds, it was nonetheless enough to startle me into complete wakefulness for the rest of the period — especially when I saw the wide eyes of the handsome basketball player locked quizzically on me when I awoke.

At this distance removed from such a dark night of the soul, I do not wish to recover in memory the frightfulness of it; I have pulled down the window shade and done my best to expunge it completely. Moreover, it would be of interest only to another ex-lush. Behind the shade, the details have not festered nor reached out to trouble me. They are viewed with regret and a sense of loss for the seventeen years which might have permitted me to become a writer, a thing I much wanted at one time, but they are not mourned and wept over. They have really and truly been mostly forgotten, save when — with sadly shaking head — I recall some dreadful episode and say to myself: "God, how awful I was!"

They tell you in Alcoholics Anonymous and elsewhere that each drunk has his own "bottom" to hit, and that these "bottoms" are layered at all levels — the very lowest being the gutters of Skid Row, or jail, or periods in the psychiatric wards. As for my own "bottom" — well . . .

I was about sixteen when my Grandfather Steward, the country doctor, died, and from his office in Jerusalem, I had stolen about twenty-four quarter-grain tablets of morphine sulfate, feeling obscurely even then that the day, the night would come when they would be needed. When that night arrived, I was alone in my apartment. The whisky bottle was almost empty. I could not see the walls of the room but only a blurred kind of swimming movement enclosing me. I remember my violent sobbing, lying face down on the floor with the dust from the carpeting sharp in my nostrils. And suddenly

---

wide eyes of the handsome basketball player. Manuscript reads "wise eyes," an apparent typo.
the details . . . are viewed. Though Steward asserts that he is no longer troubled by his period of alcoholism, his shift to the passive voice in this paragraph seems to suggest a continuing need to distance himself from his past.
Jerusalem. Jerusalem, Ohio, where Steward lived as a child with his sister and parents before his mother died. His paternal grandfather lived nearby (Manuscript, 43).

I knew that this was the night of my destruction; I could face life and its problems no longer. And sobbing still, I wriggled slowly toward the kitchen on my belly, pulling against the carpet with the flat of my hands.

I had a two-fold goal. One, the bottle of tablets (had I been in my right mind, I would have suspected that twenty-five or more years of shelf life would have rendered them harmless), and the other, the hypodermic syringe with which I had been daily injecting myself with massive doses of thiamin chloride, B12, so that my ragged nerves could face each new day's old pain.

Blinded with tears, shaken and sobbing, I pulled myself to my feet by the oven-door handle on the kitchen stove. From force of habit I took a small pan, put a little water in it, dropped the syringe and needle in, and set the water to boil to sterilize the instruments. Then—swaying and unsteady, as I looked down at the water bubbling in the pan, I felt a great light burst with me. Just why the hell was I bothering to sterilize the needle when I was all set to commit suicide? What has a corpse to fear from staphylococcus?

And so from my horrid despair, I leaped suddenly to a peak of laughter— and holding my sides, gasping for breath and with tears streaming, I roared and roared until I collapsed weakly on my bed. Death averted: or, happy days are here again.

Well, not immediately. But within a week, I had gone to my first Alcoholics Anonymous meeting, and though it took me some time before I stopped "slipping," on August 10, 1947, I had my last drink—and have had none since.

There is no need to analyze the methods of AA nor the people I knew there—all ex-drunks, all with even more horrific stories to tell than I. We leaned on each other; we did "twelve-step" work helping out our "babies." We even sometimes had to help our "sponsors" when they slipped. But you could not fool your fellows in AA. In them was none of the cold Olympian detachment of a physician who had never gone through the hell of alcoholism. These men and women had suffered, been ruined, and recovered. They knew all the answers and tricks: hiding bottles in toilet water-tanks, under mattresses, or out the window on a string. As I had, they had lied, cheated, and injured others. They had guzzled for every conceivable excuse—because they had lost money, or made it; because their wives, husbands, or lovers did not understand them, or because they did; they felt tired, or exhilarated; they wanted to be sociable, or to drown their sorrows in solitude.

Part of the AA philosophy turned me away—the resolve to put your life in the hands of a "power greater than yourself." To most members, this meant God. But I found a group in Chicago, the Water Tower group, made up of hard-bitten radio announcers, commercial artists, and such like. This group changed the "power" to mean the stuff in the bottle rather than God, and that was acceptable to all of us.

AA does not turn its members into crepe-hanging missionary zealots, nor windy evangelists. Nor do its members pursue the ones who backslide. One of my "babies" put his head in an oven in Beeville, Texas. He had become convinced he could handle alcohol and started drinking again. And I saw a former "sponsor" dead drunk in front of my tattoo shop in Chicago and turned away from him—because you cannot (nay, must not) try to talk to them when they're drunk.

After three years of attendance at AA meetings, twice a week, I made an alarming discovery. The meetings came on Monday and Thursday nights, and I found that the only time that I thought of drinking was following an AA meeting! The Thursday meetings made the weekends hard for me. Against all the advice of old AA members, I decided to stop going to the "confessionals."

"Oh," they said, "you'll slip for sure if you stop coming to the meetings!"

"I'll have to try it," I said.

It worked. Gradually, the very thought of alcohol receded until it was no longer there. This took about a year. At the end of that time, I asked myself if I were strong enough to keep alcohol around the house for my friends. Tentatively, I got a bottle; as long as I kept it out of sight, it did not bother me. Today I can pour it with no qualms or tugs—but if I think about it, I miss my three favorites: sherry, sauterne, and Benedictine.

I am not recommending stopping the meetings to any AA member who might chance across this method! Occasionally there are flares in the media—"New method to help alcoholics"—such as the report some time ago, prepared by a man later revealed to be also on the payroll of a large distiller, in which he said that alcoholics could learn to drink again. Nor do I hold my breath waiting for the synthesizing of that enzyme said to be lacking in the blood of every alcoholic—the magic enzyme which digests the alcohol, rendering it harmless and nonaddictive. If it ever were isolated and made injectable, I would be afraid to try it.

I have sometimes said that should a terminal illness afflict me, I'd go back to drinking and smoking. But I really would not—knowing that it would turn me into a maudlin mess whose leaving of life would be sodden and sordid. No, if the illness strikes, I would ask my physician instead for a Brompton's cocktail—originated in Britain—in which there are painkillers mixed with

Brompton's cocktail. Formula containing morphine and cocaine developed at the Brompton Hospital in London in 1920 as a pain suppressant for terminally ill patients.

euphorics and (I guess) even heroin or some such, so that clear-minded and happily, even in blithesome spirits, I could go forth from my waiting room to meet the "feller in the bright nightgown," who has been tracking me ever since I was born.

Source: Manuscript, 78–92, 162; omitted (except for a line on page 34) from *Chapters*. Steward borrowed part of his description of AA from his *IDJ* essay "On Alcoholics Anonymous" (November 1944).

"feller in the bright nightgown." Name for death used by the American actor and humorist W. C. Fields (William Claude Dukenfield [1880–1946]).

Chapter Ten

WHITHER NOW WILT THOU FARE?

1948–56

By the autumn of 1948, when I was thirty-nine, most of the writing projects in the area had come to an end. After the editorial chore on the *World Book*, I worked preparing a sales device for it ("*The Lookies*—We never guess; we look it up.") for grade-schoolers, being bossed by an edematous witch named Carmen with dyed black hair. Then transferred my "allegiance" to *Compton's Encyclopedia*, much to the dismay of the World Book, which thought I would, like the sea, render up its dead and its secrets unto the enemy. They need not have worried. I found Compton's a kind of loosely run organization under the fumble-fingered editorship of an ass named Clarence S., a closeted queen who was also a very model for the double-breasted suit.

That too came to an end, and I was left with nothing to do. Then my father died, sitting at stool, from taking amphetamines too soon after a binge. I did not go back to his funeral, for money was low. Nor would I return to Loyola University, for I still remembered the summer of suffering with Irene the madwoman and the nonprotective callousness of the dean in that regard. Accordingly, after Labor Day in September, I wandered casually and a bit uncertainly into the dean's office at DePaul University, told him of my background, and asked if there were any openings. This was perhaps the most unorthodox way of approaching a teaching position that he or I had ever ex-

---

Whither now wilt thou fare? Line from a lyric celebrating the victory of English forces led by Edward III over the Scots at Halidon Hill in 1333: "Thou boastful barley-bag-man, thy dwelling is all bare. / False wretch and forsworn, / whither wilt thou fare?"

The Lookies. The workbook that Steward developed remained in print, with updated illustrations, until 1960.

like the sea, render up its dead. Cf. Revelation 20:13.

Samuel M. Steward, Ph.D., Associate Professor, English

DePaul University yearbook photograph of Steward, 1952.
(Courtesy of DePaul University Archives)

perienced. Usually there had to be references, recommendations, a study of one's transcripts and past experience. But Theodore Wangler was at any rate a gentleman.

"We'll do all that later," he said somewhat toothily, a tall man, fair-haired, and either Germanic or Scandinavian in origin. "Meanwhile, I'll take you on probation—and pay you just according to the number of hours you teach. If you work out, we'll then discuss a more permanent arrangement."

"Fine," I said, and with a secret sigh sank once more into the life described by the old sardonic self-criticism voiced by so many teachers: "Those who can, do; those who can't, teach." Conceived by the written word, bred in books, nurtured on the petty gossip of faculty teas, the teachers of the late forties were wholly out of step. No matter how well informed they thought themselves, their reactions were unrealistic, walled in by their training and background. And I was one of those, despite my thinking otherwise—lying happily in my rut, gurgling at the sky, kicking my heels happily at the sinking sun.

DePaul seemed to me a notch downward from Loyola. The two schools were rivals in everything they did, but the Jesuit school seemed more worldly and aristocratic, its students drawn from a wealthier and more sophisticated group than the humble ones at DePaul. There, the background was largely working class, educated in parochial schools and faultily equipped with an intellectual dowry that diminished in scope and intensity as each year passed. Loyola had attracted teachers more competent and intelligent, whereas this one — with its greater emphasis on athletics — seemed a haven for misfits, neurotics, and drunks. And the English department had — instead of the cool clear razor mind of Zabel — the kowtowing yesmanship of an exclusively local inbred product, by which one meant that the department which he now chaired was the same one that had awarded him his PhD — with one MA on the examining committee. But the school did have a wondrously successful campaign under way for a new gymnasium for their basketball team!

It had long been my practice, when it fell to me to teach a course in freshman English, to give small oral quizzes to the entering students — not really formal quizzes, of course, but little sessions of questionings designed to see how well informed they were, what they had in their associational backgrounds — small IQ tests, in a way. To my dismay, I found a class of freshmen, forty in number, not one of whom had ever heard of the poet Homer, and of course not of the *Iliad* or the *Odyssey*. I concealed my shock and by stages moved on to mechanical questions: "How many of you," I finally asked, "know how to change a spark plug?"

To my chagrin, about thirty hands went up, both girls and boys.

Once more I decided to let the fog rise around me, and this time I did it purposively. I had now been away from alcohol for over one year and was much more in control of myself than I had been formerly. Here and there I dropped a word — yes, I had known Gertrude Stein and Alice B. Toklas; yes, I had written a novel (hinting of something dark in connection with it) but since *Angels on the Bough* had published no fiction under my own name (true enough — I'd written nothing at all!); yes, I had known Thomas Mann, Thornton Wilder, André Gide, and others. Paris was a wonderful town to live in. Algeria was a strange exotic place. No, I did not go to the movies — except in rare cases when there was a good science fiction one; and yes, I read a lot of science fiction. Write it? (A small quirky smile.)

The technique worked wonderfully well; by the time I had taught there a couple of years, I was classed as a "character," a personality. The campus paper interviewed me, publishing some of my wisecracks; the "literary" jour-

---

I'd written nothing at all. In 1948, Steward was actually in his fifth year of writing monthly essays for the *Illinois Dental Journal* (see pages 185, 240–41).

DePaul University yearbook photograph of Steward and students in his Arts Club, 1952. (Courtesy of DePaul University Archives)

nal also carried a profile. By student request, I formed the Arts Club—a kind of loose discussion group acting without president or officers "so that we would not be diverted from discussion of the arts by any increment of politics" or power plays. And my classes grew more and more popular, until usually each term they had to be closed at eighty or a hundred persons, despite the fact that I worked them hard.

But indeed, I must have been a small thorn in the flesh of several. The dean of men—a colorless mollusk named Powers—used to stalk into a class and announce (after a show of getting my permission):

"All students will be required to attend Mass tomorrow morning at eight o'clock."

After he left I would look at the class a moment and then say, "This university is declared in its charter and catalogue to be a nonsectarian one, open to all. I am sure that Father Powers simply forgot to add to his announcement the fact that if any of you are Jewish or Protestant, you are of course excused from tomorrow's attendance."

Then I resumed, fully aware that some one of Powers's spies would report to him as soon as possible what an upstart I was. For the same "nonsectarian" reason, I refused to open each class with prayer, saying that I considered it a very private thing—but if each separate student wanted to pray silently before class, he was more than welcome to do so.

Some years in from my arrival, a blow fell. Wangler was replaced by Powers as dean of the college—and from the start, I began to sense disaster of some sort. Of course, he did not like me—I never knuckled under. I was then teaching a course in the modern novel, teaching it just as I had for Zabel, using the same modern authors. But Zabel was not there to shield me. And finally came a call asking me to see Father Powers.

I went to his office. "Sit down," he said. I noticed the absence of his calling me "Dr." It was foreboding, because in all small schools such as the two I had been associated with in Chicago, one is always "doctored" to death. Prestige is a continual concern and worry.

"You are currently teaching a course in the modern novel," he said, coming right to the point as would Captain Bligh, whom he faintly resembled—at least in Laughton's interpretation. "And reports have reached me that it is a very seamy thing . . ."

I opened my mouth, but he went on.

". . . and that several students have been compelled to go to confession after reading some of the material you are requiring."

"Their faith must be pretty weak, then," I said sardonically. "And what do they do about the newspapers and television and advertisements? Are they spending all their time in the litter box?" (The term for "confessional" was not original with me; Huysmans first used it.)

I was ignored. "What reason do you have for not including fine Catholic novelists like G. K. Chesterton and Hilaire Belloc?"

"In any field of criticism outside the Catholic Church," I responded, "those writers are classed as proselytizing propagandists and about as modern as a Victorian antimacassar. But if you want me to include other modern Catholic novelists such as J. K. Huysmans with his *Against the Grain* or any of the novels of Sigrid Undset or Evelyn Waugh or Graham Greene, I'd be happy to do it. Then the students' hair would really stand on end."

Ignored again. Chances are he had never heard of the ones I mentioned. "Part of the complaint also seems to be that you actually enjoy teaching the raunchiest parts."

"I never refer to them in class, nor read them aloud," I said hotly. "Such

---

Captain Bligh. William Bligh (1754–1817), skilled but volatile captain of the HMS *Bounty*, some of whose crew mutinied in 1789 near Tahiti. The portrayal of Bligh by Charles Laughton (1899–1962) in the 1935 film *Mutiny on the Bounty* contributed to the popular caricature of Bligh as a sadistic tyrant.

antimacassar. A doily or other cloth placed on upholstered furniture originally to protect the fabric from Macassar oil, a popular styling oil for men's hair in the nineteenth century.

things can be taught with discretion and are certainly no worse than your courses on marriage and divorce and sex education, where the instructor refers to sexual intercourse with a condom as being nothing more than mutual masturbation."

"I do not intend to defend the Church's right to speak frankly when a priest discusses such matters authoritatively," he said coldly.

We parted from that interview, each of us seething, and the cloud that I had seen on the horizon had become appreciably larger and more menacing.

Of course, there were rewards in teaching—but they were small and spaced far apart. I did my best to ring up the curtain for some of those students—and sometimes I succeeded. You would have to be fashioned of stone, indeed, to be able to resist the enthusiasm and the glow with which one now and then approached you and said, "I have just discovered the poetry (or the prose) of such and such, and man—that cat can really write!" This happened perhaps twice a quarter—hardly enough to live on, and certainly not bankable. Or the excitement when I arranged for those who wanted it the experience of "supering" on the stage of the Chicago opera or with some visiting ballet. And to be perfectly truthful, there were a half dozen contacts between certain handsome male students and their beloved teacher. But all of these things must be listed as intangible profits.

Materially the situation was awful. The salary on which I existed as an associate professor in 1950 was about $4,500 a year. I was often down to my last thirty-five cents by the time the bimonthly paycheck arrived and sometimes had to borrow. There were of course no retirement or pension plans at such a small school and certainly no organization into unions.

I was once again reminded of the points I had made many years before in my article on the lay faculty. For laymen at this college were salaried not so much on their educational accomplishments and qualifications as on their marital status and the number of children produced for Mother Church—a highly immoral view, it seemed to me, but nonetheless rigidly followed. At the particular campus where I taught, there were only about five or six single persons—of whom one was Karola Geiger, a charming old-school German Fräulein with a doctorate, who was kept on what amounted practically to a starvation salary, for she sinned in two ways: she was unmarried and a woman. I continued to see salary raises for every teacher as he produced a new baby, while Karola's salary and those of John S. (speech; alcoholic) and Theodore K. (speech; homosexual) and Arthur L. (Jewish; homosexual) and myself (why bother with a characterization if you've come this far?) remained the same.

Someone evidently got very angry with the pay-scale situation, because an anonymous letter was sent to the North Central Association of Colleges. The letter, it was later learned (by reading backward from North Central's indictment), criticized DePaul because 1) it had no scholastic endowment, thus being roughly in the position of a newspaper hoping to survive through its subscriber list alone, without advertisements; 2) it had an unfair pay scale (discriminations were cited: Geiger, Steward, others); 3) it was concentrating a fund drive on building a new gym, whereas the library was in deplorable condition both with regard to holdings and physical plant; 4) it advertised itself as nonsectarian yet in official announcements took for granted that all students were Catholic, making no exceptions for Protestants or Jews; and 5) it sometimes had a holder of only a master's degree on its boards giving oral examinations for the degree of Doctor of Philosophy. There was great weeping on high and in Zion when North Central put the school on probation for a year, but many of us were secretly pleased. No one ever found out who sent the letter.

Many of us began to feel that small inner wave, that nearly unfelt ripple, that carries a doubt and a question: Might it not be time to be considering a move to some other place? Or another occupation? Added to that feeling in myself was another: the quality of students had deteriorated so much by 1952 that many entering freshmen could barely read — and as for writing a good sentence: well, that was one of the things you could learn in college, wasn't it? I found myself going back to the high-school techniques of diagramming sentences, but even that seemed not to help. I no longer had the boozy tolerance in me that used to last as a gentle secondary drunk until the first shot at noon; instead, I found myself more and more being forced to take a half tablet of some amphetamine to be able to face the classes that I came more and more to dislike.

To amuse myself, I had been doing a number of things. Since it had fallen to me always to be the gondolier in the ballet of *The Nutcracker* when it came to Chicago, I once went down to South State Street and got a small anchor tattooed on my left shoulder, the one that faced the audience as I "poled" the barque of the princess across the stage. And on Saturday afternoons for three years, I took the same life class at the Art Institute, always taught by a

---

weeping . . . in Zion. Cf. Isaiah 30:19.

gondolier in . . . The Nutcracker. As a faithful "super," or extra, in Chicago ballet productions, Steward had the first claim on the role of gondolier whenever *The Nutcracker* was performed in the city (Manuscript, 13).

charming little woman, Salcia Bahnc, who seemed not to mind putting up with me and who turned me into a fair sketcher—never an artist. And also, on one of my visits to see Alice Toklas, I met Jean Cocteau in 1950 and fell in love with his line drawings of sullen young men. Putting that new enthusiasm together with the Art Institute classes, I purchased a Vibro-tool and took to engraving Cocteau-ish designs (most of them pornographic) on aluminum drinking "glasses."

These things are mentioned because when put together, they explain why the radical change in the direction of my life, when it came, took the form it did. To these more obvious but wholly unconscious "steps in preparation" must be added other clues and impulses from the past. And certain new ones must be unveiled.

Most males when they approach forty or fifty—or somewhere between the two—experience a kind of grand climacteric that upsets them almost as much as the menopause does women. It is during this critical time, when one's rational nature and inner judgment seem clouded or greatly diminished, that most of the so-called self-determination moves take place—a man quits his job or does something silly; he has seen his life disappearing behind him and nothing but fog ahead, and he gets frightened. The male homosexual seems particularly vulnerable in this regard.

Part of this may have been working in me. I know that the impulse from the Imp of the Perverse was also there, turning me against my regimented life and making me burn intensely with a new hatred for all authority, especially in the form of that piece of blubber named Powers. I had always disliked and defied authority and chafed under it—but it grew worse by geometric progression during this time.

Once in the 1930s I wrote a small novelette called *The Golden Egg*, in which I remarked upon the three signs of wickedness which one of the characters had—socks rolled down to the ankle instead of flopping loosely, sideburns two inches longer than usual, and a tattoo. There was a vague suggestion of evil or wickedness to the idea of tattooing; of course, I knew nothing at all about it, except that I had seen a few tattoos on people, and they were always a little frightening to me for some reason. But had I not a small anchor on my shoulder already, for my "role" as gondolier in *The Nutcracker*?

Salcia Bahnc (1898–1979). Noted expressionist painter and illustrator who was born in Poland and received her first formal training at the Art Institute of Chicago.
Jean Cocteau (1889–1963). French novelist, playwright, film director, and prominent member of the circle of avant-garde artists in Paris after World War I.
Vibro-tool. An electric engraving tool.

But as a university professor of English, I knew nothing about the means and methods of tattooing. How to learn this arcane and mysterious art? Into this wholly unconscious and amorphous stew came an enzyme or a catalytic agent—whatever it should be called—in the person of a small guy in his mid-twenties, himself tattooed heavily all over his body, whose real name I never did learn. He called himself "Larry Rogers," and he was a complete tattoo buff. No—turn "buff" into "nut." He was the first of a long line of nuts that I was to encounter during the next fifteen years. Larry thought, ate, slept, talked about nothing else save tattooing. It had become an obsession with him—uncontrollable as it always was when it actually took hold of a person. Reluctantly, under his urging, I interested myself more and more—still not even remotely considering the possibility of becoming a tattoo artist.

One gloomy rainy day in 1952, he called to tell me that old Mickey Kellett, a wino tattooist in a flophouse, wanted to sell a footlocker filled with acetate stencils, old pigment-encrusted machines, and some "flash"—designs to be hung on the walls. With some misgivings, I went with Larry down to the Skid Row of South State Street, found Kellett in a fleabag hotel, bought the smelly stuff for thirty-five dollars, and took it home.

Then I purchased a correspondence course in tattooing put out by one Milton Zeis in Rockford, Illinois—and learned next to nothing from its pages. Becoming a tattoo artist that way was like trying to learn to swim from a book in your living room, so I went to Milwaukee to the old Grand Master of tattooing, Amund Dietzel, plunked two twenties down in front of him and said, "I'd like to ask you some questions about tattooing." That did it. He talked steadily for three hours and showed me endless tricks. I learned more in that time than I ever did from Zeis's course, which cost well over a hundred dollars. Within a month, I had put on my first tattoo in the privacy of my apartment; within two months, I was working part-time with a wino named Randy Webb in the Sportland Arcade on South State Street.

Three blocks down from the south edge of the Loop, this part of State Street had been an embarrassment to the city council and the elegant merchants of North State Street for many years—arcades, burlesque shows, pawnshops, cheap clothing stores, flophouses one after the other, stewbums asleep in doorways, bottles everywhere, dried urine streams on the slanting sidewalks. Of all the arcades on the Skid Row jungle of South State

Amund Dietzel (1891–1974). Legendary Norwegian-born tattoo artist who settled in Milwaukee in 1914 and worked there until the city banned tattooing in 1967.
Sportland Arcade. The Sportland was located on the west side of the 600 block of South State Street on a site now occupied by the north building of Jones College Prep High School.

Street, the Sportland looked the dingiest. The others had glass fronts and fluorescent lighting and bright new pinball machines, lunch counters, and fine glass doors. The Sportland looked dead. The flyspecked and streaked windows had not been washed in many months, and the arcade inside was long and dark and dirty. Built against one wall was what looked like a small three-walled construction shack with a slanting roof. It was open on the front side; an extensible baby gate closed it off from the public. It was nine feet square.

Randy Webb, with whom I would share this space, would have to be seen to be believed. He was a little old man with yellow-brown hair, dressed in filthy clothes and a dirty wool shirt, toothless because an irate customer on whom he had once put a five-legged black panther had swatted him and knocked his plates out. They broke on the floor and were never replaced. He had one of the worst complexions I ever saw in my life, the result of his inordinate wine drinking. His face was covered with rum-blossoms — big scarlet and purple and yellow pustules which he was fond of squeezing, popping out about a quarter teaspoonful of pus and matter. His nose veins were purple and broken in many places with resultant spots of purpura, and his eyes were red-rimmed and rheumy. He was the nastiest-looking person I had seen for a long time, as well as the slyest and craftiest backstabber on the whole street.

He hated me from the beginning, of course; I threatened his lazy drunken existence and the source of his Muscatel money. (Twenty-one empty pint bottles of wine were once found behind his chair in his shop.) He owned nothing in the shop — all the equipment had been lent him by Mickey Kellett, who by then was taking a cure for alcoholism at the Kankakee state asylum, having been found one night in a flophouse "lobby," naked with a gun, saying the FBI was out to get him and would never take him alive.

There were many aches at first — distressing situations with Randy and Mickey, when he returned from Kankakee, and squabbles over the quality of antisepsis in the shop. (Randy used none and would even spit on a fresh tattoo, rubbing the saliva well into it, saying, "Oh, you cain't infect 'em nohow" — but many came back infected.) Within the first six months, I had learned more dirty tricks of below-the-belt in-fighting than I had ever known before. It was necessary for survival. Then he and Kellett tried to take over and were themselves evicted — only to set up shop on the second floor of the

Kankakee state asylum. Founded in 1879 as the Illinois Eastern Hospital for the Insane; now known as the Samuel H. Shapiro Developmental Center.
There were many aches. Steward provides a detailed description of the maneuvers that Webb and Kellett used to antagonize him in *Bad Boys*, 24–35.

Fleetwood flophouse, right above me, and be evicted again from there after three weeks of drunken revelry.

With Randy shaken out of his money tree, I made the shop as clean and inviting as it could be. I gave out cards to everyone who got tattooed; there were instructions printed on the back and address and so on on the recto. To sailors in those days I always gave several cards to pass around at Great Lakes. And I kept my prices at approximately one-half of what the others charged. It worked: the trickle of customers began to increase until it was a stream, a river, and on some Saturdays a torrent.

But I was still teaching!

Obviously I could not tattoo under my real name and still continue to teach at the university. Earlier, I had written monthly articles — on topics of my own choosing, everything from Gertrude Stein to how to cook a wolf — for the *Illinois Dental Journal* and had used the name of Philip Sparrow. I took it from "The Boke of Phyllyp Sparowe," a poem by John Skelton in the early 1500s, a lament for the death of a pet sparrow belonging to Jane Scroupe which used to pick crumbs from her cleavage — a Rabelaisian hodgepodge of buffoonery and erotic hints and much fresh charm. For my tattooing, then, I became Phil Sparrow.

Such a situation was bound to produce interesting side effects. In the little roofed shack, I always wore a bulky turtleneck and some "seafarer" dungarees with wide bell-bottoms. And I had to be continually alert. Time after time I would glimpse one of my students entering the arcade to wander around — and would always have to run to hide under the stairwell where the mop sink was. But once I had my back to the front of my shack, bending over some machines; I straightened and turned to look directly into the eyes of Bruce Stewart, one of my superior students!

You would not be able to blame him for failing to recognize me. I was out of my usual ambience of the classroom — no double-breasted suit, no bow tie, no glasses, no textbooks. What on earth would a university professor be doing in a tattoo dive on South State Street?

This curious double life went on for two years, cautiously. I wanted to be

monthly articles . . . for the Illinois Dental Journal. Between January 1944 and July 1949, Steward wrote fifty-six quirky essays for this obscure journal for dentists, which was edited by his personal dentist in Chicago. See *Philip Sparrow Tells All: Lost Essays by Samuel Steward, Writer, Professor, Tattoo Artist*, ed. Jeremy Mulderig (Chicago: University of Chicago Press, 2015).

sure that I would be able to earn a living with tattooing. For two years, then, I got two salaries—and profited. And in the spring of 1954, my take from tattooing exactly equaled in one week what I made in one month of teaching!

There had to come the separation from the university—a thing I dreaded. I knew it could not be much longer postponed. Although I had told only a very few trusted colleagues about my new venture, I had the uneasy feeling that more persons knew about it than I had confided in, that it might not be more than a matter of a few weeks until the administration found out about my outside activities also.

The matter was settled just before Easter in 1954. Classes had closed for the vacation when the secretary rang the faculty building, asked for me, and said Dean Powers would like to see me for a few moments.

just before Easter in 1954. In the narrative given here, Steward has antedated the sequence of events by two years (William T. Powers did not become dean until the 1955–56 academic year) and has apparently fictionalized the details of his final meeting with the dean, for his journal—written contemporaneously with the events—tells a quite different story. In the fall of 1955, Steward writes in the journal that he has "never been so tired of anything in all my life as I am of teaching" and contemplates applying for a leave for the fall 1956 term. On February 23, 1956, he learns, ominously, that his salary for the coming year has been frozen at $4,800. At his final meeting with Powers, on March 29, 1956, the dean tells him that his contract will not be renewed, and when Steward pushes for an explanation, Powers says simply, "Shall we say for outside activities?" Despite his unhappiness at DePaul, Steward was devastated. "I staggered back to the faculty house (white-faced, I presume) and . . . sat for 20 minutes staring at the wall. . . . All I could see was the appalling loss of face in having nothing to do except be a tattooer." His thoughts turned to Stein. "The thing that will be hardest to accustom myself to, of course, will be . . . the diminishment of Gertrude's 'sense of importance to yourself inside yourself.' At the age of 46, to be forced outside of one's habit patterns and one's 'prestige' is a serious thing." During the remaining weeks of the term, Steward vacillated between periods of anxiety about the loss of his academic career and the inescapable fact that he had come to detest teaching, "the futility of it being broken all too rarely by the reward of finding an intelligent single one whom I could watch grow." Ultimately his inherent resilience won out. "I have adjusted to many things in my life, and this is merely another," he wrote in his journal. Yet once he had submitted his final grades and formally ended his connection with DePaul, the doubts returned: "All of a sudden I discovered a new and frightening hollowness within. . . . This first bleak look at the future is a hard and depressing one. All that little prestige is now gone; I'm not a 'university professor' even at such a pipsqueak poverty-ridden school as DePaul; I'm only a tattooer" ("Journal of a Tattoo Artist," 309, 320, 326–27, 350 [November 1955–June 1956], Kinsey Steward Collection). For the sequence of events that appear to have made his tattoo business known to officials at DePaul, see Spring, 231–35.

I am not psychic nor in the least likely to have visions. But intuitions are something else again, especially when they have a great number of details on which to rest. Before I went to see Powers, I sat down at the typewriter and on a half sheet of college stationery typed out a two-sentence resignation, dating it a week past, saying that for health and personal reasons, I was resigning from the university, to take effect at the end of the term. I folded the note and put it into my jacket.

The air seemed electric when I entered the office. Poor Carol Dooner, the secretary, could not look me in the face. Feeling strengthened in my intuition, I walked to the dean's office and looked in, smiling.

"You wanted to see me?" I said. No name, no "Father," nothing.

"Come in and close the door." No name, no "Doctor," nothing.

"You are teaching the modern novel again," he began. I noticed a small fleck of white spit had collected at the corner of his mouth. "And I—"

"Hold it just a minute, Fatty," I said pleasantly. At that, he looked as if he were going to burst—his checks puffed out and his skin darkened. I extracted the letter from my jacket. "I meant to give you this last week, and it slipped my mind."

I put the paper on his desk and got up to go.

"Just a minute, damn it," he bellowed. He opened the note and scanned it. "You were about to get fired anyway," he grated.

"For what reason?" I said innocently.

"You'll have to ask Father Kammer," he said. Kammer was chancellor, downtown branch.

I was at the door, and turned.

"Fuck Kammer," I said pleasantly, and was immediately sorry I had. The two "k" sounds coming together stopped the explosiveness I had hoped to achieve; it was like trying to slam a door with a heavy door-check on it. The drama was wasted.

Well, that was the end of twenty years of teaching—given up without any great sorrow or regret. I stumbled on until June with my classes, hardly interested at all any more, and on the last day gave a group of seniors a beautifully planned and fashioned lecture. It ended with four literary references

on the last day. Steward's last day in the classroom was May 25, 1956. "A small gasp went up when I said I was retiring from teaching," he wrote in his journal, noting also that in the preceding eighteen months he had given 3,181 tattoos ("Journal of a Tattoo Artist," 342–43 [May 1956], Kinsey Steward Collection).

to such things as "Nay, I have done, you get no more of me" and Housman's
"To an Athlete Dying Young"—but finishing importantly with the last two
lines of Milton's *Lycidas*:

> At last he rose, and twitched his mantle blue;
> Tomorrow to fresh woods and pastures new.

I did not quote the four sets of lines; I merely gave the references. How
many of the students looked them up I never knew . . . nor any longer cared.

Source: Manuscript, 244–65; omitted from Chapters.

"Nay, I have done." The first four lines in Sonnet LXI from the sonnet sequence *Idea* (1619),
by Michael Drayton (1563–1631), are "Since there's no help, come let us kiss and part. / Nay,
I have done, you get no more of me; / And I am glad, yea glad with all my heart, / That thus
so cleanly I myself can free."

"To an Athlete Dying Young." Though out of context, the most applicable lines from Housman's 1895 poem would seem to be these: "Smart lad, to slip betimes away / From fields
where glory does not stay, / And early though the laurel grows / It withers quicker than the
rose" (ll. 9–12).

Lycidas. Pastoral elegy (1638) by John Milton (1608–74).

Chapter Eleven

DR. PROMETHEUS

1949–56

In 1949, when I was teaching at DePaul, I made the acquaintance of a guy in the speech department named Theodore, who came to me one day in the shabby halls of the university and asked without preamble, "How would you like to meet Dr. Alfred C. Kinsey?"

I was flabber and gasted. "Good heavens," I said, "you don't mean to say you know him!"

He nodded. "Long time," he said. "Matter of fact, I was the one to help him get started interviewing in Chicago."

This was just after the publication of *Sexual Behavior in the Human Male*, when Kinsey's star was high, and his name was on everyone's lips. It would be too much to say that the Stonewall riots in 1969 — a landmark of rebellion in the gay movement — would have been impossible without his pioneering studies, but had he not lived and labored, it would perhaps have been necessary to invent him. He truly brought fire and light to the world in 1948 with his findings about homosexuality and the sexual mores of the American

Prometheus. In Greek mythology, a titan who created human beings and then gave them fire, which he had stolen from the gods.

Alfred C. Kinsey (1894–1956). Biologist turned sexologist whose landmark studies of male and female sexual behavior (1948, 1953) were based on more than 10,000 confidential interviews conducted by him and his team of researchers.

his findings about homosexuality. From his interview data, Kinsey concluded that heterosexuality and homosexuality are not binaries but instead occupy opposite ends of a continuum of sexual identities and behaviors that many people experience during their lives. Though preliminary and incomplete, Kinsey's research radically altered public thinking about homosexuality at a time when it was rarely discussed at all.

male. Freud as intuitive creator, Havelock Ellis as arranger and synthesizer, and Kinsey as scientist and investigator accomplished the liberating enlightenment of our century regarding sex.

So Theodore arranged it, and Dr. Kinsey came to my apartment. The interview would last an hour, Theodore said, although sometimes they ran longer if the interviewee had a lot to say.

I opened the door to a solidly built man in his fifties wearing a rumpled grey suit. He had a friendly face. His greying buff-colored hair stood in a short unruly pompadour; his eyes were sometimes blue and sometimes hazel. He had a rather sensitive but tense wide mouth above a somewhat bulldog or prognathous jaw, which in turn jutted out above his ever-present bow tie.

Indeed, Theodore had been a bit misinformed. The interview lasted five hours, and it seemed to me that I answered thousands of questions—although there were in reality only a few hundred. The thing that amazed him most of all was that he found I was a "record keeper"—something all too rare, he said. But I had an accurate count on the number of persons I had been to bed with, the total number of "releases" (as he termed them) with other persons, the number of repeats, and all the usual statistical information, taken from the Stud File that I had kept on three-by-five cards from my very first contact many years before in Ohio. My information, like Kinsey's, was coded, but not so unbreakably or exhaustively. I showed him the file; he was fascinated. At the end of the interview, he looked at me thoughtfully and said, "Why don't you give up trying to continue your heterosexual relationships?"

I abandoned my phony "bisexuality" that very evening. Poor Emmy. We never went to bed after that.

The interview marked the beginning of a friendship that lasted until his death from overwork in 1956. I became one of the "unofficial collaborators" for the Institute for Sex Research. In the days when he was still alive, no one could officially work for the institute who was not of the "majority sexual orientation"; all his associates had to be married, preferably with children, or else be absolutely asexual. He felt that otherwise the reliability and objectivity of the research might be tainted or compromised.

Unofficially, then, I steered people to him or him to people, gave him samples of my literary production, ranging from sentimental sex stories writ-

Institute for Sex Research. Established in 1947 at Indiana University and now known as the Kinsey Institute for Research in Sex, Gender, and Reproduction.

ten in high school to a translation done as a labor of love of Genet's *Querelle de Brest*, and a "dirty" novel of mine that was too much even for Jack Kahane in Paris in 1938 when he had the Obelisk Press. I deposited in the archives dozens of typewritten stories that used to circulate in such form before the explosion of pornography in 1966. And I gave him all the artwork I had done (he used to give me duplicate photographs from his collection which I would turn into line drawings in the Cocteau manner or make watercolor washes thereof). I also turned over to him the chapter of my doctoral dissertation in which I had discovered Cardinal Newman's homosexuality, as well as the sexual-action Polaroid pictures I had taken in the early 1950s when those cameras first made their appearance. The Polaroids, like bread cast upon the waters, came back to me eventually in a more beautiful form — eight-by-ten photographs blown up and reproduced by Kinsey's official photographer, Bill Dellenback. I managed to find copies of my two early books, *Pan and the Fire-bird* and *Angels on the Bough*, to add to the library. Later on, at their request, I sent the institute all of the Phil Andros novels I had produced, together with a bibliography locating the hundred and fifty stories I had written for European and other magazines and all the ephemera and reproduced artwork I had done.

translation . . . of Genet's Querelle de Brest. While in Paris in 1950, Steward bought a wildly expensive copy of the 1948 edition of *Querelle* illustrated by Jean Cocteau and subsequently wrote an English translation, for which he attempted unsuccessfully to find a publisher in Europe, since the book was banned in the United States. See Spring, 135–77.

a "dirty" novel of mine. See chapter 15. Gertrude Stein hadn't liked it — "the ending was horrible, everything cut off that poor fellow" — and summarized the manuscript's problem by telling him, "You tried to do Henry Miller but without the gusto" (*Dear Sammy*, 56).

Jack Kahane (1887–1939). Founder of the Obelisk Press in Paris, through which he published works by distinguished authors like Henry Miller and James Joyce that were banned in the United States because of passages of sexual explicitness.

explosion of pornography in 1966. See note on relaxing of censorship, page 211.

Polaroid pictures. Steward bought a Polaroid Land Camera in February 1951 (Steward to Alfred Kinsey, TLS, February 21, 1951 [Kinsey Steward Collection, Box 1, Series 1]). The Polaroids he took of sexual encounters in his apartments are reproduced in Justin Spring, *An Obscene Diary: The Visual World of Sam Steward* (n.p.: Antinous Press/Elysium Press, 2010); the originals are in the Yale Steward Papers.

like bread cast upon the waters. Ecclesiastes 11:1.

Bill Dellenback. Professional photographer whom Kinsey met in 1948 and hired as a full-time staff member the following year (James H. Jones, *Alfred C. Kinsey: A Life* [New York: Norton, 2004], 605–6).

Phil Andros novels. See chapter 15.

stories I had written for European and other magazines. See chapter 15.

Alfred Kinsey in Steward's Chicago apartment. Polaroid by Steward, about 1951. (Courtesy of the Estate of Samuel M. Steward)

Kinsey favored me in return with the most flattering kind of attention—never coming to Chicago without writing to me in advance to arrange a meeting. In the eight years of our friendship, I logged (as a record keeper again) about seven hundred hours of his pleasant company, the most fascinating in the world because all his shoptalk was of sex—and what is more interesting than that? He taught me some of their "little language," the shorthand speech which he and his associates used, so that at lunch or dinner in public places they could still discuss the most hair-raising matters: "h" for homosexual, "ht" for heterosexual, "s/m" for sadomasochistic (one he originated that spread widely), "tv" for transvestite, and several others. Thus one of the group might say: "My history today liked GO better than Z, but AG with an H really made him ER," each letter being pronounced separately. Translation: "My history today liked genital-oral contact better than that with animals, but anal-genital with a homosexual really turned him on."

In those early years, he had one of the warmest personalities I had ever met—a cordial gregarious man as approachable as an old park bench and just as much of an accomplished con artist as I was later to become in my tattoo career. The "con" approach was deliberately cultivated by him so that he could win the trust of the person being interviewed; in like manner, he took up smoking and drinking (very, very gingerly) to put his interviewees at ease. His warmth and approachability were further improved by his talent for talking to the most uneducated hustlers and prostitutes and pimps in their own language, no matter how coarse. It gained trust for him among the suspicious ones, and word of his honesty and secrecy opened doors for him that would have remained closed forever to a more academic attitude.

I learned many things from him—and in a sense, some degree of "transference" took place in me. Though there was a difference of only about fifteen years in our ages, after the initial interview he became for me a sort of father figure, as he did for so many. Several women said, innocently enough, that they had been frigid until interviewed by Kinsey. In him, I saw the ideal father—who was never shocked, who never criticized, who always approved, who listened and sympathized. I suppose that to a degree, I fell in love with him, even though he was a grandfather. Of course, there was never any physical contact between us except a handshake.

Many persons would ask me: "Is he queer?" I told him this.

"And what do you answer?" he asked.

"Well," I said slowly, "I always say, 'Yes, he is—but not in the same way we are. He is a voyeur and an auditeur. He likes to look and listen.'" Kinsey laughed, but a moment later I caught him observing me thoughtfully. I may have hit closer to the truth than I realized.

I learned also never again in my life to use the word "normal," which I once thoughtlessly employed in front of him. He jumped on me. "Just what do you mean?" he said. "Usual? Usual for whom—you, me, the rest of the world?"—and he scolded me roundly. From that moment, the word was sliced from my vocabulary and replaced with something more exact, but clumsier, such as "majority practice." But I partly redeemed myself by quoting Gide's phrase for him, which he had not heard until then, the one about "your normal is my abnormal."

And little acts were also corrected. Once while I was visiting him in Bloomington, we went to lunch and stopped in a men's room first to take a leak. Afterward I washed my hands.

"Why did you do that?" he asked.

Somewhat confused, I said, "I guess because I was brought up that way—to wash my hands after handling myself."

"your normal is my abnormal." See note on "In the name of what God," page 113.

"Ah *hah!*" he said triumphantly. "A victim of the Judeo-Christian ethos of the Old Testament! Don't you realize that it would be much more sensible to wash your hands *before* handling yourself? The Old Testament says you'll be unclean 'until the even' if you touch yourself. But think of today's door handles and all the other things you've touched during the past four hours."

Again, at lunch at the Indiana University Union, as I think it was called, there was a small container of monosodium glutamate on the table. I sprinkled some on a fingertip and touched it to my tongue.

"Did you ever notice," I said thoughtfully to the table at large, at which were seated Kinsey, Wardell Pomeroy, and Paul Gebhard, "how closely the taste of monosodium glutamate resembles that of semen?"

There was a moment of dead silence, and the enormity of my gaffe turned me rosy as I slowly realized that I had spoken to three presumably straight heterosexuals.

Kinsey grinned. "I do believe," he said, "that not a single one of us here has ever noticed the similarity, but your remark will be noted for future reference."

Everyone laughed. "I thought," I said, "that certainly this time I might trap someone into admitting he was a club member."

He grinned. "I mustn't say. We must preserve the confidentiality of the research."

When the time came for the appearance of the volume on females, we chuckled over his statement in the introduction that since the orgasm lasted only seconds, it had been necessary to film the act and that the institute had in its archives filmed records of the orgasms of fourteen species of mammals—the amusing part being that in 1953 the Indiana University regents could still be shocked—and that somewhere among the fourteen was of course the human animal. Similarly, we enjoyed the insertion into the female volume of perhaps one of the most detailed and thorough expositions up to that time of the technique of erotic arousal and contact, a genuine *ars amatoria* or *Kama Sutra* in English.

Kinsey from the very beginning gave me free access to the archives and

Wardell Pomeroy (1913–2001). Kinsey Institute associate and coauthor with Kinsey and Clyde Martin (1918–2014) of the landmark studies of male and female human sexual behavior.
Paul Gebhard (1917–2015). Kinsey Institute associate who succeeded Kinsey as director after his death in 1956.
ars amatoria. Guide to male-female relationships and sexual practice by the Roman poet Ovid (34 BCE–18 CE).
Kama Sutra. Ancient Sanskrit text on love, desire, and sexual practice.

library of the institute, which even in 1950 was rapidly catching up with—nay, overtaking—the fabled Vatican collection of pornography. At the present time, the institute's collection of erotica—literary and artistic—is much larger than that of the Vatican. And in this "Gorgeous Gallery of Gallant Inventions," this "Paradyse of Daintie Devices," the light-bringer to mankind, Dr. Prometheus (née Kinsey), turned me loose to ramble and enjoy and feast to surfeit. Each time I went to Bloomington, I saw a thousand new things I had not seen before.

"Turned me loose," however, is not quite an exact phrase. The security and the protection of the materials at the institute were intense. On the first tour Kinsey gave me, I noted that our progress was considerably slowed by the fact that each door had to be unlocked to enter and then relocked behind us. The interview material, contained in an elaborate mark-and-placement code which Kinsey had invented, was carefully guarded. The code itself took about a year to learn and had been submitted to the best cryptanalysts of the military—who all pronounced it unbreakable unless the secret of the positioning could be learned. To protect the material further, only about four persons knew the code; if they were to be together at the same time in, say, California, each had to take a different plane, so that the code would always survive an air disaster.

Kinsey and I had known each other about a year when he proposed an "arrangement" to me. He was extremely scrupulous about the confidentiality of his "subjects" and never set up assignations of any kind—but his interest in sadomasochism had reached a point of intolerable tension. He knew that I had experimented in that arena and he wanted to find out more. This was in 1949, long before the leather mania had codified and ritualized itself into leather-drag posturings, studied gestures, and codes of dress and behavior that Genet had partially described and analyzed earlier in *Querelle de Brest*.

He therefore asked me to fly down from Chicago, and from New York he invited a tall mean-looking sadist, Mike Miksche, with a crewcut and a great personality. Mike was a freelance artist, doing fashion layouts for Saks and other Fifth Avenue stores; and under the name of Steve Masters (S. M.), he produced many homosexual ink drawings for the growing s/m audience. We were to be filmed in an encounter.

this "Gorgeous Gallery of Gallant Inventions," this "Paradyse of Daintie Devices." Titles of two late sixteenth-century anthologies of undistinguished English poetry.
Mike Miksche. On his Stud File card documenting the encounter with Miksche, dated May 31 and June 1, 1952, Steward wrote, "Tall handsome sadist. Two pms [afternoons] of movies. Whoo!" "A great personality" is his sly reference to Miksche's sexual endowment.

It was quite an experience. For two afternoons at Bloomington, the camera whirred away. Kinsey prepared Mike by getting him half-drunk on gin — an advantage for him but a disadvantage for me, since I had stopped drinking and could no longer join him in his happy euphoria. While we were sitting under an apple tree in Kinsey's garden before the festivities began, the Imp of the Perverse made me look down at one of Miksche's stylish brown English riding boots (black had not yet become the leather boys' standard color) that had a bit of lacing at the instep. I plucked at one end of the lace and untied it, saying, "Humph—you don't look so tough to me."

That was a deliberate challenge, of course, for which I paid dearly again and again during the next two afternoons. Mike was quite a ham actor; every time he heard Bill Dellenback's camera start to turn, he renewed his vigor and youth like the green bay tree, and at the end of the second afternoon, I was exhausted, marked and marred, all muscles weakened. During the sessions, I was vaguely conscious of people dropping in now and then to observe, while Mrs. Kinsey—a true scientist to the end—sat by and once in a while calmly changed the sheets upon the workbench.

At the end of the last session, when my jaws were so tired and unhinged that I could scarcely close my mouth, let alone hold a cigarette between my lips, Mike got really angry and slapped me hard on each cheek, saying that I was the lousiest cocksucker he had ever seen. I could have killed him at that moment. I sprang from the bed and ran to the shower; he followed me, but I was still seething. Later that evening, Kinsey left Mike and me in separate parts of the library to do some reading; suddenly Mike appeared, wild-fire-eyed and excited—having stimulated himself with some typewritten s/m stories—and had his way with me on the cold cement floor of the library stacks.

When Kinsey heard of the encounter, he laughed and said, "I hope the blinds were closed."

Mike Miksche later bore out the theorizing of Theodore Reik, Wilhelm Stekel, and Kinsey himself that sadists were perhaps not as well balanced as masochists, for Mike—after attempting and failing to turn his directions

---

like the green bay tree. Psalm 37:35.

Theodore Reik (1888–1969). German psychoanalyst and student of Freud whose books include *Masochism in Modern Man* (1941).

Wilhelm Stekel (1868–1940). Austrian psychologist and student of Freud whose studies include *Sadism and Masochism: The Psychology of Hatred and Cruelty* (2 vols., 1929).

to heterosexuality by getting married—jumped into the Hudson River one winter day and committed suicide. His great talents as an artist and his good intellect were lost to the world too soon.

Kinsey delighted in trying small jests and tricks on me, whether to test me or just to amuse us both, I do not know. One sample will suffice.

By far the most sexually attractive person to me in the Kinsey entourage was Clyde Martin, the handsome young dark-haired statistician—happily married and unavailable. During one visit, Kinsey fixed things so that Clyde and I were left alone in the same room while he changed his shirt and gave me a good view of the polished marble of his arms and the well-defined plateau of his chest—while I looked and suffered and tapped my foot against the chair rung, a sure sign that a sexual thought was going through my head. But by then I was aware of Kinsey's sly and harmless trickery, so I made no suggestions to Clyde, which I knew would be met with amused tolerance but flat refusal.

Kinsey later asked how things went.

"Oh, all right," I said, absorbed in studying a fingernail. "Nice of you to leave us alone—but too bad that I had seen my favorite policeman just that morning and was not in the mood for anything more at the moment."

Kinsey knew that my discontent with the academic matrix was growing. When I finally told him of my decision to quit the ivied nursery—the kindergarten that took care of the children until they were able to earn a living as adults—and become a tattoo artist, he reacted with the only critical statement I ever heard him make.

"Oh my God no," he said. "I've never interviewed anyone who didn't say he wanted his tattoo off." And when he saw the tattoo cubicle in the Sportland Arcade, he said, "Oh, Sam—please be careful."

But after a month or two, his scientific curiosity began to assert itself. One day over dinner he said, "We really ought to take advantage of you."

"How so more than you already have?" I asked, sardonic.

"You are probably one of a half dozen literate tattoo artists in the country—if indeed that many. And we've noticed tattoos on hundreds of persons during the interviews. But they seem totally unable to tell us why they got them, and we don't have the time to probe as deeply as we would like."

"So . . . ?" I said.

"Why don't you keep a journal?—paying particular attention to the sexual motivations behind getting a tattoo. We would really appreciate some illumination on the subject. You haven't been exactly scientifically trained in observation, but you have a writer's eye for details, and you're pretty skillful when it comes to probing—as I've seen when you were working. So keep a journal for us, will you?"

I began the journal, then, in 1952 and kept it more or less faithfully until 1958. As its pages progressed, he grew more and more fascinated with what I was discovering and flattered me by saying that I had found information which had never appeared in print before. He suggested that eventually we might collaborate on an article or monograph about it, a project that would have flattered me greatly, but one which was ended by his early death in 1956. He decided during his interviewing of the inmates at San Quentin that a question about tattooing might be added to the general questionnaire—or he said it would be added, but whether or not it was, I never knew. The journal went on and on even after he died, until it became repetitious; then it was stopped at about a thousand pages, a half million words.

On several occasions, Kinsey visited my shop, more or less incognito, and on a number of busy Saturdays spent five or six hours there. He talked to the swabbies and others, asking loaded questions that seemed entirely innocent. At the end of one such session, when we had both learned a great deal from the answers, he said, "I think every social worker or psychologist ought to spend at least five full days in field work in a tattoo shop before he gets his degree."

Toward the end of his life, Kinsey changed. As sensitive as I was to semantics, having for years played with words in the classroom, I noticed first of all a change in his speaking habits. Before this, he had always used "we" and "us" when referring to the work and research of the institute; now it suddenly became "I" and "me." Puzzled, I said nothing. But the changes were more pronounced than those in his pronouns. He was now working so hard that the strain was telling on him and his heart; he kept flying back and forth to California, interviewing in all the prisons from San Quentin to Atascadero. And once when he came to visit my new apartment on a third floor, he came up the steps painfully and slowly. He paused at the last landing and looked up at me as I leaned over the banister.

"Oh Sam," he said, panting. "What have you done to me?"

<hr>

I began the journal . . . in 1952. Steward again antedates events in his narrative. The first entry in his typewritten "Journal of a Tattoo Artist" is dated March 22, 1954, and he continued it, for more than 950 pages, until April 1961 (Kinsey Steward Collection).

Atascadero. Maximum-security state hospital near San Luis Obispo for criminals judged mentally ill.

my new apartment. In 1956, Steward moved to an apartment at 4915 North Glenwood Avenue in Chicago.

There were other changes as well. He began to illustrate what Gertrude Stein had said of Saroyan: "He cannot stand the weight of being great." Formerly, Kinsey would listen to you, nodding, agreeing, or raising objections. Now his statements became authoritative, almost *ex cathedra* pronouncements. He no longer listened quietly; instead, he interrupted, issued dicta dogmatically, often turning impatient and snappish, sometimes arrogant, and even made cutting attacks on fellow scientists. He seemed no longer to care about the tolerance he had cherished for all of his life until then. Of course, at that time there were many serious pressures on him and the institute from political, financial, right-wing, and religious groups.

It was unfortunate, but one could really see the open and receptive mind closing down upon its grains of sand. To the end, he did remain, however, an extraordinary man, an overwhelming personality. Had he been less zealous and devoted to his work than he was, he might have lived much longer. He was killed by overwork and his unwillingness to slow down. Instead of his flights to California, he should have been resting.

But then, had he done so, he would not have been Dr. Kinsey.

If one really believed in an afterlife, it would be pleasant to consider Kinsey sitting with Socrates and Plato under the shade of an ilex tree discussing the *Phaedrus*, or asking Leonardo da Vinci about his golden youths, or Michelangelo about the models he used, or Whitman to tell the real truth about himself and Peter Doyle. Questioning and questing, he would have all eternity to roam in—and if he ever came to the end, he would still be unsatisfied.

Sources: *Chapters*, 95–106; Manuscript, 274–88.

Saroyan. William Saroyan (1908–81), novelist, short-story writer, playwright, friend of Gertrude Stein, and winner of the Pulitzer Prize for drama in 1940.

ex cathedra. A Latin phrase ("from the chair") referring to a doctrine defined by the Roman Catholic Church in 1870, according to which the pope's pronouncements when he invokes the authority of his office are infallible. In secular contexts, as here, the phrase is often used sarcastically to suggest unwarranted authority.

Phaedrus. Wide-ranging Platonic dialogue (370 BCE) in which Socrates and Phaedrus present three speeches on the nature of love that form the starting point for a discussion of the prerequisites for a true art of rhetoric.

Peter Doyle. See note on page 55.

Chapter Twelve

I, TATTOODLER

1954–65

Could I have seen at the beginning of my new "career" how much fun and pleasure and profit the next fifteen years would bring, I would have regretted not having become a tattoo artist twenty years before. The world that I had joined was a tough one, and I had to grow into its toughness. It was bound up inextricably with the life on the "street" — as its inhabitants called their Skid Row. There were drunks to deal with (once in their worst form — two drunken cops, waving their guns), panhandlers, and winos — the wandering walking zombies who sometimes vomited on the sidewalks during the night. But even during those first hard months, there was a kind of eagerness of anticipation inside me every time I came up from the subway at the Harrison Street stop; I felt (and this was curious and amazing) more at home, more alive, more that I belonged here than in the phony classrooms.

My friends and colleagues were deeply shocked; they could not understand my motivations. I tried to explain that I had grown to loathe teaching, that the students grew duller and more stupid year by year, and finally that the money was inadequate. Their response in nearly every case was, "But *tattooing!*" — as if it would have been nobler to clean urinals. How could I go on to tell them that I wanted freedom, that it was a grand new way to feast the eyes on male beauty, that one could now touch the skin which you could only look at in the classroom — the arms, the legs, the chest — and there would be no one to raise an eyebrow, and that you could even in the right instances take a young man to the cot in the back room?

Very early, I discovered how impossible it was to consider a tattoo on a person objectively. You see one, and immediately you associate it — and the wearer — with some area of your past experience, pleasant or unpleasant, sexual or antisocial. The mystique of the tattoo becomes as highly subjective a matter as one's personal idea of what constitutes beauty. You are turned either on or off according to your background and associations. Consequently, generalizations about tattoos are extremely dangerous and unreliable. Your reaction to a tattoo is established only by the fashion in which your own emotions and observations, your backgrounds and personality, are fused together.

In the journal I kept for Kinsey, I noted thirty-two motivations for getting tattooed, of which twenty-five were sexual in whole or part. Of these, by far the most heavily weighted reason for getting one was a simple assertion of masculine status. The tattoo allied a man with the tough, the real, the macho, the masculine; it represented the submerged and unspoken desires of a large part of the population. Early on, I made a sign for my shop which said, "Depressed? Downhearted? A good tattoo may make you feel like a man again." And nothing could confirm the truth of it more than the sailor's remark, as he looked down at the new anchor on his biceps: "Y'know, it makes me feel just a little bigger with that tattoo a-sittin' there on my arm." How male an ineffectual little pipsqueak could feel as he looked into the mirror at the new tattoo that first night and masturbated, certain that he was at last a Man!

Another large category was decoration, which might on the surface seem to be a nonsexual motive. But a little digging showed that below that reason usually lay a deeper one: to attract the opposite sex. It took two or three years for me to find out why so many young men had their first tattoo on the left biceps rather than the right. If it were on the left arm, that arm could be hung out the window while driving a car to impress the girls. Or boys. This category naturally overlapped into that of exhibitionism. People always seemed to want to show off their tattoos. If I happened to ask a prospective customer if he were already tattooed, there would rarely be a simple "yes" for an answer. The sleeves would be rolled up, the jacket removed, or the pants dropped to show what he had—in the way of tattoos, that is.

Perhaps the most intellectual of all motivations—and certainly one beyond the understanding of any of the customers who felt it—was that of an existential act, stemming from Sartre and Camus—an act completed in silence and alone, in anguish and despair, an act which once done is done forever. With some grim humor I used to say, when asked how long a tattoo would last, "They are guaranteed for life—and six months." Many times, I

the journal I kept for Kinsey. The carbon typescript of this journal is currently in the Kinsey Institute; as Steward notes below, the original was lost.
thirty-two motivations. Steward provides detailed analyses of twenty-nine motivations in *Bad Boys,* 46–80.

have seen a young man alone in the shop flex his muscles and look at his new tattoo and mutter something like, "By God, it's there for always." At such moments, you never reminded them that the tattoo *could* be removed by a skin graft (with resultant horrid scarring and a scar on the butt from which the cover skin was taken). And even if the tattoo were removed, the memory of their one free act, their "forever act," would always remain with them.

Recorder that I was, I kept a tally of persons who returned for a second tattoo, casually probing their reactions to the first one. I asked some questions in phrasings like, "Well, did you enjoy your first tattoo? Lotsa guys tell me they went out and got fucked, or got in a fight, or got drunk, or jacked off in front of a mirror. What did you do?" Many, of course, simply laughed and made no reply at all, but certain totals appeared after about five years: those who got laid, 1,724; got in a fight, 635; got drunk (over 800 of those of the first question also said they got drunk), 231; masturbated in front of a mirror, 879. Even after making allowances for braggadocio, the proportions between the figures were interesting.

It was a psychological challenge to find ways to take a customer's mind off the fear of being tattooed—a thing I accomplished by keeping up a running stream of nonsense while I was at work or putting one of their hands on a foam rubber falsie and telling them to close their eyes. But deeper down, I saw something else happening. A curious change would take place in many persons as soon as I stuck the needle into their arms. From being perhaps surly or frightened, they might suddenly relax and begin to unfold. With the needle working, I underwent a change in their eyes. It was never possible for me to understand this strange psychic alteration, but somehow for a little while I became for them wife, mother, best boyfriend, best girlfriend, priest, confessor, counsellor, and confidant. And sometimes, if conditions were right and we were more or less alone in the shop, I would hear tumbling forth from them details which I am sure they had never before told to a living human being. It was almost as if the tattoo needle contained scopolamine instead of pigment.

This freedom in talking, this unhindered revelation, was perhaps the single most astonishing thing that I observed during the long years of tattooing. And the "talkers" were really more numerous than the completely silent ones. The explanation for this release has always lain beyond me, and such voluntary and uninhibited confessions were rarely made, it seemed to

scopolamine. Antinausea drug whose possible side effects include uncontrolled talking.

me, in any other kind of encounter except perhaps between bartender and drunk—and even those were rationalizations. The "tattoo confession" was the purest kind of self-revelation, with all faults exposed and the blame put squarely where it belonged—on the young man himself. It was a strange and rewarding experience for me—sometimes jolting me as it left them cleansed and relieved.

I was in the small and dreadful shop for nearly two years after leaving the university. But I finally found another place to operate, across the street in what had once been a speakeasy that Al Capone had frequented, having been enamored of a bar maid. A tattoo buff named Fred Bartels—who was nearly covered with designs—not only helped me move but almost single-handedly constructed my new shop. He put up a false wall to separate the front workroom from the back of the long drafty building and made for me a tattoo table and stand, with drawers for the stencils and a rack for the needles with a sunken turntable of metal to hold the ink. In general, he was indispensable. Then almost as suddenly as he had come, he was gone—having transferred his allegiance to someone farther up the street. I never knew what I had done to offend him . . . if indeed anything. Tattoo buffs are an unpredictable lot.

The new shop was about four times the size of the cubicle in the old arcade. I painted the plywood walls black—and they ran into a peaked ceiling of near-black paneling, from the center point of which hung a five-lamp old bronze chandelier. Against the dark walls the "flash"—the designs on white illustration board—stood out in great contrast. Two feet from the wall opposite my corner working area was a heavy wooden bench with iron-pipe legs, stained brilliant dark red and varnished with many coats. I ordered a window neon sign with "Phil Sparrow" written in a half circle above a red rose with green leaves; for an outside sign, I had the word "Tattoo" in lavender neon and in one corner of the window a vertical flashing red neon with the word "Tattoo." As a window display, I designed six posters on illustration board showing various styles of tattooing, with small placards beneath explaining the types: American standard, enhancement of a good body, a single tattoo on the chest, patchwork or crazy-quilt (a bad type), Oriental design, and French underworld.

another place to operate. Steward's new shop, which he occupied until 1963, was located at 655 South State Street. The entire east side of the 600 block is now a parking lot.
"Phil Sparrow." Lettering on the shop's door identified it as "Phil's Tattoo Joynt."

My sad experience with the navy had not changed my feelings for the uniform which—as Genet said of the French navy—seemed designed more to decorate the coast of France than to defend it. And so the dark blues of the swabbies sailed into my shop and let me feast my eyes while I went about my work. Most uniforms made the bodies beneath them more exciting, and for me the sailor's at that time topped the list. Was the beguiling quality caused mostly by the cut, sometimes so close to the body that it added a strange and sexual darkness to the shape beneath it? Or was there more—a kind of psychic pull which did not exist in the case of every uniform? How could a mailman's grey or a bus driver's brown seem glamorous or enhance its wearer? Finally, I decided that the navy uniform was exciting because it represented a way of life that was closed to most of us. The sailor knew far suns and seas, the bamboo huts of savages, the stone lacework of Indian castles, crystal pools and sands in Persia, white columns against dark blue Greek skies, the golden suns and fountains of red-walled Rome. And then—when he took us in his strong young arms, we felt that beneath the rough wool there beat a heart more brave and gallant than any we had ever known, that his thighs had felt the caresses of mermaids beneath the sea and his lips had tasted the brown sweet flavor of Arabian throats.

Well, that was romantic old me when I started tattooing. Ask me what I thought after ten years and fifty thousand boot sailors—fuzzy-cheeked, bezitzed, talking big, and stone broke.

But the stories! The swabbies brought with them hundreds of tales. Life was a continuing drama, with the kind of excitement one usually saw in France, where everyone went around mildly stewed all the time. I treasure thousands of memories—amused at the young "boot" sailors who came to Chicago on their first liberty with twenty dollars—their "flying twenty" they called it—expecting not only to pay their rail fare to and from Great Lakes out of that but to have a big steak dinner, get drunk, have a woman, and be tattooed. Needless to say, for about ninety-five percent of them, that first liberty was a flop.

Not all of the clientele was navy. Early on, the city boys found me, particularly the gang members—for gangs were very popular in the 1950s. And of course, those who came to be tattooed were more often than not of the work-

as Genet said. In *Querelle de Brest* (Paris: Gallimard, 1953), 197.

The sailor knew far suns and seas. In *Chapters,* Steward presents a similar version of this sentence as part of an anonymous letter received from someone who had observed him tattooing sailors in his shop (80–81).

"boot" sailors. Sailors who had recently completed boot camp.

ing classes—lower middle, or upper lower, if such things can exist in our nonstratified society. They had more of the terrible blinding beauty which the human form can at its best produce than did the bespectacled children of the university that I had left. Here were the clean-shaven tall and long-limbed Poles, the darkly glowing Italians—either the white-skin type or the swarthy, with body hair arranging itself neatly in natural patterns and silky on the wrists and backs of hands. In the ethnic stew of Chicago there were all of the European races, and I came to know them all.

Naturally, not all of them were handsome. I saw the dregs as well—kids with ichthyosis, or fish-skin, eczema, acne-deformed. But it was the personalities and persons of the gang members that I found most interesting, and gradually a kind of half-baked theory evolved from my years of contact with them. Obviously there was a war on, an unending battle between the generations. A tattoo for the gang members or the delinquents was the visible sign of either their rebellion, their manliness, or their affiliation with the stratum that was in revolt. I had to pretend to be one of them, an "older delinquent"; and since it was I who gave them the visible sign of their revolt and performed a function of which their parents (the "enemy") disapproved, they accepted me as one of them.

Haunted always by my literary past, I could not help remarking the similarity between the conduct code of these gang members and the code of chivalry. There was the same ritual search for members in both codes, who—once found—had to undergo ritual probation and initiation. Then there followed the ritual sortie—to find the Holy Grail, or to overcome the "enemy adult" today. The gang members proved their mettle by burglary, "rumbles," vandalism, drinking large amounts of liquor quickly, theft, violence, sexual exploits, even murder, but those things did not essentially set them apart from the knights of King Arthur's day. The nature of the goals differed; the aiming was the same.

In all the years of tattooing, possibly the most frequently asked question I heard was "Does it hurt?" followed by "Have you ever tattooed anyone's cock?"

There are only two professions in the world in which one man can hold another's genitalia in his hand and not be considered queer. One is that of physician; the other, tattoo artist. A conservative estimate of the number of times I put tattoos on cocks is about five hundred. When you consider that in the years of tattooing, I put on about 150,000 tattoos (quite a few acres of skin), five hundred amounts to about only one-third of one percent.

You could easily tell when someone wanted a tattoo on his cock. There was a lot of hemming and hawing and much sidling about the room, until finally the customer would come out with a question about whether I would tattoo "any place" on the body.

A small sailor asked me that question in the second week of my "career," and I was almost as nervous as he was, for I sensed what he meant. Then he said he would like to have a small heart at the base of his penis with a ring going clear around it, so that it would look like a finger ring set with a heart-shaped stone.

"What do you want with a design like that?" I asked, curious.

He almost giggled. "So that I'll always have a heart-on," he said.

I set about the preparation of his penis, having closed the shop and set up a screen. The penis is usually flaccid (unless you have a real masochist to deal with) because the client is frightened nearly out of his wits. He need not be. When the penis is soft, the sensitivity of it is much diminished, save for the glans. And most of the cock tattoos were on the shaft, which has a quality of flesh quite different from that of the glans. The corpus cavernosum is not overly sensitive, nor does it bleed as much as the glans—which produces such a gush that the pigments are washed away, and the design has to be gone over several times.

The sailor who wanted the ring was nervous, and so was I. In order to tattoo the penis, one has to grasp it tightly on the sides with thumb and second finger, pulling down with them while pushing up on the urethral canal with the index finger; the skin must be taut, or the needle will not penetrate. I was quite as surprised as the sailor to see the reaction of the penis when the needle approached. It almost turned to jelly; it was endowed with a life of its own, seemingly—much to our astonishment. As the needle drew near, the organ jumped first one way and then the other, shrinking and trying to draw back into the belly in completely involuntary and uncontrollable movements.

On many other occasions, however, the organ remained hard, suggesting that the customer was either a crypto-masochist or a fully developed one. Many times, ejaculations occurred while work was in progress, even on an arm or a shoulder.

On the penises I have tattooed, I have put many different designs, some of them amusing—such as the boy who wanted a thermometer on his, with red fluid showing in the tube "so's I can take the temperature of the holes

corpus cavernosum. One of the two masses of spongy tissue in the penis that fill with blood to produce an erection.

I go into." One penis was colored entirely green; another was scaled green to look like a snake, with mouth, eyes, and fangs on the head—which was itself colored red and yellow. The most common cock design was a small fly or a small fish for "those who can't eat meat on Friday" before the Catholic Church changed its rules.

One of the most fascinating penile tattoos was done on a sailor who wanted the two words "Your" and "Name" on the shaft. Later he returned to tell me why. "I ain't bought a drink in a bar since you did that," he said, and described his *modus operandi*. "What I do, see, is go in a bar and sit down beside some guy who's about half smashed, and then after a coupla minutes I say to him, 'Say, I betcha I got your name tattooed on my cock,' and that allus jolts him and he says, 'Like hell—we just met,' and I go on sayin' I betcha and finally he bets five bucks and we go back to the head and I shows him, and sure enough there it says 'Your Name,' and I got five bucks to drink on." He looked thoughtful a moment and sighed. "Trouble is," he said, "I'm runnin' outa bars. I can't do it but oncet in one place."

In the early part of my experience with tattooing, before the leather movement began in the middle 1950s, there were very few homosexuals getting tattooed. I kept a running count of the overt or obvious ones who got a tattoo in those first years, with some interesting results: out of the first fifty thousand tattoos, only forty-three were put on recognized homosexuals. This led to a great deal of head-shaking between Kinsey and myself and to a conclusion that narcissism played a large part in one's decision about a tattoo. Since narcissism is one of the important elements of homosexuality, it might follow that many homosexuals did not want to spoil their pretty pink bodies with a tattoo, being satisfied with themselves as they were. Lines of questioning revealed their reasons for disinclination: One said, "I can't imagine myself being permanently satisfied with one design—I'd be wanting to change it after a little while." Another was sure he couldn't stand the pain, and a young Chicago elegant said, "Really, m'dear, it's too low-class for words. I couldn't stoop that low." (Just for the record, he turned out to be a coprophage, but that doesn't matter.) Still another in a Brooks Brothers suit said that he had always rejected frills and decorations—in his clothes and his life in general—and therefore naturally he disapproved of such fripperies as tat-

before the Catholic Church changed its rules. In 1966, the Catholic Church dropped the long-standing requirement that Catholics abstain from eating meat on Fridays.

toos. And finally, one perceptive person said that he was afraid of the revelation a tattoo might make of his sexual inclinations.

Beginning about 1954 or 1955, the so-called leather movement began, a more or less serious pastime which quickly created a conduct code and a set of ritualised behavior patterns (and a specialised dress—the all-leather costume drag) which has persisted until the present. I had been experimenting with s/m in the 1940s and was nearly done with it when its great popularity began. In those early days, it was extremely dangerous, for if you followed the heady scent of a leather jacket on a brawny truck driver during a drizzling night and took him home, you were never certain that you might be alive the next day. Limits on the s/m encounter had not yet reached the point of mutual agreement between the parties.

The s/m boys, however, started to appear in the shop—and with them, the small percentage of homosexuals getting tattooed increased rapidly. Most of the tattoos on the s/m crowd were masculine symbols—tigers, panthers, daggers entwined with snakes. Things grew so confused I had to abandon my separate tally of the homosexual customers. Unfortunately for the image of the homosexual, those of that persuasion who got tattooed were usually more vocal (unless they were true masochists), reacting to the small needle pain more violently than did the heterosexual customers.

Of the many homosexuals who fooled me for a while, there was Ed, a sailor from Great Lakes Naval Training Station. Because of some defect in his skin or because of the laundry he had to do as a "boot" (thus wetting the tattoo too much while it was healing), the first coloring of his rose did not take well. He came back to have it recolored. Then he disappeared for four years during his navy hitch. When he returned just before his discharge, he had a great many tattoos. He came in the last time with a buddy of his, and in a double scroll under a flower he asked for the names Ed and Chuck. They had successfully been lovers in the navy for four years without having been discovered. Ed proudly showed me the decorations on his cock which he had got in the Orient—a small "6" and "9" on the underside of the glans, separated by the frenum, a delicate octopus on the ventral side of the shaft and several other tiny designs.

A young Polish homosexual aged about nineteen brought in a curious design for his arm. It was an outline drawing of two men kissing, but their profiles had melted into each other so that the nose of each was in the cen-

I had been experimenting with s/m. Steward understates both the intensity and the duration of his interest in sadomasochistic sexual encounters.

ter of the other's head. At first I objected, saying that he was advertising his preference and might someday regret it. "What would your mother say?" I asked. "She'd know at once you were gay."

"Oh, she already knows," he said. "She don't care. Matter of fact, she said that my goin' out with boys saved her a lotta money and was cheaper'n givin' me the bread to take girls out."

There were other examples of advertising, some subtle, some direct. On the buns of one young man I once printed "Screw" on the left side and "Me" on the right, with appropriate arrows. On another I put a rose tree, the idea having come to this particular hustler from a fake photograph he had seen: the rose tree began in the cleft of the ass near the anus, branched out onto the gluteus, and gracefully wandered up the spine with flowers here and there, branching finally into two divisions at the shoulders, each ending high on the peak of a deltoid. It was a charming *divertissement* for those who screwed him.

Another hustler "model" who operated in northern California had a snake's head about an inch below his navel, with the body of the snake curling down and under his scrotum and the tail coming up the other side. He later said that he was glad he got it because "no one ever forgets me once they see that design." Tattoos do have their place in the business world.

Tattooing, although it flourishes during depressions and wars, has always had America's basic puritanism ranged against it. It has been considered faintly evil, criminal, and nasty. Right Wingers and Little Old Ladies denounce it, seeing it as the *cause* of criminal behavior or believing it to be prohibited by religion (it is in orthodox Judaism, but only there). They are incapable of realizing that if convicts and murderers happen to have tattoos, the damage was done before the tattoo was applied. A tattoo does not turn a man into a criminal any more than it turns him into a saint. But for the puritans of the world, tattooing is strange, dark, and evil, a mysterious subculture, and should therefore be outlawed.

It is, of course, no such thing. But the aura of mystery remains. Tattooing is merely the last of the unchanged folk arts, a highly lucrative calling for the exceptionally skillful practitioners, and the most superb substitute for cruising that ever has been invented. If you become a tattoo artist, you will never have to go searching into the bars or the baths again, for then you will find, as I did, that . . . all the beauties will come looking for you.

The fascination of my discoveries in the wilderness of motives for getting a tattoo lasted for the first four or five years and then began gradually to diminish. Kinsey died in 1956, but I continued the journal until 1958. Toward the end, it turned largely into a mere sexual diary, a record of my own exploits in the shop, and was then abandoned for lack of interest. My own copy of the journal was inadvertently destroyed a few years ago, but Kinsey's copy is safe in the archives of the Institute for Sex Research.

About 1958, I became acquainted with the members of a photographic studio in Chicago—several more or less talented people living under a kind of communal arrangement directed by a balding popeyed galoot with no conscience whatever—the truest case of "anomie," complete lack of morality and scruples, that I had ever known. In those veiled and shadowed days before the great relaxing of censorship that came in 1966, no pornography was permissible, so this studio photographed handsome young men—weightlifters, athletes, hustlers—in posing straps and sold the pictures in sets to a clientele of homosexuals numbered in the thousands.

This entrepreneur saw—from the visits to my shop—that there was money to be had in such an enterprise as mine and got me into a kind of arrangement with him, whereby I would steer extremely handsome customers of mine to his studio to be photographed, and he in turn would send me the cream of the crop of hustlers whose pictures he had taken.

The one member of his household who showed a great interest in tattooing was a handsome well-made young man who had studied fine arts and had a degree from Indiana University. His name was Cliff Ingram, and I gave him several tattoos. And then the bug bit him: he decided that he wanted to become a tattoo artist himself. By stages he changed his name, discovering that *Ingram* really came from the Anglo-Saxon "hraefn," which meant "raven," and

continued the journal until 1958. See note on Steward's chronology, page 198. The Kinsey Institute also possesses Steward's journals of the summers of 1953 and 1954 in San Francisco, an additional 144 pages (Kinsey Steward Collection, Box 1, Series 2).

a balding popeyed galoot. Chuck Renslow (1929–2017), photographer and founder of the Kris Studios in 1950 (on which the aging Steward relied for hustlers); of the first gay leather bar, the Gold Coast in Chicago, in 1958; of the International Mr. Leather competition in 1979; and of the Leather Archives and Museum in Chicago in 1991. Steward was sexually attracted to Renslow, who was twenty years younger and did not reciprocate. Their falling out is indicated by the way Steward depicts Renslow here and by his deliberate refusal to mention him by name (in chapter 15, Steward pretends to have forgotten his name). See Spring, 266–70ff.; and Tracy Baim and Owen Keenan, *Leatherman: The Legend of Chuck Renslow* (Chicago: Prairie Avenue Productions, 2011), 71–82.

relaxing of censorship. In *Memoirs v. Massachusetts*, the Supreme Court in 1966 held that to be judged obscene, a work must be shown to have no social or artistic value whatsoever—a test that narrowed the definition of obscenity established in 1957 by *Roth v. United States*.

that *Ing* was a Germanic sea god, and *ramm* Old High German for "raven." Thus several possibilities gave him more reason to use the bird name than I had to use the name of Sparrow. So he became Cliff Raven — tattooing here and there and even setting up a weekend shop in Rantoul, Illinois, near the Chanute Field Air Base. Cliff and I became very good friends, so much so that during several Christmas seasons when I was making my annual visits to Paris to see Alice Toklas, I left him or his friend in charge.

Every year there were rumors about the Illinois legislature changing the age limit for tattooing, and one could hardly blame them. The jaggers up the street — those old carny winos and drunks — paid little or no attention to the law saying that eighteen was the minimum age and consequently were tattooing kids down to thirteen and fourteen. And mothers everywhere were screaming. Since I was the only tattoo artist who was listed in the yellow pages of the phone book, I got all the calls and complaints — and spent a good deal of my time trying to convince irate parents that I hadn't tattooed little Johnny on the ass.

New York City had closed its tattoo shops in October 1961 because of an outbreak of hepatitis, although the blame was never flatly put on the tattoo artists (there was also a question of oysters spawning in polluted sewage waters on the east coast). And the winds of change began to be felt in Illinois, with the result that in 1963, a law was passed forbidding the tattooing of anyone under twenty-one years of age. Both Cliff and I found it very amusing that the tattoo law followed by a full year the Illinois law removing penalties for homosexual contacts with persons over eighteen; you could screw them at eighteen, we said, but you couldn't tattoo 'em. Logic was never a large part of any collective legislative brain.

I closed my shop when the law went into effect, and for the years 1963 and 1964, Cliff and I went on weekends to Milwaukee to tattoo. This created a somewhat delicate situation with the Old Master Dietzel, my mentor and teacher — but he seemed not to mind. His reputation was firmly estab-

---

Cliff Raven (1932–2001). Graphic artist turned tattoo artist who popularized the Japanese style of tattooing in Chicago and later in his legendary tattoo studio in Los Angeles.

the Illinois law removing penalties for homosexual contacts. In 1962, Illinois became the first state in the nation to decriminalize consensual oral-genital and anal sex.

I closed my shop. Because Steward's primary clientele had always been eighteen-year-old naval recruits completing their basic training at the nearby Great Lakes Naval Training Station, the city's new age restriction on tattooing had the effect of instantly decimating his business.

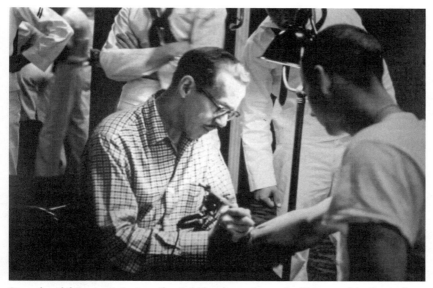

Steward as Phil Sparrow tattooing sailors in Milwaukee, 1963 or 1964. (Courtesy of the Estate of Samuel M. Steward)

lished, and all Cliff and I got was the overflow of sailors, but there seemed to be enough to put money in everyone's pockets. Our shop there was in a mirrored room that had formerly been a barbershop in a hotel on Third Street.

And then that hotel was torn down to make room for a parking lot. We had to vacate the barbershop for the last three weeks of our lease, and those were spent in perhaps the most elegant tattoo shop ever — a great fifty-foot long conference roost on the mezzanine floor of the same hotel, deeply carpeted, furnished with rich leather lounge chairs, mirrored around the wall. The sailors who came to us there were open-mouthed with astonishment when they first entered — and they came in great numbers for the final weeks of our Milwaukee period in the early months of 1964.

Once more I was at loose ends — ruined by parking lots for automobiles. My restlessness now seemed to be centered in Chicago. I had come to despise its cruel winters and its equally heartless summers — too cold by far, too hot and muggy. Most of my old friends in Chicago were no longer there, and Emmy Curtis had died in 1962 in a nursing home. The photographic studio had sucked me dry of ideas — for stories, drawings, tattoo designs, and all else — and had opened a tattoo joint as an adjunct on the very day after I closed my shop in Chicago.

It was perhaps time once more after this long interval to rise and twitch my mantle blue. Alice Toklas was still alive but very feeble, and on one of my last visits to see her I began to consider the possibility of a shop in Paris. Preliminary investigations had revealed there was no tattoo artist in all France; and French law would have permitted me as a foreigner to work there, since the law stated "as long as the profession is not overcrowded." I had met Jacques Delarue, who was the author of a book on self-applied underworld tattooing in prison, and he was helpful and encouraging.

But on one of those trips to case the town and its locations, I suddenly became aware of a drawback—a barrier so insurmountable that it could not be conquered. Although I knew French and could speak it very well, I had never mastered the argot of the city—the special language of the underworld and lower classes which many Parisians themselves did not know, and as I wandered in Montmartre and listened to the speech of Pigalle and the "milieu," I knew that I was not prepared. Either I would have to become a master of argot, or I would need someone in my shop who was familiar with it and who could be a kind of security guard. For I was not being merely paranoid in imagining that I would be easy prey to someone with a knife who wanted to rob me. Furthermore, I realized that I would not be able to understand a conference between two thugs who suggested my quick demise. Such things often happened in the City of Light.

Reluctantly I gave up the idea of Paris. And where else to go?

Well, I had spent several summers in San Francisco—and that was a sailor's town, wasn't it?

I went to Paris to see Alice Toklas during the Christmas season of 1964 and then early in 1965 went on to California, to San Francisco, to case the area with regard to opening another tattoo joynt and also to find a place to live.

Wandering around the Tenderloin in San Francisco one chilly evening in February, I ran into a former Chicago acquaintance, a small plumpish person named James Klaja, who had emigrated to the Golden State a few years before. During that first meeting, he babbled ceaselessly about how his study of

---

rise and twitch my mantle blue. Steward also cited this line from the pastoral elegy *Lycidas* (1638), by John Milton (1608–74), on his last day of teaching (see chapter 10).

Jacques Delarue (1919–2014). Historian, member of the French national police, and author (with Robert Giraud and Robert Doisneau) of the classic book on underworld tattooing, *Les Tatouages du "Milieu"* (Paris: La Roulotte, 1950).

Pigalle. Legendary red-light district in Paris.

Zen had made him walk on Eddy Street that evening, telling him something was about to happen, etc., etc., in the best nutty California fashion. He was living in Berkeley and invited me to his house for dinner.

The next evening, I found my way with great difficulty to Berkeley and at dusk arrived at Klaja's small house, built in someone's backyard, a house-behind-a-house, a "cottage" in northern California terminology. It was a nice dinner—squab, wild rice, kumquats, a good salad. During the course of the meal, he said that he was leaving for Europe in March, to stay a year and a half.

"What will happen to your house?" I asked.

"I dunno." He shrugged. "They'll rent it. I suppose."

I was galvanized. "*I'll* rent it," I said. And I went immediately to the front house and spoke to a very fat person named Eva and her ancient father. I rented the house and would arrive in mid-April.

Back in Chicago, I packed all my books and household furnishings—a great task, and one which with its tensions started me to smoking again, after I had been off the weed for a year and a half. So, feeling like a pioneer, I arrived in California—where I knew no one except Klaja and a nutty motorcycle-ridin' fifty-year-old travel agent named Milt Holtz. And when I saw the neighborhood of my new location in daylight, I discovered that it was smack in the middle of a black ghetto.

Oh, well, I thought—a man can be happy any place. And stayed right where I had landed.

Sources: *Chapters*, 78–94; Manuscript, 259–73, 289–303, 340–41.

Chapter Thirteen

FAREWELL, MY LOVELIES

1948–65

When I left Chicago for California, I found the roots that had to be pulled up had gone very deep. It was not possible to leave the lovely dirty old city without taking note of some of the bodies I remembered best of all. Each of them answered some demand of my being or one of my different selves.

I was in no sense a case of multiple personalities—like the three faces of Eve or the extraordinary young man with some ten or twelve differing selves. But—although the simile is not a good one, nor very imaginative—I did in a sense have an old artichoke heart, and the various pen names I used in the things I wrote, my Sparrow name as a tattoo artist and later the Andros name as a writer, were like the separate leaves that are capable of being stripped away. But what was at the center? The tough and dangerous inedible strings or the soft and delicate "heart" at the very bottom? Or perhaps there was nothing at all there, under any name whatsoever.

As the years went on, I passed into the land where Everyman must eventually go, that of the older human being. The carefree life of one's prime and the ease with which romantic encounters had been so carelessly and happily made—those things vanished so slowly that one was scarcely aware they were diminishing. But go they did, leaving a kind of bittersweet afterglow, a flickering tapestry of golden memories, from which now and again one arose with nostalgia and a barren pleasure.

No question: one had to begin to purchase, or do without—and here again in Chicago, the studio which had pimped for me helped enormously.

three faces of Eve. Title of a 1957 film starring Joanne Woodward (1930–) as a woman with dissociative identity disorder, directed by Nunnally Johnson.
the studio which had pimped for me. Chuck Renslow's Kris Studios (see note on page 211).

They sent me many young men who answered my needs, and the affection that developed in me for a few of them rounded out the picture of my desires—from sleek and compact Latin to blond and stalwart Nordic. Each of them fulfilled a fantasy of mine, and I am grateful to them all.

There was Guido—a dark and brooding Italian with the sullen moods and romantic charm of a Latin Heathcliff, and no thundercloud shot of the young Olivier against the storm-sky of *Wuthering Heights* ever surpassed Guido in beauty and passion. At twenty years of age he was still engaged in the perfection of his small body; he exercised and lifted weights, and his small frame carried a classic musculature which I had seldom encountered before.

I came as close to falling for him completely (in limerence, to use the new term for lovesickness) as I had ever done with anyone and for somewhat over four years saw him at least once a week and sometimes more. When it came to a tally of the money spent on him—down payments on cars, reduction of debts—I was startled. Yet why not? The money was flowing into the tattoo shop in a golden stream, and it might as well have been spent on Guido as on anything or anyone else.

In a story about Guido, "Jungle Cat," I said what I had always believed—that the body of a man was the most beautiful creation in the world and that every sculptor since the beginning had praised it above the female form. And Guido's body was perfect. In movement or repose it was as flawless as a Chinese poem, a sonnet by Keats, a concerto by Mozart. When he was active, moving his arms or legs, his muscles flickered into excited life. To see him pick up a book and watch the counterpoint of his muscles turning against each other was like listening to a harp arpeggio; to see him bend to tie a shoelace was better than Beethoven. In repose, with a forearm flung across his eyes, the side muscles running above his ribs looked like the two hands of a jealous lover clutching him from behind; and the black curls of his armpits were more entrancing than the head of Medusa. His long slim brown fingers repeated in miniature the beauty of his body, exquisite as a carving in topaz.

Olivier. Laurence Olivier (1907–89) played Heathcliff in the famous 1939 film adaptation of the novel, directed by William Wyler.

in limerence, to use the new term. The word was reportedly used in writing for the first time in 1977, the year before Steward wrote (*OED*).

the money spent on him. On his Stud File card titled "Payments to Hustlers," Steward recorded "ap. $3000" paid to Guido for 157 encounters between 1960 and 1964.

"Jungle Cat." *Der Kreis*, June 1962, 29–39, published under the name Ward Stames (see chapter 15).

Medusa. In Greek myth, a monster with writhing snakes on her head in place of hair.

His feet were high-arched and perfect, his skin clear and unblemished and tawny with the residue of the Mediterranean sun. The eyelashes hardly belonged to a man's face; they were long and black, and beneath them, intense dark eyes looked out. The eyebrows grew in a straight black line clear across the bridge of his nose, dipping slightly downward in the middle — calm, but with mobility in them. At moments, one end would shoot upward like a startled bird from cover, extraordinarily expressive. Guido was all youth and firmness and silk, and he turned the shabby old back room of my shop into a place where we were alone on the isles beneath the wind with the warm dark night around us and the ice-cold moon above.

Yah — facile, romantic! I was never in love, perhaps because I preferred a multifold experience rather than a long commitment to a single idealized love object. But I came close to the edge of danger with Guido. Had I the capacity for love, or was I intended to be a solitary with such poverty of spirit that I could never enlarge myself to take in another? Was I too much an egoist? The most dangerous of all egoists is the one skilled in what seems to be self-effacement, one whose outer kindness and gentleness really mask a complete and total centering on self, with a thorough indifference to others.

So — Guido nearly tore down the granite wall. John Donne said, in a well-known passage from which Hemingway chose a title, that no man was an island, entire in himself, that we are all a part of the whole, and that no one should ever send to ask for whom the bell tolls, since "it tolls for thee." This is all wrong. It is obvious today that each man is an island, eternally sealed away from his fellows, whose mind-workings — even the simplest — he can never know. And no matter how much in love, in limerence, Everyman remains isolated and alone. Let us change, then, the last part of Donne's quotation to "And therefore, baby, don't bother to send to learn for whom the bell tolls; as long as thou canst hear it ringing, you'll know it's *not* for thee."

And perhaps my ghetto wall crumbled a little more with Friedrich — Guido's extreme opposite. Here was the great-thewed bridegroom — blond, Nordic, Austrian, blue-eyed, a weightlifter and once a Mr. Illinois, perhaps the single most photographed "model" of the 1950s and '60s. Seeing him, one would hardly think he was a male prostitute, a hustler — tall, with corn-silk hair and innocence on his forehead. His chest was tremendous, bulging — to think of it limited and contained by the frail fabric of a white cotton T-shirt

John Donne (1572–1631). English poet, essayist, and cleric. The "well-known passage" is found in "Meditation XVII" in his *Devotions upon Emergent Occasions* (1623).
from which Hemingway chose a title. For Whom the Bell Tolls (1940).

gave you a feeling of unreality. His upper arms were as brawny as those of Hercules; he was bursting with health and blond godliness. In summer his tan was red-gold deep and the charm of his body's radiance as blinding as an electric arc. In the gym he frequented, all the small types veered toward him as if he were the true magnetic north—but he avoided them all. What seemed to be arrogance and stiffness in his nature was really shyness, perhaps a basic insecurity, for he was not very well educated. But he had the disease of beauty, which in its progression rots the soul and destroys the will. Something happens to innocence when—as you walk unclothed on the beach, or clothed on the street—you know that every third person, male or female, would like to go to bed with you.

It was not unreasonable to assume that occasionally Apollo or Hercules, tiring of their loves on Olympus, would now and then come to earth again and momentarily assume a human form to make love to us poor mortals. And having sex with a god is quite a jolt to one's universe; it takes some little time thereafter for the nebulae to stop their spiral whirling and for the stars to settle down into their familiar and accustomed constellations.

This young god (masquerading this time as a send-over from the pimping service) had arisen one afternoon from the bed—and as my sight gradually returned, I watched him standing in front of my full-length mirror, idly flexing his great muscles, treating me to a view of the tanned and incredible landscape of his back, his torso, those great-columned legs lighted with the soft luminance of the golden hairs that covered them. I watched the poetry of his movements as muscle answered muscle, springing into indolent or rapid life as he ordered his body to do his bidding. His profile was godlike as he tilted his chin upward, and godlike the full-face front as his eyes, half-smiling, looked at me from under the sweep of his golden hair, bleached by the summer sun until the end points seemed tipped with silver. His massive tawny shoulders tapered down the wonderful terrain of his torso to the slender waist, ending in the smoky gold of the softly curling hair.

So he posed and moved, and posed again. How had it happened that he should have liked and trusted me? True, I had put forth a great effort to understand him. I talked to him only about himself and his golden-brown body and arranged mirrors so that he could see himself in action (for I knew there were no mirrors on Olympus—and moreover, I quickly recognized his narcissism) and was generous with his fees. And while he posed, I pulled forth from the caverns of my mind the symphonies he did not hear and read the poems he could not see. Then I thought of the right thing, the best comparison to make (although I had said it before to others and had only half meant it), and I said, "You remind me of some young god who has just stepped down from the frieze on the Parthenon."

The blue eyes, and the blank blank look as the synapses failed once again to connect. "Whatdyuhmean—the freeze on the parking lot?"

Ah well, there, Freddie (more "American," he thought, than Friedrich), who cares about the Parthenon or the parking lot? After I left for California, he became a Chicago cop, I heard, and in moments of musing, I wondered just how he managed to handle the scene, where daily he might have met or been recognized by his previous "scores." Would he scowl and pass by, swinging his nightstick, never acknowledging a murmured greeting of any kind? Or would he have sought out his former clients and perhaps suggested a bit of blackmail, despite the "legality" of things in Illinois? What did the police chief say about all those poses of his in tiny cache-sexes, those profiled bulges behind wet thin cloth? Or did he know? And what did Friedrich's erstwhile scores say of him? Perhaps they blackmailed *him*, thus feathering their caps by saying they had had a cop in full uniform.

And moving on . . . there was thirty-two-year-old Roy Robinson, toothless, a bum, a hanger-on in the tattoo shop, con man, thief (he burglarized my place three times and was always stealing whatever he could make away with to pawn). But he had a very skilled and useful mouth and furnished me with an extraordinary sensation—for a price, although I never touched him sexually. Roy was continually having wife trouble of one sort or another; whether she knew of the services his toothless gums performed for several, I never learned. But one chilly autumn night in Chicago he jumped into the cold water of Lake Michigan, and that was the end of Roy—as mixed-up a person as I had ever known, and perhaps the most dishonest, truly afflicted with anomie—no moral sense, no obligations, no loyalties, one who, as a current saying had it, would have sold the blood in his mother's veins for a buck. In ten years of knowing him, I was never able to trust him. Yet there was something that made you like him while you pitied him—and he was

---

frieze on the Parthenon. Famous marble frieze depicting a procession of citizens, removed from the fifth-century BCE temple on the acropolis of Athens in the eighteenth century and currently displayed in the British Museum.

the "legality" of things in Illinois. In 1962, Illinois had become the first state to decriminalize consensual anal and oral sex.

cache-sexes. A small cloth or garment worn to cover the genitals.

Roy Robinson. Steward's Stud File card documents 227 encounters with Robinson between 1957 and 1964.

helpful in many ways around the shop, cleaning and sweeping and mop-
ping.

And farewell, too, to my skinny aesthetic friend Reggie, who hated his last
name so much because of its easy confusion with that of John Dillinger (shot
by the FBI outside the Biograph Theatre in Chicago) that he dropped it and
used his middle name thereafter. Reggie was a ballet dancer, not a very good
one—but acting on my advice, he began to study Labanotation very early
in the game and became an authority on it. If you needed oral gratification,
Reggie had just what was satisfying to work on, being excessively equipped;
but having pleasured himself, he could never bring happiness to his partner,
which led to our eventual parting. Reggie was exceedingly effeminate, but
sometimes one could put up with swish if Nellie had something everyone
wanted. And Reggie did.

Wandering in these pleasant forests and preserves of a highly selective
memory brings me to a trio—for you could not know one without knowing all. The one I knew especially was Larry, who had two identical-triplet
brothers, Louie and Lester. In 1963 they were all eighteen, and that was the
year that Larry—hearing from a benchmate in the factory where he worked
that I had to do with hustlers—got my name and address. And so one evening, a gawky six-foot-two adolescent came to see me, knowing nothing
about anything. When he left, putting on his windbreaker, there dropped to
the floor a lightweight imitation meat cleaver about four inches long with
handle, weighing perhaps three ounces. I burst out laughing.

"To protect yourself?" I finally managed, and he nodded and escaped.

I still know Larry, now in his mid-thirties, and Louie and Lester too;
they were all three naked one night in my apartment, to my great confusion, and they all had a thin white line across their bellies where they had
been cramped together before birth—or as Larry explained it, "There wasn't
womb for all three." The father vanished on seeing the trio pop out, and the
mother in great dismay consigned them for high school to Boys Town, from

John Dillinger (1903–34). Notorious gangster and bank robber who was shot and killed by
federal agents in July 1934.
Labanotation. A system of symbolic notation to designate movements in dance.
I still know Larry. The Stud File card for Larry documents 141 encounters between 1964
and 1972. He remained in contact with Steward, who became the godfather of his son, and
at Steward's death he wrote that he felt "a large hole in my heart. . . . Sam was my friend
and mentor, the father I never had" (ALS to Michael Williams, April 11, 1994 [Yale Steward Papers]).
Boys Town. Famous orphanage for boys founded in 1917 in Nebraska by Catholic priest
Edward Flanagan (1886–1948).

which they escaped twenty times in two years. Curiously, each of them was a kind of drifter; Larry himself in fifteen years held over forty jobs and had been married three times, with one shack-up. Louie was similarly rootless and twice divorced, and Lester was homosexual, which should say enough about his general qualities of permanence and fidelity. Thus Larry was bi, Louie hetero, and Lester homo, a curious division; and as the old wives might have it, perhaps they shared one soul among three. Their sibling rivalry was intense, and they claimed to get "flashes" of intuitive knowledge from each other, no matter how widely separated. But they were really identical, except Larry's bent to the left, Louie's to the right, and Lester's straight down. Or up. And it was Louie who in a phone call many years later said to me, "You seem to be a focal point around which so many lives revolve. Ours, too. You'll always be there."

Hah!

Then there was Bob Berbich, whom I cruised in a bar at the end of World War II. He was in a sailor's uniform, and both of us were drunk. "I'd like to go witcha," he said, "but I'm broke."

Magnanimity! "Oh, thass all right," I said loftily. "This time's on the house, account you is one of our boys in blue."

He learned soon enough that all was free in my place, and so he began to take advantage of it—and our knowing each other went on for innumerable times. Sixteen years after our first meeting, he reciprocated. But in all those years, Bob really answered several of my needs; he was successively a sailor, a motorcycle delivery messenger, a taxi driver, a night steelworker, and a uniformed guard. In my growing preference for the blue collar instead of the white, these occupations were just what I needed for my fantasies.

And just possibly for his too. He was not very bright, and his language was "dese" and "dose." But he loved the glory hole I put into the door of the head in my tattoo shop and made good use of it. What odd little imaginings passed through his brain, his three pounds of dimly conscious meat, as he stood facing the plywood two inches from his nose, I'll never know—nor, I guess, would I be very much interested.

Then there was a Mom-infested person with a grave and horrid stammer, a tall lean handsome guy with a good face and a growing fascination with psychic masochism. His name was Tom, and he was one who owned both a motorcycle and a concert-size harp, who combined narcissism and exhibitionism within himself. On him I put five large tattoos—an eagle on the

Bob Berbich. The Stud File card for Bob Berbich documents 233 encounters between 1948 and 1964.

chest, panthers and daggers and dragons and such-like on his arms—and helped him cut the silver cord which bound him to Mommy, whereupon his stammer largely vanished. He was a grand person and extremely good-looking; I regret that my demand for the real thing in a sexual encounter—not the sort of play-pretend activity he enjoyed—so extinguished his desire and upset him that he fled back home to New York and was not heard from after that.

There was also a remarkable hustler whose nickname was "Cherokee." In those days, he was considered the best. He was perhaps the most professional hustler I had ever known—with perfect bedroom manners, cooperative, unshockable, and with an intuition which never failed him. He always seemed to know exactly what to do to bring comfort and surcease from pain to his clients—and quite possibly his good reputation rested on that. If toward the end of his career he began somewhat to run to fat, he nonetheless maintained his list because of his manners and because his clients were sentimentally attached to him. He extended his hustling career until he was well into his late thirties—and perhaps, for all I know, he may even yet be occasionally selling himself in the vasty desert of the Midwest where he lived.

And finally, my cops.

The first was a guy whom I had possibly met in the Lincoln Baths before I stopped drinking. I do not know how he got my name and telephone number; perhaps I gave them to him while I was drunk; perhaps someone else passed them to him. I remember that the circumstances of our getting together were rather mysterious—a phone call or two, and then a visit. He gave me the name of "Bob McDonald," but I did not think it was the right one. Since I was cautious, after our first romantic encounter, I looked into his wallet while he went to the bathroom to see if McDonald were his real name. Imagine the shock when the wallet opened on a Chicago police badge, number 4468. He came back from his ablutions, and it took all of my histrionic abilities, developed in twenty years in the classroom, to keep my voice steady, to be polite, to say yes, I would like to see him again. When he left, I collapsed trembling into a chair.

I need not have worried overmuch. He reciprocated in every possible way—and we knew each other for six or seven years. He never revealed his job, and I rather enjoyed the "status" that having a cop gave me. In 1956, I got a sad phone call from him. He had been in an accident and a leg had to

my demand for the real thing. Steward refers to a craving for sadomasochistic sexual encounters that went beyond mere role-playing.

be amputated; in a heavy depression, he announced his departure for California, and I never heard from him again.

The second cop was a tall handsome young man, rather slender, for whom every attractive police uniform in the world seemed to have been designed. He was on the Milwaukee police force for a time, and his name was Jim; I tattooed him in Milwaukee and furnished him with gin as he walked his downtown beat. The Milwaukee winter uniform was sexually very attractive to me — the dark-blue coat had a double row of brass buttons rising to curve outward toward the shoulders and a high tight collar to enclose the neck. He was completely hetero — but even so, at that time something was askew in his head, for he confessed to me that with women, and also when masturbating, he could rarely develop an erection. That uniform of his which he wore so jauntily, with the cap pulled so low that the bridge almost covered his eyes, made me foolish enough to spend a considerable amount on Jim-baby; and although his problem was the same with me as with his women, it did not keep him from orgasm and enjoyment.

The third cop was a tattoo buff — or at any rate one who enjoyed the feel of the needle. I tattooed him in the shop (and made him the protagonist of a story by Phil Andros). His name was John, and for all I know he may still be on the Chicago police force. After carefully quizzing him to see that he completely understood the then-new Illinois law regarding homosexual encounters, I asked him if he considered the tattoo shop a "private place."

"If the door were locked, and you went into the back room behind the curtain," he said.

I locked the door and we went into the back room behind the curtain. Afterward he asked if he could see me again, and delighted, I said yes.

"I was just wondering if sometime you would mind showing up in uniform," I said, for he had been in plainclothes (with his gun) when he came into the shop.

"Does that make it better?" he asked.

"N-no, not n-necessarily," I stammered, trapped in an unanswerable question.

"It sort of adds the frosting on the cake, huh?" he said, twinkling a bit.

"Exactly."

made him the protagonist. In the manuscript, Steward writes that this cop was the model for his story "The Peachiest Fuzz" (*Der Kreis*, August 1964, 29–36), originally published under the name John McAndrews (see chapter 15).
a "private place." The 1962 Illinois law that decriminalized sodomy still prohibited lewd acts in public places.

And that was the way he showed up from then on. I liked Johnny; he was a wild one—and since there was no way to get in touch with him (discretion for his job with the fuzz!), I had to leave Chicago without giving him my address in California.

The fondness I had for the police was an indication, I suppose, of the deeply buried residue of guilt from my childhood which accounted for my psychic masochism. One can never get entirely rid of those doleful shreds and tatters of the early impressments—in my case, the stern and austere puritanism of my Methodist maiden aunts and my narrow upbringing. And the policeman—well, he was the single point at which the law touched the individual, the ultimate authority, and when he was young and handsome, he could hold me in his hands and shape me like clay. If cops could only realize how deeply attracted many of us are to them, they would never have to go horny again. If they were in uniform—and perhaps only then—they could find comfort on any park bench, or in the shadows of any alley, or in the warmth of many expensive apartments. But the uniform would have to be in sight or be worn—cap, gun belt, and boots at least. Without the symbols of power, a naked cop would be just another naked body.

There were others in my life—even some with whom for a while I shared myself and opened my mind and heart. The Stud File is full of cards and names and bits of coded information. The glass jar is packed with snippets of crinkly hair taken from my favorite persons, for when I was seventeen I knew I was going to be seventy. And there were going to have to be tangibles to which the imagination and memory could be tied, devices to stimulate nostalgia and the remembrance of things past. I was getting ready for the days when the "island spirit" would be truly alone, without youth to visit me or to be ensnared—when the sort of happiness which Sophocles described might descend, the ultimate freedom from the "mad master" of sexual desire.

Sources: *Chapters*, 119–29; Manuscript, 321. With the exception of the second paragraph, which appears only in the manuscript, the text of this chapter follows the version published in *Chapters*, for which Steward altered most personal names and deleted an anecdote in the manuscript that could not be included without leaving clues to the identity of the person involved.

The glass jar is packed. Beginning with his encounter with Rudolf Valentino as a teenager, Steward collected pubic hair from sex partners throughout his life, sometimes attaching it with cellophane tape to the back of corresponding Stud File cards.
which Sophocles described. See note on page 52.

Chapter Fourteen

CALOR DI FORNI

1965–70

Folk etymology says that "California" derives from "calor di forni"—heat of the furnace, according to the usage of Catalan missionaries in 1769. Another source says the name comes from that of an earthly paradise mentioned in an early sixteenth-century Spanish romance, *Las Sergas de Esplandián*.

Whatever.

In San Francisco, there was but one tattoo artist—an all-around con man, generally given to puff and bluff. For a long time, he had been the undisputed ruler of the "art" in the city, keeping all others out by any number of ruses and devices. After twelve years of experience in the dog-eat-dog world of tattooing, the cut-throat unethical practices that I had seen in Chicago, I should have been prepared for anything—but I wasn't. This "artist" was called variously "Mr. Kleen," because of his great to-do about antisepsis (yet no one had ever seen his autoclave going; he kept cups and saucers therein), or "The Speed King," perhaps because of the rapidity with which he slapped on his tattoos. And what tattoos, and what prices! Mr. Kleen used only black and red—or if the customer hollered loud enough, a touch of green. A small tattoo for which I might have charged two dollars was ten in his shop.

With great naiveté, then, I told the Speed King of my plans, saying that I hoped he wouldn't mind the competition. Oh, not at all, he said, with a false and sunny smile.

Las Sergas de Esplandián. The Adventures of Esplandián, by the Spanish writer Garci Rodríguez de Montalvo (d. 1504), described a fictional island called California, a name subsequently used on maps drawn by early explorers of the west coast of the Americas.

I went to the Board of Health to get a copy of the San Francisco ordinance. Part of it was mimeographed, and there were an added two pages — on carbon flimsy. The carbon stated that the minimum age for tattooing in the city was twenty-one. I remember that I was somewhat astonished when I heard the woman say, "Hell, I've been expecting you for several days." I should have been suspicious then, but I wasn't.

Curiouser and curiouser! Everywhere in Mr. Kleen's shop were signs saying "You must be eighteen." Instead of going to City Hall and checking the printed ordinances, I accepted the Board of Health one. It was not until a couple of years later that I discovered, or was forced to conclude, that the Speed King had bribed a woman in the office to type up a phony "ordinance" for me to keep me from being a competitor in the city.

After some delays, I opened my shop in Oakland, near Seventeenth and San Pablo, in a greatly run-down section of the inner city, next door to a pawnshop. Charles Gain, then deputy police chief in Oakland, had assembled a full dossier on me as he investigated my background. Included were disapprovals from several businesses in the neighborhood — a furniture store across the street from my projected location had complained that a tattoo shop would "run down the area." You had only to look up and down the street to be much amused at their objection.

"Why do you use the alias of Phil Sparrow?" asked Chief Gain.

"You mean my professional name?" I countered. "It's easier to remember. More picturesque."

"I can't keep you from opening your shop," he said, riffling through the papers. "I can only say that I think you may regret it — and that you won't keep it open long."

Milt Holtz had at this time been undergoing a series of reverses and tensions in the travel agency in which he worked and was glad to use a hammer in my shop to relieve his frustrations. He was a big ungainly man with a large heart — not too intelligent, since all his life he had had a form of dyslexia: he had to spend five full minutes reading a page in a book, because everything appeared to him backward and upside down. Consequently, he had barely made it through school and never read anything unless he was compelled.

Finally, however, the shop was ready. I named it the Anchor Tattoo Shop so that the name would stand first in the Yellow Pages of the phone book.

Curiouser and curiouser! Exclamation by Alice in *Alice's Adventures in Wonderland* (1865), by Lewis Carroll (1832–98).

near Seventeenth and San Pablo. Steward's Oakland tattoo shop was located at 1727 San Pablo, in a block of storefronts that have since been remodeled and renumbered.

It looked much like my place in Chicago—black plywood panels eight feet high, topped with six feet of wall painted dark Chinese red, a lighted sign outside with black "circus" letters spelling "Tattoo" against a yellow background, an expensive Formica workbench of my own design, and a large display window with my drawings illustrating tattooing techniques. A false wall cut off the rear of the large room, and the building extended forty feet behind the wall—a back room as large as the one in Chicago. It was an elegant place—but alas, it was in Oakland! There was "no there there," as Gertrude Stein once said.

The sailors who occasionally found themselves in Oakland rather than the more glamorous Baghdad-by-the-Bay were a different breed, too. In Chicago, the swabbies were mostly boots; in Oakland, they were largely "old salts." They had been to sea; they had got all the tattoos they wanted when they were at either Great Lakes or San Diego, and by now they had developed enough common sense not to want any more decorations.

The business did not exactly languish, but it became more a hobby than an occupation, and the "take" was cut to half of what it had been in Chicago. I developed a small homesickness for the old dirty windy city and found it difficult to get used to the absence of the tall Chicago buildings to which I had been so long accustomed.

There was no denying that I had landed in Berkeley at a tumultuous period—the Free Speech Movement was in full swing, and the student riots and protests over Vietnam were shortly to follow. Formerly, while in Europe, I always noticed that when I told anyone I was from Chicago there was a slight stiffening of the body, or even a tiny drawing away from me, as though I might have a tommy gun concealed somewhere. And now, Berkeley achieved for a little while the same worldwide notoriety that Chicago had for so many years. But the riots and the student tumult had little effect on me, except when the protesters massed at the Oakland army induction center, a building only a block away from me. Then I feared for my plate glass windows, but my luck held—they were not broken more than once or twice.

I began to feel, however, that living in California and tattooing there were merely a matter of more of the same—the same routines and clientele that there had been in Chicago. The young men still wanted the same old tradi-

---

There was "no there there." From Stein's *Everybody's Autobiography* (1937): ". . . what was the use of my having come from Oakland it was not natural to have come from there yes write about if I like or anything if I like but not there, there is no there there" (ch. 4).
Baghdad-by-the-Bay. Nickname for San Francisco popularized by writer Herb Caen (1916–97) to suggest the city's natural beauty and cosmopolitan character.

tional tattoos, for the movement toward decoration to cover the whole body had not yet begun. In Oakland, I showed Ed Hardy some of the preliminary steps of tattooing; he went on to become one of the two best in the country, specializing in the Oriental style. I was pleased to have had a small part in his development.

But as 1970 drew closer, there was a change. More hippies began to come into the shop—and with them came additional problems. I had always been careful enough about antisepsis and autoclaving the needles or sterilizing them in a pressure cooker at home—since my autoclave was a huge old-fashioned one large enough to hold a collie, and the noise and popping of steam it made were enough to frighten anyone entering the shop. But the majority of the hippies had had hepatitis—for the joyful needle passed around the happily humming circle all too often carried the little bugs from one vein to another—and hepatitis demanded an extra-long time for sterilization.

Then, too, about 1968 I was discovered by the Hells (no apostrophe) Angels. This group of aging rebels suddenly found that in my shop they could get their symbols—the winged skull with "Hells Angels" written curving above it and the chapter name underneath—for about one-third of the amount they would have to pay elsewhere. And as with the youth gangs in Chicago, the word flashed around; in a sense, I became the "official" tattoo artist for them all. They came from Livermore and Stockton, Richmond and Fresno and San Francisco, even as far away as "San Berdoo" and included, of course, most of the members of the Oakland chapter, led by their "prez," Sonny Barger. They wanted not only the skull with wings but other designs which were arcane and esoteric—at least until the Angels started getting all their publicity. I put on many swastikas and iron crosses; the jagged "SS" symbol; the 1%—which referred to someone's saying that only one percent of all motorcyclists were outlaws; the brown pilot's wings—indicating that buggery on a man had been performed; or the red wings—to mean cunnilingus on a menstruating woman; or black wings—the same on a black woman; "13" for the letter M—a marijuana smoker; "DFFL"—Dope Forever, Forever Loaded; "666"—the number of the Beast in the Apocalypse, because a minister had referred to Sonny that way; and others, perhaps transient in meaning, but

[Don] Ed Hardy (1945–). Art student mentored in tattooing by Steward who subsequently studied tattooing in Japan and carried tattoo designs into a popular line of clothing.
[Ralph] Sonny Barger (1938–). Biker, author, and cofounder of the Oakland version of the Hells Angels motorcycle club.

enjoyed by a few for a while. Even as tightly knit a group as the Angels had wheels within wheels. I shall never forget my astonishment when I tattooed a long philosophical quotation from (I think) Khalil Gibran on the inside of Sonny Barger's right forearm, beginning "I had rather die yearning . . ."

At first, the Hells Angels were terrifying to me, although I did my best to conceal it. Then gradually with them I came to acquire a kind of special status, so that I could indulge in kidding and badinage that I am sure would have resulted in a broken jaw were a stranger to have tried it. After all, while they were sitting in my chair and I was holding the needle against their arms, I was the boss—a little of that "confessional" attitude that I had first noticed in Chicago appeared in the Angels.

A sample of the sort of thing I could get away with successfully: One of them, judging from the remarks of the others, was especially endowed with what was reputedly the biggest schwanz in the Bay Area. One night while they were commenting on that, I opened a drawer and took out one of those small rubber finger-stalls that doctors sometimes use when investigating the prostate; it was rolled like a condom but of course was only about a half inch in diameter.

"Here," I said, tossing it to him. "Take this and go have a wild time tonight."

The laughter of the others was loud. He turned red and raised his arm against me, but I ducked and laughed. I must have been either very sure of myself or very foolhardy—but in nearly every case, I accurately judged just how far I could go with them.

They were very jealous of their "colors," by which they meant their winged skull and their designs. One evening I had closed the shop and gone home from Oakland to Berkeley, when about midnight I got a call from Sonny Barger.

"Can you come down to the shop again and open up for a special job?" he asked.

"Jaysus, Sonny," I protested. "It's late, and I just got home."

"We'll make it worth your while," Sonny said. "Can you come?"

Grudgingly I said yes and went back down to Oakland. There were four or five Angels waiting in front of the shop, and they had in their grip a young man much banged up, with a black eye and bloody nose. I opened the shop, and they explained.

"I had rather die yearning." Line from the poem "A Tear and a Smile" (1914, original in Arabic), by Lebanese-born poet Khalil Gibran (1883–1931), whose work reached new heights of popularity in the 1960s.

"He's got our tattoo on his arm," Animal said. "And he ain't no Angel."

Yes, there it was on his forearm—crudely done and carrying the sacred words around it.

"Cover it up," Zorro said. "Black it out completely."

"Hold on a minute," I said. "Technically this is mayhem. Tattooing under duress. He'll have to sign a release." I wrote one out in a hurry, stating that the undersigned wanted to have his tattoo blacked out. "Is that so?" I asked.

The frightened young man gulped and nodded and signed with trembling fingers. I blacked out the design, with each of the Angels taking turns in holding the needle briefly and jabbing it as hard as he could into the skin. After Sonny paid me, they threw the young man into a small enclosed truck and climbed in after him. I heard later what happened. They drove him into the country to a deserted spot, knocked him around some more, and then each of them sodomized him. Afterward they stripped him naked and dropped him on the freeway.

Although I often had requests for the Angels' tattoo, I never applied it unless the customer was accompanied by a member I knew. Telling the non-Angel what had happened to the interloper was usually enough to discourage the would-be romantic who wanted the skull and wings.

I tattooed not only the Angels but their "mamas" and their "old ladies." In three years of working on them, I had only one unpleasant experience: When members of a rival gang showed up, some frantic mama slipped into the back room to call the police. I am sure that things could have been settled without one of the fights for which the Angels were famous—but the fuzz were understanding and did not blame me for the rumble—which in any case was averted. Yet I always had the feeling whenever I saw a group of them entering the shop that their presence put me on the thin edge between disaster and catastrophe. They certainly kept my insides awash in adrenaline whenever they came a-callin'.

Despite all the news articles and studies by neo-Freudian psychiatrists and others about the Hells Angels, the fact remains that they were tough and mean and had to be handled with extreme care. In any one of their fights, there was no such thing as sportsmanship; if one Angel got punched out, it was part of their creed that all the others around—whether three or thirty of

Zorro. William Mark "Zorro" Mitten (1940–85), Hells Angel charged with accessory to murder in 1972 for his role in disposing of the bodies of two motorcycle enthusiasts from Georgia who were killed by the Angels ("2 Slaying Victims Found on California Ranch Left Georgia for Life with West Coast Motorcycle Cultists," *New York Times*, November 5, 1972, 41; People v. Mitten, 37 Cal.App.3d 879 [1st Appellate Dist., 1st Div., 1974]).

them—would jump on the one who had attacked their brother. A fair fight was unknown; the Marquess of Queensberry never existed.

I did have a distinct admiration for Ralph "Sonny" Barger—an intelligent person, cool and thoughtful. He was about six feet tall and could manage, if the occasion demanded, to be as shaved and clean-cut an American male as you would want to see—even handsome in those days—and the acknowledged and admired leader of the gang. I did not dare to let him suspect, however, that I would greatly have enjoyed one romantic encounter with him or Zorro. Now it's too late.

Perhaps to the present moment I would still be sitting in the Anchor Tattoo Shop in dingy Oakland, fiddling with the soldering of needles and the mixing of pigments and the bullshitting of customers, were it not for three events that changed everything—perhaps for the better, perhaps not.

I was strong-armed three times in the shop by our black brothers. A quick movement, a thick black arm around the neck while a hand fumbled in my pocket for my wallet (and his confederate unhooked and made off with the small color TV set)—leaving me weak and shaken and so nervous I could hardly call the fuzz. And the second time—not so violent, but stealing my wallet from the place where I thought I could safely keep it. And the third—

But why bother? I decided that three times was enough and that perhaps on the fourth occasion I would not be so lucky—that there might be a knife or a bullet, and who would want that? The shop next door—a pawnshop run by an elderly Jew named Herman Cartun—had been several times victimized, and between my own second and third experiences, poor Herman was shot and killed.

Milt Holtz helped me to tear down the place that he had helped to build. He viewed my decision favorably.

"I've been thinking you should have quit a couple of years ago," he said. "This area is much too dangerous. It's really not worth it, is it?"

No, I decided—it wasn't. In March 1970, I locked the door for the last time and retired to my house in Berkeley. Phil Sparrow, in effect, was killed,

Marquess of Queensberry. The nineteenth-century Marquess of Queensberry rules—actually written by John Graham Chambers (1843–83)—were the first codification of rules for boxing and are the basis of the regulations governing boxing today.
Herman was shot and killed. The newspaper account of this incident reported that on December 7, 1966, Cartun was shot in his shop by two men who fled as he staggered after them with his own gun. Steward reportedly knelt over his bleeding neighbor and called the police at his request ("Pawnbroker Slain During Gun Battle," *Oakland Tribune*, December 8, 1966, 21). Steward's narrative here suggests that he closed his shop soon after this event, but as he notes below, he actually continued running his business until March 1970.

destroyed, wiped out of memory, off the books. I left no forwarding address with the post office and became Samuel Steward once more.

For the first few months I was miserable, until I discovered the cause of my unhappiness and succeeded in rationalising it. I had lost every semblance of "authority" I ever had. In the classrooms while I was teaching, I had been subject only to the "suggestions" of a department head or dean, and in the tattoo shop, I had been absolute boss for fifteen years. If I didn't want to tattoo a person — if he were too drunk or obnoxious or offensive — I would tell him to get the hell out, using the "tone of authority" which the years of teaching had developed. Now all of that was gone. No one had to do anything I ordered; in fact, there was no one to order. And I came to understand why so many executives of corporations or persons in positions of authority crumbled and declined and even died when that was taken away from them.

I had the chance at last to look around me at Berkeley, finally forced to the opinion that (excluding the university) it was the home of the second-rate. During all the years when the town was in tumult, the protest years from 1965 to the early '70s, I had been sitting in comparative isolation in the other-world of Oakland and my tattoo shop, conscious of the confusion only when the nearby induction center was the focus of the marchers. But by the early 1970s, Berkeley had cooled off considerably. The drug culture had begun to settle down to the relatively harmless use of pot — which only insidiously and slowly weakened the will and the urge to work of its heaviest users. Heroin had been discouraged among the university students. And the fashion of LSD had passed — the great drug of hope, the mind-expanding magic that would turn everyone into Einstein, Mozart, or Leonardo, that would make Everyman a genius. Nothing had turned out the way it had been predicted. The hallucinogens helped their takers to produce rock noise, psychedelic posters in fluorescent inks, artsy-craftsy belt buckles, puka-shell necklaces, copper bracelets, zodiac pendants, elaborate roach-holders and joint clips — all the eternal and enduring kitsch of the half-talented and ignorant who (knowing nothing of the past) had to reinvent for themselves even such symbols as yin and yang. In Berkeley there were spawned rock groups with weird names and mayfly lives, playing at tiny clubs to ears no longer functional because of too much din; and here flourished the little presses, publishing the arcane incomprehensible nonsense of young "poets" talking to themselves in public. Here people repaired merry-go-round horses and made stained-glass lamps. The sidewalks of Telegraph Avenue were lined with street merchants

displaying their crudely fashioned wares on blankets, and the "1965 look" —
the long straggly hair, the full beards and mustaches, sandals — persisted in
many pockets and communes long after it had become old-fashioned everywhere else. Unwashed clones still quoted Chairman Mao long after he had
fallen into disfavor and been abandoned even in China. If you wanted to see
the scruffy barrel-bottom scrapings of the 1960s, you should come to the
Land That Time Forgot — Berkeley.

I neither approved nor disapproved of this; I merely observed, with whatever detachment I could summon. I listened to the arguments from the
heavy pot smokers that they could stop at any time, that they really didn't
need the eight or ten joints a day — but I also saw Danny S., one of the heaviest users, grow forgetful and apathetic and watched his will to work and
make a living weaken and disappear. And what of Pete S., another heavy user,
who got within a centimeter of passing his bar exam, only to turn aside and
start to manufacture pot pipes for a living?

And I was certainly not without my own sins. In *The Magic Mountain*,
Thomas Mann describes how the inhabitants of the tuberculosis sanitarium
at Davos in Switzerland passed from one amusement, one consuming fad or
fashion or diversion, to another — from eating different kinds of chocolates
to drawing geometric figures blindfolded, from amateur photography to collecting stamps or phonograph records or wildflowers. All these things Mann
described with one phrase that lingered permanently in my memory: "sinking back into the great dullness."

Until my reason reasserted itself and the long years of preparation for
these do-nothing days could be put into effect, I fell victim to Mann's disease. With me it took the form of collecting clocks, all the kinds and types I
could afford, until my house had thirty-one of them, striking synchronously
on Sundays when they were wound and reset, and drawing gradually apart as
the week progressed and the springs unwound. Who can say to what extent
this interest in watching the visible passing of time had been influenced by
my early reading of the excursion on the subject of time in Mann's master-
work?

Another example of the mindless "sinking into the great dullness" took
hold of me: I built electronic gadgets and instruments from kits and instruc-
tion books furnished by a company called Heathkit — a color TV, a stereo
music center, digital clocks, intrusion alarms, even doorbells that could be

"sinking back into the great dullness." Steward refers to the chapter "The Great Stupor"
("Der grosse Stumpfsinn") in Mann's novel *The Magic Mountain* (*Der Zauberberg*, 1924).

programmed to play tunes (I chose *Gaudeamus igitur* because of its melancholy view of youth and because old Dr. Anthony had loved it).

Thus my life arranged itself—and Phil Andros, springing full-grown from my temple, like Athena from the brow of Zeus, was a pleasant surprise, helping me to pass the time. In him and through him for several years, I relived not only the adventures of my own youth but those of several others I had known—hustlers mostly, or bank presidents or priests, judges and policemen, young gangsters and motorcyclists, fetishists and narcissists, musicians and photographers, factory workers and interior decorators—the whole vasty world of the homosexual, cutting across all social strata, uniting the different temperaments, occupations, and levels with the consuming interest in one thing which the old word dealer, Erimos, in my very early story, had sold to the petitioner who came to him, the one word embracing all passions and pleasures for all of us: Man.

Sources: *Chapters*, 132–35; Manuscript, 341–53, 357.

Gaudeamus igitur. "So let us rejoice," a traditional academic song consisting of a Latin text with medieval origins paired with an eighteenth-century German melody.

Chapter Fifteen

BECOMING PHIL ANDROS

1927–78

When I got to college, I thought vaguely that it might be nice to be a journalist and make a career of writing—so I enrolled in the School of Journalism in the College of Commerce. Alas, for the requirements thereof! Dull things like economics and sociology as subjects proved not to my liking, and after one miserable term, I transferred to the College of Liberal Arts, there to stay, stoutly defending it against all comers like the colleges of Education and Commerce.

As an undergraduate, I had little time for writing; themes and term papers kept me busy until my junior year, when I managed to be accepted as one of a dozen students in a writing course of Claire Andrews. There for him I wrote the ten stories and sketches that were later to appear in *Pan and the Fire-bird*, privately printed (subsidized by Ben Musser) and published in 1930. The prevailing tone of the ten sketches was homosexual, and rather obviously so—ranging from "Nomad" and "Saihtyp" (Damon and Pythias) in "Silence on Earth" to "Amor Profanis" and "Libation to a Dead God"—the latter addressed to none other than Rudolf Valentino—and "The Word Dealer," in which in a tortuously worded ending, a young homosexual buys the word "man" to make himself happy and fulfilled. All the sketches were filled with anagrams in the Cabellian manner—"Diblio" for "libido," and "kircp" as the

Damon and Pythias. In ancient Greek legend, friends in the fourth century BCE whose faithfulness to one another was tested and proved when Pythias was imprisoned and condemned to death. Damon volunteered to take his place so that his friend could return home one last time; Pythias returned as promised to face execution, and the tyrant who imprisoned him was so impressed by their dedication to one another that he freed both.
the Cabellian manner. A reference to the subtle sexual implications of language and imagery in works by the American fantasy writer James Branch Cabell (1879–1958).

name of the fire-bird—a word which almost anyone can rearrange at any time.

But the most startling thing about *Pan and the Fire-bird* was the daring—or foolhardiness—that would lead one to have such a book published in 1930! I seemed not to care in the least about the tone or content, nor did anyone else who read it at that time. Perhaps it was too avant-garde for most reviewers, although one in Texas, of all places, did suggest that the homosexual flavor of it would make it "welcome in certain circles." One can only conclude that the general naiveté of the public at that time—the feeling among red-blooded Americans that such things might be talked about and written about but were never actually performed by anyone—was all the protection that it needed.

I was at that time managing the graduate seminar rooms on the third floor of the library and vividly recall one charming encounter caused by the book's publication. I had long noticed a six-foot-two hunky stalwart with sleek black hair and sensual lips who came regularly to the third floor to work, and one Friday evening he approached my desk in the corridor at about five minutes to closing time. His name was Marcus; he was from Bellefontaine, Ohio.

"What are you doing this evening?" he said.

"Nothing," I said.

"Your name's Steward, isn't it?"

I told him that it was.

"I've got some wine in my room over on High Street. Like to have some?"

"Sure," I said, and off we went.

We had a few glasses in his tiny room. It was hot, and a small electric fan was whirring. Suddenly he reached over and snapped off the desk lamp. The streetlights threw a leaf pattern on the thin blowing curtains and faintly illuminated the room. Marcus reached up and began slowly to unbutton his shirt.

"I've read your book," he said. "And I've got something for you."

Such rewards supplemented my patterns of hunting with great regularity for the next few years in the university. There was no monetary profit to *Pan and the Fire-bird*, but the fringe benefits were enormous. And perhaps the most delightful thing about all of them was that in nine out of ten cases the ones who approached me were straight-arrow guys who just wanted to experience a little, the very kind that I relished most of all.

---

too avant-garde for most reviewers. Steward's book in fact received a host of positive reviews, in such newspapers as the *Detroit Free Press*, the *Boston Globe*, the *Oakland Tribune*, the *Sacramento Bee*, and the *Minneapolis Star* and *Tribune*.

Aside from a couple of small stories in campus publications, nothing else creative was attempted or achieved until the summer of 1933, when again sitting at a desk in the graduate rooms, I wrote, by hand on long yellow sheets, the novel which later was to appear as *Angels on the Bough*—the book which brought about my dismissal from the State College of Washington. Aside from the stir it caused in Washington, its appearance did not greatly interrupt my comfortable obscurity. It was reviewed rather enthusiastically in the *New York Times*, where the critic called it a novel of great promise and compared its writing to that of Virginia Woolf and Henry James—heady praise indeed for a beginner.

And Gertrude Stein praised it as well, saying in *Everybody's Autobiography* that it was a good one, that it was clear and had in it more than clarity, that my clear line created something, and that there was something in it that made literature. But at the same time, she told me in 1937, when I was visiting her in Bilignin, that I shouldn't teach if I were going to write. "You can't write and teach, you know," she said fiercely, shaking me by the lapels. "The worst thing to do if you want to write is to teach and here's why. You teach all day and then that word-finding part of your brain is worn out and you can't find any words to put down on paper because that part of your brain is empty. It would be better yes much better to be a butcher."

Not only did I spend the next fifteen years teaching—and thus diminishing my urge to write—but for most of those years I was lost in the bottle, and no man can write while he's smashed. You can't even see the keys, let alone hit them.

Excuses, excuses! But despite the drinking and all the other cop-outs, I did manage to write a considerable amount. The truth may have been that what I wrote was of no value at all—either commercial or literary. Even before I had departed from Columbus, I attempted a soap-opera potboiler under the name of Eva Lo Baily, calling it *The Piper Pays*, and had the consummate nerve to submit it to the *Ladies' Home Journal*. It was turned down, of course. In 1934, I chronicled my religious experience in a novel called *Journey through the Night*, which Caxton accepted as a sequel to *Angels*. But

reviewed . . . in the New York Times. See Stanley Young, "Trouble in Academe," review of *Angels on the Bough*, by S. M. Steward, *New York Times Book Review*, May 31, 1936, 7, 15.
And Gertrude Stein praised it. See *Everybody's Autobiography* (1937), chapter 4. In an earlier letter to Steward, Stein had written, "The book came and I have just finished it and I like it I like it a lot, you have really created a piece of something, by the way how old are you, I have just finished it and I am not sure that I am not going to read it again" (Stein to Steward, ALS, June 16, 1936, Stein Letters).

they wanted me to work on it, to make it jibe with *Angels*; by then I was losing interest in religion, so I never did it. In 1936, during the Davis and Elkins teaching summer, there was a novel about Parke Allen at Hallie-hurst—a heavy gothic thing centered around the mysterious old house, a novel in holograph called *Splendid in Ashes* . . . never published. And in 1937–38, I wrote a novel about homosexuals in Chicago, a fearsome thing ending with a murder by some "dirt" and the subsequent actual emasculation of the protagonist. I did this in two versions—one with dirty language, and one using euphemisms. Gertrude read the first version in 1939 and said of it that the dirty book began very well, the church scene was very good, and then it went on and I varied the dirt quite a good deal and that was not easy, and the thing that was wrong with Wendell's and Saroyan's and my novel writing was that we were all haunted by the spoken word.

My dentist in Chicago was William P. Schoen Jr.— "Dr. Pretty" as I called him, a name which did not please him overmuch, although it was quite apt; he was very handsome. He was also the editor of the *Illinois Dental Journal*, and while I was at his mercy in the chair one day in 1943, he talked me into starting a series of articles for his journal, giving me free rein to write on any topic I chose. So I began, using the same name I was later to use as a tattoo artist, Philip Sparrow— "Philip" instead of "Phil," since it was more dignified.

For six years and over sixty articles I enjoyed the outlet that the Sparrow articles gave me — opportunities to air my loves and prejudices, likes and dislikes, foibles and fripperies, reminiscences and tributes—to Stein, Mohammed Zenouhin, Dr. Anthony, Chicago, Paris, the Comic Spirit, and many others. Gertrude Stein never saw any of the articles (though many were done while she was still alive), but Alice Toklas saw most of them and flattered me by liking them, saying they were filled with "Sammish impishness" and my "best whimsy and pretty lightness." Eventually I grew weary of writing them and with a calculated gesture ended them by writing "A Modest Proposal," in which Philip Sparrow suggested that on the next anniversary of the Civil War's end, the South quietly secede from the Union. I said many unpleas-

---

haunted by the spoken word. Steward pokes gentle fun at Stein's characteristic departures from normal spoken language in her own writing.

Illinois Dental Journal. See note on page 185.

over sixty articles. In addition to his monthly essays as Philip Sparrow, Steward also wrote six articles for the journal's annual book-review issue under his own name.

"Sammish impishness . . . best whimsy." See Toklas's letters of December 31, 1946, and April 18, 1948, in *Dear Sammy,* 157, 163.

ant things about the South—that it was a grudge-bearing Poor Loser, that it had contributed little to the American scene save the mint julep, the race horse, and bourbon. The exchange list for state dental journals had carried the article into the Deep South, which exploded in anger and dismay at such insults. The result was that the Illinois Dental Society passed a resolution against Sparrow and his writings, ordering him to cease and desist. As usual, I was in trouble again . . . and enjoyed every minute of it.

It may come as a shock to some of the younger members of the homosexual community to realize that the freedom of expression obtainable in any adult bookstore (read "pornography") was not always there—that, as a matter of fact, such emporiums of lust and wickedness were opened only after 1966.

Before that time, what happened? We were all hunters, looking on every page for expressions that would be meaningful to us, relishing the hidden allusion, the double meaning. The college students of the 1920s delighted in the works of James Branch Cabell, who was for that generation what Tolkien was for the 1960s—except that Cabell was juicier, and when the candles went out and the fair ladies began to comment on the length of Jurgen's sword or his staff—or he to praise the lovely scabbards which they had—well, we all tittered and slyly underlined the passages or made a page-reference note in the back of the book so that we could find the hotspot again.

There was some homosexual writing done in the 1920s and '30s, but it was a sad and sorry thing. A firm named Greenberg published much of that early stuff—mostly novels, all of which ended unhappily with the homosexual "hero" committing suicide or being killed in some way; thus sin was punished and middle-class virtue triumphed, and America could go happily blundering on its hypocritical puritan way.

Dr. Kinsey at one point gave me the name and address of *Der Kreis* (The Circle), a trilingual homosexual magazine published in Zurich, and I sub-

the length of Jurgen's sword. Steward alludes to Cabell's most popular novel, *Jurgen: A Comedy of Justice* (1919), the target of a protracted but ultimately unsuccessful prosecution for obscenity.
A firm named Greenberg. The publishing house of Jay Greenberg was the leading distributor of gay and lesbian novels in the 1930s—works, as David Bergman writes, that "presented gay men as harmless creatures more in need of pity and sympathy than fear and scorn" (*The Violet Hour: The Violet Quill and the Making of Gay Culture* [New York: Columbia University Press, 2004], 50).

scribed, even sending them a few little scratch-board sketches and a poem or two, which were published. Through the 1930s and '40s, *Der Kreis* was the only homosexual magazine generally available. It began as the *Freundschafts-Banner*, a small mimeographed four-sheet under the direction of Anna Vock, a lesbian fondly known as Mammina, who had founded it in Switzerland and maintained publication for thirty-five years in the face of capricious laws sometimes enforced and sometimes not. After several changes, Mammina handed the leadership over to "Rolf" (Karl Meier, a well-known Swiss actor). When I first knew the publication, it was a thin little thing of about thirty-six pages (more in some issues), the first half in German, the latter half divided between French and English, the English section added only in 1954. In each issue, there were at least four pages of half-tone photographs — handsome young men, all discreetly covered, no frontal nudity allowed. And yet approximately every fourth issue of the magazine was withheld by US Customs as obscene — one of the most perverse and scandalous homophobic judgments ever made, solely on the grounds that the publication was homosexual.

And what stories they were, those little vignettes in *Der Kreis*! Sweet and sloppy, with lots of hand-holding and sidelong glances and deep heartfelt sighs. Most had sad and sentimental endings; sometimes everything worked out all right, but the stories ended before anyone got into bed or did much except sigh romantically and grin at each other. Yet in an effort to attract American subscribers, the work of a few notable Americans began to appear in the English section. Paul Cadmus sent photographs of his paintings

Mammina. Steward's early history of *Der Kreis* is slightly inexact. Anna Vock ("Mammina," 1884–1962) started publishing the *Schweizerisches Freundschafts-Banner* (Swiss Friendship Banner) in April 1933 following the demise of the similarly named *Freundschafts-Banner*, which had issued nineteen hectographed numbers in 1932. The new publication was printed rather than hectographed, boldly carried Vock's name on the masthead, and would appear continuously for the next thirty-four years (Hubert Kennedy, *The Ideal Gay Man: The Story of "Der Kreis"* [Harrington Park: Haworth, 1999], 8–9).

After several changes. From 1937 through 1942, the publication bore the name *Menschenrecht* (Human Rights). At this point, Vock retired and passed editorial responsibility to Karl Meier (1897–1974), a successful actor and cabaret performer who under the pen name Rolf had been a major writer for the journal since May 1934. With the January 1943 issue, Meier gave the publication a new double name acknowledging its readership in French-speaking Switzerland — *Der Kreis / Le Cercle* — as well as a new focus on gay rather than lesbian contributions (Kennedy, 17–18, 23–24).

Paul Cadmus (1904–99). American artist known for his exquisite drawings of the male nude and his satirical depictions of American life.

and drawings, and George Platt Lynes sent his "non-profit-making ventures" as he called them—his excellently lighted, inventive, and beautiful photographs of extraordinarily handsome young men—at first allowing them to appear under his real name and finally switching to the lens name of Roberto Rolf. Of writers, James Barr (Fugaté), author of *Quatrefoil* and *Derricks*, was the best-known American.

In 1958, I met Rudolf Jung—or Rudolf Burkhardt, as he appeared in print—the English editor of *Der Kreis*, who came from Zurich to the United States to try to uncover new contributors and to introduce himself to those he had known only through correspondence. Rudolf was a charming German expatriate who since World War II had lived in Switzerland—roly-poly, walking with a slight limp, and speaking excellent English with just a whisper of "zis" for "this." And he was an extraordinary flatterer. He came to my tattoo shop in Chicago, and we were immediately simpatico, so much so that I invited him to stay in my apartment for the remainder of his visit. And he coaxed and cajoled until finally I said yes, I would write him a little something—"at least an essay, if you don't feel like writing fiction"—for the English pages.

So began a close association with *Der Kreis* which lasted until its demise in 1967. Rudolf drew me deeper and deeper into its workings during those nine years, wheedling more than fifty short stories, essays, poems, and line drawings out of me for the magazine and often asking me to help him rewrite some of his own things. Since Rudolf's list of contributors was small, I used pen names to make it seem larger. "Donald Bishop" contributed sociological things such as "The Negro Homosexual in America," "The Bull Market" (on hustlers), "What's New in Sodom?" (on Chicago after the change in laws regarding homosexual contacts), and "Pussies in Boots" (a sardonic article on the leather movement). For poetry in the manner of Housman, I became "John McAndrews." Some stories were written under "Ward Stames" (a simple anagram of my name); "Thomas Cave" produced more thoughtful

George Platt Lynes (1907–55). Successful commercial photographer of the 1930s and 1940s who also produced a large body of homoerotic photographs, unpublished during his lifetime, that he left to the Kinsey Institute.

James Barr (Fugaté). James Fugaté (1922–95), author (using the pen name James Barr) of gay-oriented fiction and essays during the 1950s and 1960s; best known for his novels *Quatrefoil* (1950) and *The Occasional Man* (1966), his story collection *Derricks* (1951), and his play *Game of Fools* (1955).

Rudolf Jung (1907–73). Writer, editor, and translator who began working for *Der Kreis* in 1951 and became the editor of its English section and Karl Meier's secretary and close associate.

and reflective stories, sometimes in the Thomas Mann manner. "Phil Andros" was not yet born. None of this was financially profitable, since I did it all for nothing, but I enjoyed the outlet again and the usually pleasant comments that my stories brought in.

Eventually the confinements and restrictions of *Der Kreis*'s policies developed great feelings of claustrophobia in me. Anything explicitly or even tacitly sexual had to be removed because of the danger of being charged with prurience or obscenity. The hand-holdings and sighs and glances came to seem utterly unreal in a world where people sucked and fucked. I had rather delicately expressed such feelings to Rudolf from time to time. Now I was firmer.

"This is the gah-damnedest crap I ever laid eyes on," I said, shaking a recent issue under his nose.

"Ah yes," he said. "I felt you were growing a little restless."

"I wanna write about real life," I said.

"Well," said Rudolf, "there's Kim Kent in Copenhagen. He's got two magazines—*eos* and *amigo*—in Danish, German, and English. Why don't you send him something? I haven't told you about him because I don't want to lose you. If I give you his address, will you still write for us?"

"Yeah, yeah," I said. And so I sent Kim Kent a story called "The Sergeant with the Rose Tattoo," which he entered in a short-story contest he was having at the moment, and it won a fifty-dollar first prize. Big deal. Kim was as adept at flattery as Rudolf was—the sure mark of an editor who wants contributors for nothing.

Meanwhile, back at the raunch in Chicago, in 1962 tattooing was about to be closed down. Well, not closed entirely—but the age limit for it was being raised to twenty-one. This was happening at the same time that the penalties for homosexual encounters were being lifted in Illinois and the "age of consent" for male-male sex lowered to eighteen, all this through the single-handed efforts of Kinsey. Tattoo buffs commented about the law raising the tattoo age limit to twenty-one—which automatically cut out all the boot sailors from Great Lakes; they felt that the mark on the psyche of an early homosexual experience might be more damaging than an anchor tattooed

Kim Kent. Pen name of Knud Rame (1935–), Danish founder of the homophile magazine *eos* (1958–75) and its German/English version *amigo* (1962–75), which became "the voice of Denmark's homophile subculture during a period of virulent anti-homosexuality" in the 1950s and 1960s (Robert Aldrich and Garry Wotherspoon, *Who's Who in Contemporary Gay and Lesbian History from WWII to Present Day* [London: Routledge, 2001], 342–43).
the age limit . . . was being raised. See chapter 12.

on the arm. I avoided the argument, but I sensed the closing of the doors and began to think of doing other things.

The owner of the photo studio whom I had known since 1958 and who sent me handsome hustlers was in the shop one day. To this guy, I was idly turning over in conversation various flaky possibilities about what I might do when I closed my shop at the end of 1962. "I might move the tattoodling business to Paris," I said, remembering that in my first story for Kim Kent I had already done so. "Or to San Francisco. Or I might go back to writing," I added wistfully.

"Nuts," said he. (Why can't I remember his name?) "You're too fuckin' old to write."

Well!

I was galvanized. Spurred to action. Nothing that anyone could have said would have sent me more quickly to a typewriter. Forgotten were the years of listening to my internal critic who had been whispering daily that I was burned out, that I had nothing more to say, that everything had been said already. And to hell with even the question of money—I'd write just to please myself, and Kim Kent and Rudolf.

It was while writing for Kim that I invented the character of an intelligent, widely read, and sophisticated hustler. Phil Andros was thus born, and his name had a small joke in it. "Phil" came from the Greek "philos"—to love; and "andros" was the Greek word for man. Thus "Phil Andros" could be either "lover-man" or "man-lover." (Not many of Phil's readers were able to pull the name apart to discover the word play.) We even found a picture of the imaginary author, who was supposed to be of Greek extraction, with black curly hair, six feet tall, and handsome as the rosy-fingered dawn. His exploits in the first twenty-five stories were largely confined to the Chicago, San Francisco, and Dallas scenes—and were about eighty-five percent true experiences which either I or my friends had had with hustlers.

Most of the stories were composed, or begun, on the train between Chicago and Milwaukee during the time that Cliff Raven and I were tattooing on weekends there, where the age limit for tattooing was still eighteen. Every Friday afternoon, I boarded the old North Shore electric bearing a tablet of yellow legal paper and began to write. The hour's trip gave me a good start on a Phil Andros story—all tailored for Kim Kent. For most of 1963–64, I sent him a story each month and occasionally still sent one to Rudolf. Once I even sent one to *Der Kreis* under the name of Phil Andros. Old Rolf, the chief

owner of the photo studio. Chuck Renslow. Steward persists in not identifying him, pretending here that he has forgotten his name. See note on page 211.

editor, nearly had apoplexy: "I will not have that beast's name appearing in our pages!" was his gentle way of rejecting me.

Very early, I considered the different ways of telling a story, and decided — for verisimilitude — to narrate them in the first person. (Edgar Allan Poe, according to the best critical analyses, gained belief more easily for his stories by using "I.") And to that technique I added the "eponymous" — of having the narrator-hustler's name of Andros appear also as that of author. The method seemed to work. I stumbled around with two or three inconsequential stories at first — and then finally with one hit on what was evidently an archetypal theme: how a white guy (not Phil) submitted himself as a sexual "slave" to a black guy, in order to atone for past sins of whites against blacks. Sometimes Kim Kent got five or six letters a month commenting about his stories or his magazine. Imagine his surprise when "The Blacks and Mr. Bennett" brought him over a hundred letters! Phil Andros was thus "established," the readers clamored for a sequel, and I went on writing.

I wanted Phil to be as honest with himself as he was with his clients and to progress and develop. In the earlier stories, he was not sure of his own sexual identity, only gradually becoming completely homosexual. He was the antihero turned hero by a curious twisting of fate — his Greek good looks joined to an educated brain in a macho body, the whole overlaid with an ability to empathize and feel compassion. And so he began his wanderings, like those of Ulysses, through a world peopled with a diversity of "clients" — bank presidents, young gangsters, college boys and professors, weightlifters and policemen, fetishists and motorcyclists, millionaires and narcissists, factory workers and interior decorators — something for everyone. I tried to give Phil an advantage over most hustlers I had known — to make him observant and literate, able to relate what he saw with wryness and sometimes venom, with an unconcealed pleasure in the things belonging to passion and gentleness for things of the intelligence and the spirit.

The success of Phil Andros in the Danish magazines was astonishing. He was called the "American Jean Genet" — although that *certainly* was wrong! He was complimented in letters for a kind of writing that was new and different in plot and style, far removed from the well-worn patterns of the unhappy homosexual novels of the 1930s and '40s, before the Great Explosion of pornography.

Despite the comparative freedom of expression allowed in the Danish magazines, the early Andros stories were not hardcore but closer to soft porn. Nearly every one was preceded by a cautionary note from Kim Kent: "warn our more sensitive readers against reading this story," "for grown-up readers only," "our firm belief in our readers' maturity the only justification for having printed this," "no pleasant children's tale," and so forth. The stories weren't really all that extreme, but Kim Kent was protecting himself against possible repercussions, even though Denmark had relaxed its antiporn laws almost to the vanishing point. Phil had a great deal more freedom than in *Der Kreis*, yet there was no use of four-letter words.

In the United States in the mid-1960s, a case came before the Supreme Court, one intended to settle the question of obscenity addressed by the famous Roth decision of 1957. The nine quarrelsome old men now came to the conclusion that obscenity required a work to be utterly without any redeeming social value.

Whammo! There was a thoughtful pause whilst the country digested that—and came to the conclusion that of course there was a revelatory and redeeming social value to even the lousiest suckee-fuckee books. The gates were opened. The flood began. Suddenly all the old four-letter words (and some new ones) appeared in print, almost overnight. Publishers no longer had to write prefatory notes condemning what they were printing; they could merely suggest the social significance of erotica, and lo! all was satisfied. The court's decision had more holes in it than a colander, and publishing houses sprang up like mushrooms after rain.

One of the older homosexual presses which had been weaseling its way carefully between the markers was the Guild Press, presided over by a jolly rotundity who had been in trouble with the law before and had even voluntarily committed himself (it was alleged) to the mental ward at St. Elizabeth's Hospital—whence he ran his press with the insouciance that Leigh Hunt had shown a century and a half before, when he continued his literary works while in prison. In 1966, a New York bookseller put me in touch with this Jolly Roger, suggesting that if he wanted to upgrade the reputation of his press with some softcore hardcover homosexual literature, he ought to consider adding Andros to his list.

a case came before the Supreme Court. Steward refers to *Memoirs v. Massachusetts* (1966). See note on relaxing of censorship, page 211.
Guild Press. Major publisher of gay fiction and erotica from 1962 until its demise in 1974. The press was founded by H. Lynn Womack (1923–85), Steward's "Jolly Roger," who held a PhD in philosophy but lacked both acumen and ethics in his business dealings.
Leigh Hunt (1784–1859). English journalist and friend of many of the leading literary celebrities of his day. Jailed in 1812 for libeling the Prince Regent, Hunt was lodged in an unused prison infirmary consisting of a suite of rooms that he famously decorated with extravagance.

Collection of Phil Andros stories published in 1982, with cover
illustration by Tom of Finland. TOM OF FINLAND (Touko
Laaksonen, Finnish, 1920–1991), Untitled, 1982, Graphite
on paper, © 1982 Tom of Finland Foundation.

And so $tud was born—eighteen connected stories from *eos* and *amigo*,
gathered together and called a novel. A contract was signed over $250, gal-
leys were read in 1966, and Phil—now in California—waited breathlessly
for his book to appear. It didn't. Dead silence from the Jolly Roger in Washington, DC. No response to a dozen letters; the runaround on phone calls.
Three years went by. Phil later learned that the J. R. had run out of money
and couldn't pay the binder.

Availing myself of the three-year escape clause in the contract, I permitted J. Brian in San Francisco to bring out an oversize paperback edition in 1969. Immediately, a sleazy three-volume paperback set with dreadful pictures was produced by the Jolly Roger's press, without Phil's name anywhere to be seen. Finally in that year, he evidently found the money to pay the binder: the hardcover edition of *$tud* — with a jacket by the pimp's mignon — was remaindered as soon as it appeared. The book somehow developed an underground cult status for reasons that are far beyond my analytical ability to see, although I never made a nickel out of it beyond the initial $250.

Naturally, that was the end of any dealings with J. R. After closing my tattoo shop in Oakland in 1970, I amused myself by letting Phil Andros try his hand at some writing that was more hardcore than the earlier stories, and seven novels, including Danish and German versions, came from Phil's typewriter, all about his adventures as a hustler — in San Francisco as a cop, in Rome with the Italians, on a search for a perhaps nonexistent twin brother, and as a movie star in pornies in San Francisco. Frenchy's Parisian Press in San Francisco published *My Brother the Hustler*, *San Francisco Hustler*, *When in Rome, Do . . .* , and *The Joy Spot*, all in the early 1970s. Kim Kent in Copenhagen published a handsome trilingual edition of *The Joy Spot* under the title *Ring around the Rosy*. The porn market being what it was, Phil was not surprised to see a pirating of *San Francisco Hustler* (with "Biff Thomas" billed as the author) under the title of *Gay in San Francisco*. Only the characters' names were changed — to protect the thieves.

If anyone thinks he may get wealthy by writing such stuff, forget it. The going rate was any amount from $400 to $800 — a one-time payment, no royalties — while the publisher cleaned up anything from twenty to thirty thousand on each title.

"Why did you write them?" several acquaintances asked me. I had a standard reply: "To bring pleasure to lonely old men in hotel rooms at night."

J. Brian. Jeremiah (or James?) Brian Donahue (1942–85) published gay erotica in the 1960s, maintained a stable of models and hustlers, and in the 1970s produced pornographic gay films with a modicum of theme and plot. See Spring, 338–40.

the pimp's mignon. Chuck Renslow's lover and business partner, Domingo Stephen ("Dom") Orejudos (1933–91), successful Chicago dancer and choreographer better known for his erotic illustrations of hyper-masculine men in the attire of the gay leather movement, often published under the pen names Étienne or Stephen.

Frenchy's Parisian Press. The Gay Parisian Press (formerly Frenchy's Gay Line) was founded by Roland Boudreault, a French Canadian in the adult entertainment business (Spring, 345).

In 1971 or thereabouts, I visited an old friend of mine, Jim Kane, who was then living in a small cabin on the side of a mountain in Manitou Springs, Colorado, and while there I wrote what I initially called *A Love Letter to Gertrude and Alice*, a personal memoir about Gertrude Stein and Alice Toklas. A New York agent sent it around, but to no avail; it was not until I attached to it my thirty-six letters from Stein and twice that number from Toklas that it became acceptable to a publisher. Houghton Mifflin brought it out in a handsome edition in 1977 under the unwieldy title of *Dear Sammy: Letters from Gertrude Stein and Alice B. Toklas, Edited with a Memoir by Samuel M. Steward*. And since of necessity I had to mention my life as a tattoo artist therein, reviewers everywhere pounced upon variants of the headline "Tattoo Artist Publishes Stein-Toklas Letters"—a once-in-a-lifetime lead.

Some very pleasant things happened to me after *Dear Sammy* was published. People from whom I had not heard for thirty—even forty—years got in touch with me: former students from Helena, Montana, and others from Chicago—and a few new friends were made. Among the scores of letters that were forwarded by Houghton Mifflin was one especially fine one from Douglas Martin—who had changed his name to that from an Irish one. He addressed me rather formally as "Dear Dr. Steward" and then went on to reminisce charmingly about the past at DePaul—recalling my bow ties, how students had called me Mr. Belvedere, the founding of the Arts Club and my introducing them to ballet, art, symphony, and such like. He told me what he had been doing in the intervening nearly thirty years and used the dropped-hairpin technique of informing me that he too was a club member (as if I had not known it from the beginning!) by saying he had seen an interview with me in *The Advocate*, the largest homosexual newspaper. And he ended it by saying, "I remember talking with a group of students before one of your classes. We were remarking on how great we thought you were when one girl asked, 'Do you think he knows? Do you?' Dear Sammy: I had to make sure that you knew." Such a letter left me awash in a puddle of sentimentality, and Doug and I became good friends through our correspondence.

Another rewarding friendship was formed with Martin Greif, owner of

Mr. Belvedere. Character in the novel *Belvedere* (1947) by Gwen Davenport, adapted in a trio of films that appeared between 1948 and 1951 starring Clifton Webb (1889–1966) as the British nanny in an American household with three boys. In addition to a slim physique and dapper bearing, Steward and Webb's character shared a preference for bow ties.

Martin Greif (1938–96). Editor, publisher, and author of books on a wide range of topics, best known today for *The Gay Book of Days* (1982), his entertaining guide to gays and lesbians throughout history.

the Main Street Press in New Jersey, who wrote me a moving letter of trib-
ute. His brilliant mind and his outrageous sense of humor brought us close
together very quickly by both letters and phone calls. It would be very enjoyable if I were spared long enough to read *his* memoirs. A paper stock with
asbestos instead of rag content would have to be found to contain them;
otherwise, the volume would doubtless shrivel and burn.

After the appearance of *Dear Sammy*, a writer's block descended on me
like a force field, cutting off all contact with the creative impulse. I had always
been the kind of person who, finishing one thing, had to wait until I could
see it in print, hold it in my hand tangibly, before I found it possible to begin
something else. Thus it was not until the autumn of 1978 that I was able to
approach the loathsome typewriter, uncover it, and type the sentence:

> In winter, the snow sometimes fell thick in Woodsfield, melted for a day
> under a feeble sun, and froze again during the night.

But once the plug came out, it seemed that there could be no damming of
the flow.

Sources: *Chapters*, 107–18; Manuscript, 305–20.

Chapter Sixteen

OKTOBERFEST

1970–81

Every October, two friends of mine in Oakland (we are all in the same age bracket) throw an Oktoberfest—a pleasant little gathering of middle-aged queens (and a few young ones) who come to drink, eat brownies heavy with marijuana, and gossip. The usual attendance is around twenty, but there were thirty-three at the most recent one—a kind of sardine situation for Jon and Harvey's apartment.

As usual, I griped about going. Once I was there, everything was fine—but the psychological and physical effort necessary to pull myself together, to make the decision to go, was increasingly difficult for me. If I were still drinking, it would be much easier—but to be stone-cold sober amidst a group of euphoric drunks who think they're being witty was getting harder to bear. Don drove me—a friend since my earliest days in Berkeley who had chauffeured me everywhere, a big man and very strong.

"Eat some brownies," he counseled.

I wore a shirt and tie for the occasion, knowing that I would be the only one there so formally dressed—and I was. And then (with my necessary cane, for a hip replacement looms in the future), I sank onto the leather sofa at one end and listened. The group had divided itself as always into small-talk units of two or three, and fragments of the conversation eddied around.

Said a sixty-year-old with bouncy jet-black hair arranged in a Prince Valiant hairdo: "Personally, I think the Accu-jac is the greatest invention since the wheel." And to someone's query about what it was, he explained, "A

Accu-jac. A masturbation machine marketed in the 1970s, consisting of a long, flexible tube connected to an electrically powered suction mechanism in a case similar to a large fishing-tackle box. Steward's Accu-jac is in the Yale Steward Papers.

human . . . er . . . milking machine. After everything's over, you turn it off. It doesn't go on talking."

From another angle: "The ego should have a cutoff switch when you're cruising, for only the id is working then . . ."

And another: "I liked what he said on the tube about chickenhawks: I can't imagine having an affair with someone to whom you have to explain what you're doing or gasp physiological instructions such as 'higher' or 'lower.'"

Or: "When he interviewed me for the *Sentinel*, he wanted to know why— back in the twenties—I didn't join my 'oppressed brothers and sisters in marching for our rights'! Jaysus! Marching where? For what purpose? To protest to whom? We'd have been jailed. We were too busy having fun, keeping our secret hidden. It was more amusing before the closet opened and so many came out noisy. So much stompin' around."

Beside me, someone said: "When you come, the British call it 'changing the acid.' Kinda cute."

From the depths of an armchair: "My favorite age is the far end of the twenties, just when they're beginning to rot. But I will say the only pleasure in growing old is watching the young and arrogant ones go to pieces."

Faintly, from a corner: "Astrology's just medieval claptrap. In two thousand years, they've added two new signs—or should have: the whale and the serpent slayer. Anyone who believes in astrology is right up there with the medieval scientists who swore that menstrual blood killed grass, tarnished mirrors, and poisoned iron."

From a straight chair: "I was unpacking my suitcase in Paris and Jacques Guerre was there watching me, and when I came to a box of Band-Aids he kept staring at it, and finally he asked what it was, and I told him 'little *pansements* for cuts and scratches,' and then it dawned on me: 'bander' in French means to get a hard-on, and 'aid' from 'aider,' 'to help,' so Band-Aids in French means something to help you get a hard-on."

These statements did not come bang-bang; they were picked from the gossip of a half hour. The first brownie I had eaten began to make itself known. The host's cat sat staring at me. I was not overly fond of cats, since I had long ago decided they came from outer space and would eventually take over the world.

J. Brian, the porno king of northern California who had published the paperback edition of *$tud* when the Jolly Roger had been unable to pay his bindery, approached the sofa with a curly-haired young man in tow. Brian always brought the best.

The young man had broad sweet eyelids, luxurious soft yellow hair with twining rich golden curling spirals, a subtle promising mouth, refined and expressive hands, and supple limbs. Dreamstuff of soft cornflower violet came from his eyes. I looked at him; I heard a lion roar. His body and soul were aflame and aflower in their day of perfection; he was beauty militant and all conquering. As I watched him, I felt as I used to when I was drinking: I was a prince of the world and commanded fire and flames! It was possible, I decided on the spot, to love physically with a psychic delight—as I loved flowers and white wine and soaring wings and rare perfumes—but anxiously, since human things can hurt. I concluded that in love only the aristocrats understand each other, and there is a laity that knows nothing but physical desire.

"This is Scott," Brian said.

"Hello," I said, and shook hands. Scott pulled a footstool close and sat disturbingly near my knee, which I moved aside a half inch.

"Brian tells me you've written a lot of things as Phil Andros," he said.

"Guilty," I said.

"And that you knew Gertrude and Alice and wrote a book about them, *Dear Sammy*." He inflected the title as if he were addressing me rather than naming the book. "I haven't read it yet," he went on, "but I'm going to get it, and then will you sign it for me?"

"Sure," I said. My heart was acting strangely.

"I've been collecting autographs," he said. "I've got Tennessee Williams, George Maharis, lots of others. Even Herb Caen. Will you give me yours if I get a piece of paper?"

"Well, I—" I began. "Sure," I said. "Delighted."

He was gone and came back in a moment with a three-by-five card. I wrote his name on it and then in French, "En souvenir d'une nuit de folie à St. Tropez," and signed it.

"Just dandy," he said, with a small wrinkling of his nose. "Now what does it mean?"

"It means 'In memory of a night of madness at St. Tropez,'" I said. "Let's see you explain that to your roommate."

He moved his head slightly, looking down, a charming gesture, and then there came to me one of those magic moments when the cigarette smoke vanished and the sounds of babbling were sucked down into a silence that only I was aware of, while a long-forgotten sentence from a book on Leonardo appeared in my mind: "Sometimes a gesture or an expression of youth is so charged with physical grace that it takes the heart with intoler-

---

"Sometimes a gesture." The line is from Rachel Annand Taylor, *Leonardo the Florentine: A Study in Personality* (London: The Richards Press, 1927), 487.

able tenderness, like the last fine ghost of a wave vanishing on silver sand, or the young moon shy in a jasper evening." I recalled myself with difficulty, to find him watching me somewhat enigmatically, the hint of a smile quirking the corner of his lips. And that turned me to thinking of the saintly old Arab who was once asked to imagine himself in a garden of roses and hyacinths with the evening breeze waving the cypress and a fair youth of twenty beside him, with the assurance of perfect privacy. "And what then," asked the questioner, "would be the result?" The holy man bowed his head and thought for a moment and, too honest to lie, said finally, "Allah defend me from such temptation."

"Let me give you my phone number," said Scott, and did, whereupon I passed him one of my cards.

These small exchanges did not go unnoticed by the crowd, and I saw one or two looking daggers at me. Prince Valiant gnawed his lower lip.

"I'd like to come to see you," Scott said.

"By all means." If I had had a green feathered fan, I probably would have batted my eyes at him over the top of it.

The entire episode left me in a tumult. On the way home, Don said, "You really seemed to be making out with the handsomest one there."

I yawned, pretending boredom. "Somewhat young," I said.

A few days later Scott came to see me, to get the copy of *Dear Sammy* signed. With him he brought a brochure printed in color, advertising a porno film in which he had appeared. He gave me also a large color photograph of himself, naked, with one arm uplifted to a branch, his lithe tanned swimmer's body amidst a total background of greenery — cedars and firs — his genitals barely showing before merging with the green out of which his body sprang. On the back of it, he wrote: "I enjoy your company, and look forward to more visits in the future. I hope to be as charming and witty as you are when I am past thirty!"

The net — alas! — had fallen on me, for the first time in twenty years. And I was not helped by a drama that appeared on the idiot tube that very night. It was about a female college teacher of ancient history who took in a student roomer. And the handsome student, rummaging in a closet one day, came across a scrapbook which told him that the teacher, the loner, the aloof one, was really in the past the lady member of a song-and-dance vaudeville team. She became emotionally enmeshed with the young man, and he finally

the saintly old Arab. The story is found in *One Thousand and One Nights* as translated and published in 1885 by Richard Francis Burton (1821–90). See *Arabian Nights*, ed. A. V. Williams Jackson (New York: Cosimo Classics, 2008), 10:202.

Photograph of Scott, inscribed on reverse to Steward. (Courtesy of the Estate of Samuel M. Steward)

moved out—not ever suspecting until the final scene that she had felt something more than affection for him.

It underlined the business of myself and Scott and was a miniature of the problem that looms large for every aging homosexual. In what year does a good man stop it all? It seemed somehow unfair to me that so late in life I should once more be put through the—well, agony was not the word—"annoyance" might be more fitting—of having my emotions churned once again. Could I ever approach the yellow-haired beauty? Where was dignity? Where was pride? I did not want rejection—could not endure it, perhaps. What did I want? The thing that bedevils every homosexual—the one-time physical contact, the dirty five minutes? Did I want friendship? That fades. "Love" was out of the question, and anyway, it dies. What did the student say to the teacher of ancient history? "Affection continues"—but there should

be a stronger word than affection—a special word to hold all the yearning
for what is lost, all the love for physical beauty or beauty of mind and intelligence, all the adoration that an older man can have for a younger. There was
a new word—"limerence"—lovesickness, which certainly did describe me,
for I was love-smitten. But what was it that I felt for Scott? Or what did he
feel for me—if anything?

I found myself wondering about happiness and the pursuit we make of
it—so frantic and unceasing. "If I were as happy now as I was then," we say,
sighing. But the truth is that few men have more to their account than a total
of a dozen hours of happiness in a lifetime—a fragment here and there out
of the dull and sullen roll of years. It is necessary to realize that a state of
unhappiness or frustration is the usual lot of nearly all men, nearly all of the
time. For most, life is a state of barely endurable discomfort.

Keats once wrote a letter to his brother in which he praised what he called
negative capability—a willingness to live in the midst of doubts and uncertainties without any irritable reaching out after fact and reason, never trying
to reduce our universe to a neat $x^2 + y^2$ formula. And if we could take that as
a starting point, the next step should come easily: the attempt to settle oneself into a pattern which would permit observation—even participation—
but still allow detachment, untouched in the deeply emotional sense so that
no person or thing or situation would ever have the power again to wound.
Such an action makes use of the same sort of "self-ness" that underlies our
instinct for self-preservation. We look at the label to make sure the bottle
does not contain cyanide.

To achieve this inner detachment, there must be a careful preparation,
creation, and stocking of inner resources, building them over the years—
perhaps a love of music, of books, of art, of anything in which real interest
is possible, or at the very least a treasury of memories to sustain us. Since
our emotional lives are fragmented, we should have a vast stock of tangible
things to invest our love in: mementos, memorabilia, photographs, an old
blue cloak (like Newman), a water glass his lips had touched, anything which
can stimulate us, can make us remember. And finally, when experience has

Keats. British poet John Keats (1795–1821) defined what he termed *negative capability* in a
letter of December 21 (or 27), 1817, to his brothers George and Thomas. Steward quotes his
definition almost verbatim. This and the following two paragraphs are taken from Steward's essay "Detachment," which was the first piece he published in *Der Kreis* (in 1958) and
which he reprinted as a "coda" at the end of the text in *Chapters*.
an old blue cloak (like Newman). Steward refers to a story that following an illness in Malta
in May 1833, John Henry Cardinal Newman (1801–90) refused for sentimental reasons to

multiplied itself to such an extent that you are no longer under any compulsion of any kind toward persons or things or situations, then you have the only kind of freedom worth aiming for, and the best reward.

If we cannot detach ourselves—what then? The endless empty hours of cruising bars, of suffering from the dwindling number of admirers as we grow older, of the frantic-pathetic efforts to stay young and attractive in a culture which admires youth alone, of not being able to see *le moment juste* when we must renounce the chase, the hopeless pursuit.

Had Scott with his lithe and handsome body and his color brochure wrecked everything that I thought had been built so rigid and strong? There in those glowing pages his body was laid out, his dimensions revealed, his activity everything that had come to be expected in a homosexual adult film. The mechanics of all kinds of sex were not foreign to him. But if a shy and tentative first touch from me caused his hand to fall on mine and gently push it aside, could I survive? Could I divorce old barren Reason from my bed?

Well, at any rate . . . nowadays I see Scott frequently. Once in a while we go to dinner. Occasionally he brings me a small "corsage" of chrysanthemums and tells me—laughing—that I'm his date. He visits me on his bicycle—in a tight red T-shirt and tight short red pants, his long and lovely tanned legs like a flower stem to a red calyx, his yellow hair and handsome face a part of the flower. His crinkly snippets of hair shine from a reliquary next to Valentino's.

There are times in one's life when you accept the gifts from the gods, and smile, and do not question.

Sources: *Chapters*, 130–42; Manuscript, 358–68.

---

part with his old cloak when the young man who had nursed him to health asked if he could have it. See Anne Mozley, ed., *Letters and Correspondence of John Henry Newman* (London: Longmans, 1898), 1:377.

nowadays I see Scott frequently. Steward in fact dedicated *Chapters from an Autobiography* to Scott, but by the time the book appeared, Scott had already moved on to a relationship with a physician who offered him financial support (Spring, 392).

a reliquary next to Valentino's. As a teenager in Columbus, Ohio, Steward learned that the actor Rudolph Valentino was staying at a hotel in the city, went to his room to get an autograph, and left with a swatch of Valentino's pubic hair that he kept in a monstrance for the rest of his life. He described the encounter in a 1989 interview (Carl Maves, "Valentino's Pubic Hair and Me," *The Advocate*, June 6, 1989, 72–74).

Chapter Seventeen

A BONSAI TREE, A DOG OR TWO

1973–81

Several holiday seasons ago, my sister, Virginia, asked me to go with her to pick out a Christmas present.

"But shouldn't it be a surprise?" I asked.

"You have to pick out the one you want."

She took me to a nursery where they had a large collection of bonsai trees. I almost covered my face with my hands in horror.

"Please, no . . . no," I said.

"Why ever not?" she asked.

I was ashamed. "I simply can't be responsible for any living thing," I said. "It's just too much."

She was stunned and later teased me about it.

Yet something else happened. The ancient father of my landlady, Eva, died, and her daughter got her a longhaired dachshund, a feisty little beast name Fritz. And after two years, Eva herself died. The front house was rented for one year, and then two, by two separate young married couples, both marriages breaking up. The dog was rented with the house, like a fixture. But in the third year, the renters were a couple with a large Doberman—and Fritz was homeless. I had enjoyed his company for four years, his scratching at my door every morning, without having any of the responsibility—but now he was forced on me. Either I had to take him, or I had to give him away.

For the first few weeks, I kept asking all my acquaintances if they didn't want a dog—and then gradually it all changed. I fell in love with Fritz, I was smitten, I was lovesick, I was in limerence. I began to adore every hair on his bullnecked, broad-chested, bandy-legged black-and-tan body. I taught him tricks and was amazed at his vocabulary of a hundred and twenty words and phrases.

The sudden upspring of love and affection for the little friendly beast astounded me. It was as if all my life I had been waiting for an object on which to pour out all the accumulated love that I had been storing up for so many years. At first, it was somewhat frightening, and then I succumbed completely—walking him four or five times a day (good for me, too) and adjusting my life to take care of him. And so I saw him through attacks by one of the savage free-running commune dogs a few doors away, which gave him a week in the hospital, and through various back ailments, which many long-spined dachshunds have. But alas, I could do nothing when he ruptured a spinal disc by furiously wagging his tail and his rear end in his great enthusiasm over a visitor. There was an operation (more expensive by far than the removal of my "twin" many years before) which did not work. He had to be destroyed.

For a full month, I was beset with sudden furious shattering tear-storms, more intense and agonizing than anything I had ever felt for the death of a member of my human family, unless it had been my Aunt Elizabeth. Certainly I shed more tears for Fritz than for my father, whose death had left me dry-eyed. And then I decided I had to find another dog.

It was a search that ended at a kennel in Novato, where a small beastie had been kept for sixteen months and was scheduled for destruction because his breeder felt that his front paws turned outward too much for him to succeed as a show dog or a sire. I found his stance rather charming; it reminded me of the ballet fifth position. He looked exactly like Fritz—*pointes de feu*, fire points above his eyes, tan "gloves" and all—and I called him "Fritzl." But he lacked most of a dog's instincts, because he had not had enough human love and contact during the formative weeks. He knew nothing of "fetch" or playing ball; he would not grip or tug; he could not dig (having been raised on concrete), nor did he recognize a bird. For the first weeks, his tail was always between his legs, and he crept belly-close to the floor. He had more complexes than any three of my complicated friends. Six months of love effected great changes in him—but he still remained a victim of "kennelosis," a timid-shy syndrome that nothing may ever erase. He will probably never improve further. Yet who really cares?

commune dogs. On the Earth People's Park commune that established itself two doors from Steward in the 1970s, see Spring, 382; and Bill Wallace, "Eviction Threatens Earth People's Park," *Berkeley Barb*, July 15–21, 1977, 2.
ballet fifth position. Steward seems to mean the first or second position, in which the feet point left and right.

Steward late in life with one of his dachshunds. (Courtesy of the Estate of Samuel M. Steward)

In time, I decided that "Fritzl" was not a good name for him — and it gave me a kind of ghosty feeling. I changed it to "Blackie" — oh, yes, very original! — and I resist all temptation to make comparisons between him and Fritz. Blackie calls forth great love and pity, compassion and understanding. His "incompleteness" — his "damaged" personality — creates a deeper and wider surge of love because he has been deprived of — or never known — the joys of puppyhood and playing. Are we so close because I see in him something of my early self?

Every night I switch off my telephone and, to remind myself to turn it on in the morning, drop a large long-stemmed plastic rose on the carpet. One morning, Blackie picked up the stem and like a shaggy Carmen approached me with it, sitting up on his hindquarters and pawing the air at me with his front feet.

So the two of us, fretted by life but still enjoying its pleasures, will go on cocking our respective snoots at the slings and arrows of adversity and bringing roses to each other in the mornings.

Sources: *Chapters*, 130–32; *Manuscript*, 354–57.

a shaggy Carmen. Steward alludes to the opera *Carmen* (1875), by Georges Bizet (1838–75), but more broadly to the stereotype of the female tango or flamenco dancer with a rose stem between her teeth.
slings and arrows. Shakespeare, *Hamlet*, III.i.57.

INDEX

Page numbers in italics refer to illustrations.